Looking for Leroy

① This book is a critical narrative with a thematic expression of black culture

② Or critical narrative of black culture as seen and acted upon by whites in a racist context

POSTMILLENNIAL POP

General Editors: **Karen Tongson and Henry Jenkins**

LOOKING FOR LEROY

Illegible Black Masculinities

Mark Anthony Neal

NEW YORK UNIVERSITY PRESS
New York and London

NEW YORK UNIVERSITY PRESS
New York and London
www.nyupress.org

References to Internet Websites (URLs) were accurate at the time of writing.
Neither the author nor New York University Press is responsible for URLs
that may have expired or changed since the manuscript was prepared.

Library of Congress Cataloging-in-Publication Data
Neal, Mark Anthony.
Looking for Leroy : illegible black masculinities / Mark Anthony Neal.
pages   cm   Includes bibliographical references and index.
ISBN 978-0-8147-5835-9 (cl : alk. paper) — ISBN 978-0-8147-5836-6 (pb : alk. paper)
ISBN 978-0-8147-8940-7 (e-book) — ISBN 978-0-8147-6060-4 (e-book)
1. African American men. 2. African American gay men. 3. African American
men in popular culture. 4. Men—Identity. 5. Masculinity.   I. Title.
E185.86.N394 2013
305.38'896073—dc23   2012043777

New York University Press books are printed on acid-free paper,
and their binding materials are chosen for strength and durability.
We strive to use environmentally responsible suppliers and materials
to the greatest extent possible in publishing our books.

Manufactured in the United States of America

c   10 9 8 7 6 5 4 3 2 1
p   10 9 8 7 6 5 4 3 2 1

In loving memory of
Elenor Murray
Arthur Cleveland Neal Jr.
Elsie Elenor Neal

Contents

Preface

Waiting for Leroy

The germ of the idea that became *Looking for Leroy* goes back nearly a decade. As initially conceived, many of the interventions that I attempt in this book were intended for a volume that also included many of the interventions I made in *New Black Man* (2005). Somewhere in late 2003, *Looking for Leroy* asserted itself in ways that would become familiar to me throughout this process, and demanded that it be allowed to breathe in its own space. Like suspicious, competitive, yet loving fraternal twins, the two books went their own ways. As such, *Looking for Leroy* was the first of my projects to dictate to me how it was going to live in the world: it seemed to anticipate the broadband and digital revolutions without which the project could not exist. *Looking for Leroy* implored me to go back to the lab—a lab that wasn't even built yet—and it kept me honest by keeping my critical observations tethered to the career arc of Shawn Corey Carter (Jay-Z), who announced his retirement with the release of *The Black Album* in 2003. A half-dozen recordings later, with the summer 2011 release of the Jay-Z and Kanye West collaboration *Watch the Throne*, *Looking for Leroy* finally announced that it was in fact time to, as Miles Davis once urged John Coltrane, take the horn out of my mouth.

But there were also times that *Looking for Leroy* had to wait on me—and it did so lovingly, as it allowed me to bury my parents, who departed this earth eighteen months apart in 2008 and 2009. *Looking for Leroy* allowed me to parent two demanding, assertive, brilliant, and mercurial daughters (and to sit for hundreds of hours at swim meets), daughters who have not only made me a better parent, but a better person and a better thinker. That my oldest daughter listens to Jay-Z's Pandora channel and my youngest watches episodes of *Fame* on my iPad is some small indication of how closely they shared in the creating of this book. *Looking for Leroy* allowed me to exhale, and celebrate twenty years of marriage, on a journey that my partner often reminds me that she didn't "sign up for." *Looking for Leroy* allowed me to first doubt and then rediscover my voice—and my passion for this work.

Acknowledgments

Like all of my other projects, my work is the product of the places and spaces that inspire me to think and write. There were many such spaces, but four were absolutely critical to my process: the Parkwest Crossing Starbucks, Parker & Otis (particularly during those summer mornings on the porch), the Bean Traders at Homestead Market (especially on the weekends), and finally the Beyu Caffe.

In Durham, around the country, and on the grid, I've been fortunate to be inspired and challenged by a range of folk. I'd like to thank my colleagues at Duke University, particularly the folks in the Department of African and African American Studies: Michaeline Crichlow, Stephen Smith, Thavolia Glymph, Sharon Holland, Charmaine Royal, Bayo Holsey, Paula McClain, Lee Baker, Kerry Haynie, Anthony Kelley, Karla F. C. Holloway, Charlie Piot, Anne-Maria Makhulu, Jennifer Brody, Thomas DeFrantz, William "Sandy" Darity, Maurice Wallace, and Wahneema Lubiano. Duke also afforded me the opportunity to work with some marvelous students, both on the undergraduate and graduate level, notably Dr. Micah Gilmer, Professor Kinohi Nishikawa, Professor Alisha Gaines, Brandon Hudson, Professor Bianca Robinson (my first teaching assistant at Duke), Ali Neff, Cynthia Greenlee Donnell, Professor Casey Wasserman, Professor Jenny Woodruff, Rizvana Bradley, Kesha Lee, and Amanda Boston, as well as the Duke University basketball players Nolan Smith, Seth Curry, and Andre Dawkins.

My thinking throughout this project was pushed by a group of brilliant minds; the collective work of Richard "the R" Iton (who was dropping little gems of encouragement from the very beginning), Cathy Cohen, Fred Moten, Robert Reid-Pharr, and J. Jack Halberstam are all over *Looking for Leroy*. David J. Leonard reminded me what it is like to be a *hungry* scholar—and why I needed to remember that psychic space. Loved the regular "real talk" that I got from James Braxton Peterson, Lisa Thompson, Guthrie Ramsey, David Ikard, and Jeannette Eileen Jones—real talk I couldn't get from the barbershop or the Faculty Commons. Special dap to Esther Iverem, Natalie Hopkinson, Marc Lamont Hill, Byron Hurt, Esther Armah, Salamishah Tillett, Sofia Quintero, John Jackson, Tracy Sharpley Whiting, Stephane Dunn, William Jelani Cobb, Alondra Nelson, Marcyliena Morgan, Elaine "Dr. E" Richardson, Geneva "Dr. G" Smitherman, Regina Bradley, Murray Forman, Deborah Thomas, 9th Wonder (Patrick Douthit), and Michael Eric Dyson. Shouts to the *Left of Black* crew of Jason Doty, Catherine Angst, Camille Jackson (yes, I'm claiming you), Galvin Wells, and Laura Margarita Maule. Thanks to the faculty and staff at the Annenberg School for Communication at the University of Pennsylvania, particularly Barbie Zelizer, who allowed me a magical semester of thinking and writing in Philadelphia in the fall of 2008, where I got the chance to work with some amazing students, including Professor C. Riley Snorton and Joshua Bennett.

Over the past few years I've been afforded the opportunity to travel across the country with some amazing thinkers and activists as part of the Rap Sessions touring town hall meetings, under the leadership of Bakari Kitwana. Bakari has become a trusted friend, but he also gave me the opportunity to work regularly with my childhood friend and first BFF Joan Morgan, making Mama Morgan and Mama Elsie (from heaven) quite proud. It was a piece that Joan wrote about Ice Cube more than twenty years ago that inspired me to take my writing seriously, and I hope I am giving her at least a bit of inspiration as she completes her PhD in American studies at New York University. Also thanks to Professor Treva "diva-feminist" Lindsey, who was simply my brilliant teaching assistant when I started *Looking for Leroy*; now she is an accomplished scholar and thinker in her own right, whose own willingness to think "beyond a boundary" (shout-out to C. L. R. James) forced me to do the same.

My oldest daughter was still an infant when I published my first book, and my youngest was a toddler when I published my last. Between my countless travels, weekends at the coffee shop, too many missed dinners, and so many lectures in the car about Motown, the world their grandparents grew up in, and what it means to be Chocolate in a Vanilla world, my daughters, Misha Gabrielle (Whurl-a-Gurl), now a teenager (sigh), and Camille Monet (Baby-Butterfly), have some inkling of what their daddy does. Thankfully they also have a great sense that their daddy loves them and continues to be inspired by the girls that they are and the black women they will surely become. Time doesn't go by without significant challenges, but for the last twenty-four years (twenty of them in that quaint thing we call marriage), I've faced those challenges with the same partner beside me. I often joke that I married a "big-booty Bronx Gurl," but that's real talk; when I go home at night I'm freed of all the pretensions of this world we've managed to climb up into.

I've often said throughout my career that I wanted to do work that my father would find value in. I've told the story many times before about his illiteracy, his tenth-grade education, and his love of the Soul Stirrers and the Mighty Clouds of Joy. Now, some four years after his death, I have also realized that he was my first teacher, teaching me how to feel when you're numbed by the world around you, and how to find small joys in the way someone might bend a note. There's not a day when I hear Bobby "Blue" Bland, Joe Ligon, or Sam Cooke and not get to spend a few minutes with my dad, as if he knew so many years ago that I could always find him in those notes, even when he was gone. I'm hoping I've done the same with my daughters. My mother was arguably the most difficult person I knew; our relationship got more tense as I spread my wings and she tried to keep me close. It was difficult that final year, watching her diminish; I often felt that when my father died I lost both parents, since my mother never recovered from his death (and that of her mother, my grandmother, a month prior). And yet so much about her was revealed to me at her home going ceremony—about the independence that took her from Baltimore to New York City while still a teen or the focus that led her to pursue a college education while being a working wife and mother. I see that independence in both of my daughters, and lament that, like my mother, I won't be able to keep them close either.

Introduction

I can't remember exactly when I first saw Leroy. It was likely sometime during that first season of the television series *Fame*, where the actor and dancer Gene Anthony Ray reprised the role of Leroy that he introduced in the original film version of *Fame* (1980). As a teenager growing up in the Bronx, I had few available examples of masculinity that didn't play to basic heteronormative assumptions, though there was the transgendered man who lived in the house next to my tenement building, who always elicited hushed tones among my peers and their parents. But indeed by the age of sixteen—my age when *Fame* debuted on NBC in January 1982—I had inherited enough fictions about black masculinity to be able to discern what male bodies my peers and others suspected of being "gay" bodies or quite specifically, gay "somebodies." My peers and I all needed to maintain a metaphoric distance from those "somebodies" that might not have been ontologically possible—Robert Reid-Pharr remarks in passing that deviancy does not disrupt ontology—hence the clear gesture toward unfamiliarity that the term "somebodies" suggests.[1] We needed language that also efficiently marked those gay "somebodies" as cultural and political strangers (or strangeness to my sixteen-year-old mind). Ironically, my own proclivity for wearing pastel-colored polo shirts with matching hosiery and penny loafers (with shiny new pennies intact), in an era when many of my peers were wearing Kangol hats, unlaced shell-top Adidas, and tightly creased colored Lee jeans, made me a target of the very speculative fictions that I was willing to place on the body of Leroy. Nevertheless, my first reaction to Leroy was, "This cat is gay."

Though little in *Fame*'s scripts suggested that the character of Leroy was in fact gay (there were clearly sexual tensions between

Leroy and at least two of his women teachers), there were signs that suggested, to borrow from the work of Seth Clark Silberman, a "fierce legibility" about him. Silberman describes "fierce legibility" as a vernacular that "vocalizes black masculine same-sexuality within and around black letters."[2] "Fierce," though, is a term that also resonates beyond the same-sex discourses that Silberman examines. In his essay "The Gangsta and the Diva," Andrew Ross writes, "Being fierce, in the ghetto street or the nightclub version, is a theatrical response to the phenomenal pressure exerted upon black males."[3] Taking into account Ross's notion of performativity and Silberman's focus in a vernacular framework, I evoke the term "fierce legibility" in relation to Leroy's visual legibility—his cornrows, his red "hot pants," and the lilting sway of his hips—which could mark Leroy as gay. At least this was the case for my then untrained and virginal sixteen-year-old eyes. Indeed, there was a radical quality to Leroy's queerness, the confirmation of something that was unfamiliar or not quite what it was supposed to be, since, I mean, "He's supposed to be gay, right?" Striking, for example, was the way Leroy refused to wear dancing tights throughout the series, choosing instead to wear shorts that always highlighted his muscularity and, ironically, heightened his sexual availability. In another example, when Leroy is confronted by an older brother who challenges his masculinity by demeaning his desire to be a dancer, Leroy responds, "Dancing and working is not what I do—it's what I am."

The potential of Leroy's radicalness was consistently undermined, though, by narrative devices that regularly scripted Leroy as a "post–Black Power ghetto baby." As such, Leroy easily trafficked in the tropes of the angry, disaffected urban black male —the mainstream visual precursor to hip-hop masculinities— who, of course, per standard neoliberal critiques, possessed all the potential in the world, if he could only let go of his rage and stop blaming whites for his fate. That a teenaged and likely unemployed black male might be enraged in 1982, as Reaganomics threatened to erode the very political and social gains that made a series like *Fame*—with its *Glee*-fully diverse cast—plausible, seemed beyond the scope of the show's writers. Instead we were treated to confrontations between Leroy and his white female English teacher, Sherwood (embodying a liberal retreat from the demands of black rage), whose intergenerational and interracial sexual desire for Leroy was palpable in virtually every scene they shared. The combative tensions between Leroy and Sherwood were eventually softened when she discovered that he lived by himself in a walkup tenement in Harlem (where else would a black kid live?), who also worked to support himself, while his mother lived and worked in Michigan. This revelation only heightened Sherwood's interest, even obsession, with Leroy; and let's be clear: the cornrolled, "wife-beater"–wearing, full-lipped, doe-eyed Leroy (think Tupac) was the object of everybody's de-sire, including the sixteen-year-old who sat in front of his tele-vision in the Bronx, watching these dramas unfold.

When Gene Anthony Ray died in November 2003—treated as another obscure figure from a marginal television drama from the 1980s—I was hoping that there would be some confirma-tion of the queerness that I so willingly wanted to read onto the bodies of Ray and Leroy. In fact, I was consumed by the desire to locate a body, any somebody—queer, black, and male—that could contradict what I was beginning to suspect was the reality that we all were "interchangeable fictions" scripted for the desires of the many who would deny us some semblance of humanity. Ultimately Leroy offered a view of black masculinity that is so seductive, even as a teenager, because it challenged the pervasive and decidedly unsophisticated images of pimps and petty crimi-nals—precursors to the hip-hop thugs and strip-club denizens of the early twenty-first century—that regularly circulated on commercial television in the 1980s. Leroy also contested the up-tight stereotypes of bourgeois masculinity that could be found in characters such as Heathcliff Huxtable or Frank Parrish in series like *The Cosby Show* and *Frank's Place*, welcome as they were in the televisual landscape of the 1980s. As such, I would like to suggest that Gene Anthony Ray's Leroy represented the founda-tion for a queering of black masculinity in contemporary popular culture. By "queer" I am alluding not only to the obvious ambi-guities associated with queering sexualities—it's not like there's ever been an assemblage of out black gay, bisexual, or trans men on television—but also to queerness as a radical rescripting of the accepted performances of a heteronormative black masculinity. In other words, Leroy represents a black masculinity that was "illegible" to many.

In contrast to Leroy and other illegible black males, the "legible" black male body is continually recycled to serve the historical fictions of American culture (as the state rolls tenuously into a future of continued globalization, terrorism, and privatization). Here black male bodies continue to function as tried and tested props, whether justifying the lynching of black male bodies after emancipation or the maintenance of antimiscegenation laws and Black Codes (well into the twentieth century) to discourage so-called race mixing and limit black mobility. In the contemporary moment we witness the prison industrial complex (where privatization looms large), which warehouses black (and brown) male bodies for nonviolent offenses as part of some preemptive attack on the presumed criminality of those bodies, while simultaneously exploiting the labor of those bodies for the profit of private prisons, a form of mass incarceration that the legal scholar Michelle Alexander has described as the "new Jim Crow."[4]

In her book *The New Jim Crow: Mass Incarceration in the Age of Colorblindness*, Alexander recalls leaving an election-night celebration party in 2008, a night on which many claimed a victory for blackness, and black masculinity in particular, in the election of Barack Hussein Obama as the nation's forty-fourth president—and her mood being tempered by the sight of a black man "on his knees in the gutter, hands cuffed behind his back, as several officers stood around him talking, joking, and ignoring his human existence."[5] Though Alexander was more concerned about whether President Obama's victory would dramatically impact the lives of men like the one handcuffed in the gutter, the images of the officers standing over the man suggest, for my purposes, that little will change in terms of the legibility of such men even as the president's own legibility (and illegibility) establishes him as the most accomplished African American man ever.

As Bryant Keith Alexander suggests, "the black male body is

polemical. It is a site of public and private contestations; competing investments in black masculinity that are historical and localized."[6] That the most "legible" black male body is often thought to be a criminal body and/or a body in need of policing and containment—incarceration—is just a reminder that the black male body that so seduces America is just as often the bogeyman that keeps America awake at night. Thus "legible" black male bodies, ironically, bring welcome relief, a comforting knowingness casually reflected in notions like "niggers will be niggers" (a distinctly gendered term) or "they always get away," whether they are accessed on your iPad, Android, or local Fox News affiliate. Herman Gray acknowledges as much when he writes, "black masculinity consistently appears in the popular imagination as the logical and legitimate object of surveillance."[7]

A recent study by the Opportunity Agenda, "Literature Review: Media Representations and Impact on the Lives of Black Men and Boys," makes an explicit claim—what the authors describe as a "core problem"—about the "troubling link between media portrayals and lowered life chances for black males," noting "distorted patterns of portrayal" and causal links between media depictions of black males and public attitudes toward those black males. With regard to the distortion of black male images, the report observes that there is a general underrepresentation of black males in mainstream corporate media; that when black males do appear, they are often presented with exaggerated negative connotations; that "positive" associations are limited; and that black men and their issues are always already framed as problems.[8] Such general framing of black men leads to causal links in the public imagination that create antagonisms toward black males, largely instigated by the belief that black men are criminally and violently inclined. In such a context many of the attempts to address the black male "problem" are done so with punitive measures in mind.[9] This dynamic, of course, plays out in every institutional arena from public education, the labor force, and health care (particularly mental health) to, most tragically, the criminal justice system, something that many were reminded of with the shooting death of Trayvon Martin in

February 2012. As such, black men are seemingly bound to and bound by their legibility.

This state of boundedness has not been lost on scholars, critics, and artists. For example, the legal scholar David Dante Troutt considers the implications of black masculinity functioning as a trademark in his provocative essay "A Portrait of the Trademark as a Black Man." In the essay, Troutt writes about a fictional African American advertising executive named MarCus, who believes that by creating a trademark for himself, he ensures that his "distinctive mark would enter consumption through every entrance and gradually play upon each consumer's preferences whether known or unknown, disarm their prejudices and reshape their perceptions about race."[10] Troutt is in part inspired by the examples of figures like Michael Jordan, Tiger Woods, and the late Michael Jackson, some of the most legible individual black men of the twentieth century, who "must overcome the stereotypes of personhood that are deeply ingrained in public consciousness."[11] Though Troutt's character MarCus is most concerned with the ability to "create myself, to *name* myself in public consciousness . . . and to interpret the meaning of that name" for primarily commercial purposes, the essay highlights the difficulties of challenging prevailing images and meanings of black men, even as the mainstream finds value and, indeed, pleasure and satisfaction in the consumption of those images.

The conceptual artist Hank Willis Thomas also takes on the boundedness and legibility of black masculinity, particularly in the context of popular culture and the advertising industry. Thomas began to give serious consideration to the images of black men after the murder of his cousin and roommate Songha Willis, who was killed outside a club in Philadelphia in 2000 after being robbed of his gold chain. These considerations first took artistic shape in the stop-animation film short *Winter in America*, in which Thomas and Kambui Olujimi replay the murder of Songha Willis using some of the action hero toys that Thomas played with when he was a boy. According to Thomas, the action figures helped "tell a story that's been told thousands of times before," highlighting how the everyday violence of black life has been literally reduced to child's play.[12] As the curator René de Guzman writes, the figures "show how violent play is inherent in how boys are raised," and the film "gives a tone of surreal banality that matches the commonness that the epidemic killings of young black men by their peers has become."[13] The banality that de Guzman alludes to is captured by Thomas, who in an interview with *FLYP* magazine admitted, "we didn't even have to ask whether or not the killers were black."[14]

A photo from Songha Willis's funeral became the basis for a later series by Hank Willis Thomas called *Branded*, in which he deconstructed and exposed the causal connections between popular brands and race. In *Priceless #1* (2004), Thomas uses an actual photo of his family mourning at the gravesite of his cousin, to reproduce the popular MasterCard "Priceless" ad campaign with the affecting ending tag, "Picking the perfect casket for your son: priceless." In other photos in the series, Thomas links the accessibility of hard liquor—Absolut Vodka in this case —to issues of black-on-black violence and the continued trauma of the Middle Passage. Perhaps the best-known photos from the *Branded* series are *Branded Head* (2003) and *Scarred Chest* (2004), in which Thomas imagines the Nike "swoosh" branded on the bodies of black men. Thomas's *Branded* series forces audiences to consider the connections between black male legibility and commercial brands, the distinction between a black man with the Nike insignia branded on his body—the property of Nike—and a black man without such markings. Lost in that subtle distinction are the realities of black men and boys whose presumed criminality is largely redirected for corporate profit, or at least the potential of such profit, if we consider the "cradle to pipeline" narrative that has circulated in many black communities (with those few detours to a stadium, arena, and recording studio).

In an interview in *Art Nouveau*, Hank Willis Thomas describes his recent series *Strange Fruit* as a "series of works that is questioning how the media represents and portrays black bodies, particularly with regard to their physicality. To me, popular culture influences the way we as a culture learn and perpetuate stereotypes about ourselves."[15] If Thomas's work aims to disturb the comfort of the prevailing logics about black male bodies, it is a project that I share by suggesting the radical potential of rendering "legible" black male bodies—those bodies that are all too real to us—illegible, while simultaneously rendering so-called illegible black male bodies—those black male bodies we can't believe are real—legible. Thus the act of looking for Leroy, like the search for Langston before him, might represent a theoretical axis to perform the kind of critical exegesis that contemporary black masculinity demands. As such, Gene Anthony Ray's Leroy serves as a jumping-off point to examine other illegible black masculinities in the disparate performances of the actor Avery Brooks, the rapper and entrepreneur Shawn Corey Carter (Jay-Z), the actor Idris Elba, the musician R. Kelly, and the vocalist Luther Vandross.

Chapter 1, "A Foot Deep in the Culture: The Thug Knowledge(s) of *A Man Called Hawk*," examines the extraordinary television career of the accomplished stage actor Avery Brooks. Well respected as a stage actor and professor at Rutgers University in New Jersey, Brooks was cast in 1985 in the television detective drama *Spenser for Hire*. The series was based on the popular detective novels by Robert Parker, which featured the character Spenser and his enforcing sidekick Hawk. At the time, the series offered another iteration of the burgeoning black/white buddy films made popular by Richard Pryor and Gene Wilder and perhaps most famously by the *Lethal Weapon* franchise, which starred Danny Glover and Mel Gibson as police partners. One of the first of such series on commercial television featured Ben Vereen and Jeff Goldblum in *Tenspeed and Brown Shoe* (1980).

Brooks's Hawk proved to be a breakout character in the series, in an era that was in part defined by the hypervisual presence of blackness, via conservative deployment of black pathology narratives, alongside the popularity of black crossover stars such as Bill Cosby, Eddie Murphy, Whitney Houston, Michael Jackson, and Michael Jordan, who represented distinct performances of blackness that were all marked as either cutting-edge cool or the paragon of black respectability. The popularity of the character led to Brooks's own series, *A Man Called Hawk*, which was a mid-season replacement in the spring of 1989. Though the character was entrapped in stereotypes of a menacing black masculinity often on the verge of violent expression, Brooks brilliantly invested the character with the capacity to draw on a full range of black expressive culture, often in opposition to the intent of the show's writers and producers. As such, Brooks was able to make claims on the capacity of black stereotypes—in this case that of the black male thug—to make critical interventions in our understandings of black history and culture.

Jay-Z (a.k.a. Shawn Corey Carter) could also be charged with making such interventions, though his most legible status as one of the biggest icons of commercial rap music suggests that he is part and parcel of a cottage industry of problematic images of black masculinity. In chapter 2, " 'My Passport Says Shawn': Toward a Hip-Hop Cosmopolitanism," I make an alternative claim about Jay-Z / Shawn Carter, suggesting that both entities represent fertile textual sites to extrapolate a cosmopolitan hip-hop masculinity that deftly challenges the prevailing tropes of (black) masculinity that exist in much of mainstream hip-hop culture. My reading of Jay-Z / Shawn Carter is premised on a broad reading of his career arc, beginning with his debut, *Reasonable Doubt* (1996), and extending to his 2011 recording *Watch the Throne* (in collaboration with Kanye West), as well as his transition from "street" entrepreneur to a leading arbiter of mainstream urban culture. I argue that given the rigid constructions of masculinity in mainstream commercial hip-hop and equally rigid policing processes, attention must be paid to oppositional gestures within hip-hop—gestures that, I argue, in some instances become the mechanisms for attempts to "queer" artists who do not conform. As such, chapter 2 is dependent on close textual readings of Jay-Z's work, particularly in the realm of music video, which I argue offers a richer analytical terrain than lyrical analysis.

It would not be an overstatement to suggest that David Simon and Ed Burns's series *The Wire* significantly altered the presentation of black men on television. During the HBO series' five-season run (2002–2007), characters such as Omar (Michael K.

Williams), Avon Barksdale (Wood Harris), Snoop (Felicia Pearson), Michael (Tristan Wilds), Marlo Stanfield (Jamie Hector), Chris Partlow (Gbenga Akinnagbe), and Russell "Stringer" Bell (Idris Elba) offered a compelling read of the performance of black masculinity in the late twentieth and early twenty-first centuries. Of the series' many compelling characters, it was Bell to whom I was most drawn because of his performance of what I call the "thugniggaintellectual," someone who credibly navigates a life of the mind and the life of the street.[16] In chapter 3, in the context of examining Bell's role as a thinking man's gangster and the possibilities afforded that mindset, I also examine the threats posed by that role for both the character's peers and enemies, and ultimately for the show's primary writer, David Simon. Bell's ultimate crime was to think and imagine beyond the "block," which I argue in the context of *The Wire* functions as the nation; thus Bell's ultimate downfall in *The Wire* is premised on his cosmopolitan worldview.

I have long been interested in R. Kelly's music and career. In many ways his talents as a singer, arranger, songwriter, and producer mark him as peerless among his generation of post-soul musical artists. But Kelly's career has also been marred by rumors and ultimately criminal charges related to his sexual relationships with underaged females. Though I find Kelly to be a fascinating subject and highly relevant to the focus of this book, I had little interest in examining Kelly's singular musical genius in light of the child pornography charges against him, for which he was eventually acquitted. In that I was increasingly "legible" as a scholar because of my work as a "black male feminist," I was in a quandary as to how to write about Kelly as text, when Kelly the person clearly offended my sensibilities as a feminist, as a father of two daughters, and ultimately as a human being.

On cue, Kelly offered me an out, with his twenty-two-episode music video *Trapped in the Closet*, which was produced from 2005 to 2007. Kelly's surreal examination of black interpersonal relationships in the era of HIV, down-low sexuality, myriad religious scandals, and ongoing fears of black pathology struck a chord in me. Chapter 4, "R. Kelly's Closet: Shame, Desire, and the Confessions of a (Postmodern) Soul Man," reads R. Kelly's career in the context of the soul man tradition and the myriad scandals, tragedy, and trauma that have been visited upon the bodies of many of the tradition's best-known icons, including Sam Cooke and Teddy Pendergrass. As such, I argue that Kelly is an extension of that tradition and that *Trapped in the Closet* offers an exhumation of that tradition and its deep relationship to everyday black life—the proverbial soul closet, if you will—that helps contextualize Kelly's role as a witness to and chronicler of black pathology and narratives of black respectability.

Chapter 5 offers a critique of another soul man, the late Luther Vandross. Generally regarded as the most accomplished black male singer of the late twentieth century—I'm making a distinction here from, say, Michael Jackson, who was more of an all-around entertainer—Vandross remained an enigma for much of his career. Though Vandross was referenced in a broad range of African American expression from the mid-1980s until his untimely death at the age of fifty-four in July 2005, little was known about his personal life. The shroud of secrecy that surrounded Vandross's career was in conversation with the widespread though unspoken belief among his fans that the singer was gay. Chapter 5, "Fear of a Queer Soul Man: The Legacy of Luther Vandross," reads Vandross's performance of the "queer" soul man alongside the black macho figures that come immediately before him, most famously in the case of Teddy Pendergrass and the hypersexualized hip-hop–era masculinities that come after Vandross's emergence as the quintessential voice of black romance. I argue that Vandross succeeded in part because of his willingness to labor on behalf of black respectability at a time when blackness was becoming hypervisible in mainstream culture. Vandross's career arc was complicated by the dawning of the age of AIDS. Rumors that Vandross had contracted the disease made him its visible black "victim," and Vandross himself became the primary symbol of black America's anxieties about sexuality in the post–civil rights era.

I close *Looking for Leroy* with a brief reflection on the figure of the "race man," as popularized during the previous generation in the work of the actor Denzel Washington and rehabilitated by the rhetoric of the Reverend Jeremiah Wright during the 2008 presidential campaign.

1

A Foot Deep in the Culture

The Thug Knowledge(s) of A Man Called Hawk

In the fall of 1985 the television series *Spenser for Hire* debuted on the ABC network. The main character of the hour-long drama, an urbane Boston-based private detective named Spenser, was based on a character featured in a series of novels authored by Robert Parker. Spenser was portrayed by the actor Robert Urich as an upscale version of Dan Tanna, a character Urich played in the late 1970s series *Vegas*. At the height of the popularity of Parker's *Spenser* novels in the late 1980s, much was made of how much Parker's identity informed that of Spenser. As one writer described it, both Spenser and Parker wear "polished loafers with tassels, blue denims with an open-neck shirt and expensive sport jacket." Parker and his character Spenser embodied "business casual" well before such a term existed, and in the mid-1980s such a style gave Spenser an air of sophistication rarely associated with those in his profession. That Parker and Spenser were so closely linked rendered the character of Spenser believable.

In both the novels and the television series, Spenser often collaborated with a black "enforcer" simply known as Hawk. As described by Parker, "Hawk has the same skills and inclinations, but he grew up in another way with a different set of pressures."[1] Whatever sensibilities that Hawk might have shared with Spenser and however progressive Parker imagined the character to be, the reality was that Hawk was all too familiar to audiences who had grown comfortable with seeing a big black bald man, clad in black leather, with a big black gun—a performance that has historically been known as that of the "bad (black) man." In his book *Hoodlums: Black Villains and Social Bandits in American Life*, the historian William L. Van Deburg discusses the "bad

(black) man" in the context of what he calls "black social bandits." According to Van Deburg, these figures, as constructed by
post–Civil War writers, were often "Quirky, quixotic, and prone
to appropriating white-owned status symbols as partial compen-
sation for past indignities," and were "wedded to the cause of
group freedom and saw nothing wrong with extralegal means
to balance the scales of justice." "Typically more extroverted
and colorful than the average individual," Van Deburg notes,
these "outlaws of American folk history won wide acceptance as
risk-taking representatives of an unjustly demeaned race."[2] As a
dual product of Robert Parker's imagination and the American
psyche, Hawk seemingly did little to disturb long-held popular
beliefs about adult black masculinity.

According to Avery Brooks, the actor who brought Hawk to
life on the small screen, "I've been asked many times whether I
was exactly like the Hawk character."[3] Brooks, who has portrayed
figures as diverse as Othello, Malcolm X, and Paul Robeson, is a
classically trained actor who, in 1976, earned the first MFA (Master of Fine Arts) in theater granted to an African American at
Rutgers University. At the time that Brooks accepted the role of
Hawk, he was a tenured professor of theater at the university.
None of Brooks's accomplishments were apparent to those fans
(many of them white) who approached Brooks and, as he describes it, "think that I actually carry a gun, and that probably I
was standing on a street corner somewhere and these producers saw me and asked me if I wanted to come on television."[4] In
many ways Avery Brooks is as illegible—unbelievable—to mainstream audiences as Hawk is believable to those same audiences.

When I watched *Spenser for Hire* in the mid-1980s, Hawk was
absolutely believable and riveting for me as a twenty-year-old
who imagined living a life of the mind while trying to negotiate
the demands of the social spaces I called home. Hawk seemed
to exist somewhere in between Amiri Baraka's *Blues People* and
the vestibules where my boyhood friends were selling crack-
cocaine and weed. At the time Hawk embodied what some dismissively call "street smarts," though Hawk immediately struck
me as a character who was highly literate. In his book *Your Aver-*

age Nigga: Performing Race, Literacy, and Masculinity, Vershawn
Ashanti Young writes, "literacy is not chiefly about matching pro-
nouns with the right antecedents or comprehending why Willie
and Janet went up the hill. Literacy is first and foremost a racial
performance."[5] As such, it was a performance that I found quite
alluring, as much because of the seamlessness with which Hawk
navigated very disparate social and cultural spaces, as because of
the intellectual gravitas that the character conveyed—a gravitas
that was perhaps more disarming than his bold physical presence.

Conjuring Black Male Genius

Fuck being a thug—in my mind Hawk was damned erudite: a
combination of John Shaft's street savvy, W. E. B. Du Bois's scholarly acumen, Billy Eckstine's modernist cool, Huey Newton's
politicized eroticism, Cecil Taylor's improvisational instincts,
and Tea Cake's mysticism—in other words, a cat who *had* to be
conjured out of the wellspring of black masculine genius, both
real and imagined. The novelist Martha Southgate, for instance,
notes how "Brooks's intelligence and eagerness have . . . taken
Hawk beyond what his creator imagined for him."[6] In an interview with the journalist and author Jill Nelson, Brooks says of
his character, "Hawk lives somewhere, for me, between fiction
and reality. That is to say that Robert Parker imagined this black
man, this character," but "I don't imagine black people, . . . I happen to be one, and I have studied and lived and loved them all my
life."[7] Brooks's comments highlight how the sliver of agency he
was given to shape the character had the potential to produce a
character who could be read as transformative, though illegible,
in relation to those black male characters who existed in mainstream television up to that point. Not surprisingly, Brooks's creative agency challenged the professional writers—many of them
white—who were charged with creating a spin-off of *Spenser for
Hire*, called *A Man Called Hawk*. Brooks had transformed Hawk
into a distinct intellectual property that the writers were neither
prepared nor inclined to create in the first place.

Brooks incredulously recalls being asked by producers who

Hawk really was—this some three years into the series *Spenser for Hire*. It was this real lack of imagination on the part of the producers and writers that gave Brooks the opportunity to "do something that allows me to go back home and be cool with the people I know."[8] Amidst his struggles with the writers, Brooks famously said that "if we get just one of these [episodes] on the air, it's too late. . . . All they have to do is show it one time."[9] Brooks's point was that if his vision for Hawk was ever seen by the public, even once, it would have an impact on how mainstream society might view black culture and black men in particular. And indeed, because he did get thirteen episodes of *A Man Called Hawk* on the air, I can now grapple with the constructs of black masculinity in mainstream popular culture.

In order to establish a narrative grounding for *A Man Called Hawk*, the writers were seemingly obsessed with providing a believable backstory for the character of Hawk. Set in Hawk's hometown of Washington, DC, the early episodes of the series all provide ample references to the character's past as a professional boxer, gifted child ("curiosity surrounded you like a landscape"), and special operations officer during the Vietnam War. The latter factor was used to create tension between Hawk and various law enforcement officers—notably Charles S. Dutton in the role of Hodges—who consistently are amazed at Hawk's connections to the intelligence community in Washington. There are echoes of Sam Greenlee's novel and later film, *The Spook Who Sat by the Door*, in Hawk's relationship with the intelligence community— trained by the government, but functioning independently on his own terms as the fall of the Soviet bloc looms in the 1980s.

The writers also felt the need to domesticate the character, not surprising given the historic construction of the "bad man" as a figure who thrived on independence and actively resisted control. As such the attempts to domesticate Hawk—conscious or not—can be read as attempts to limit the narrative agency of the character and by extension, the creative agency of the actor Avery Brooks. Ronald A. T. Judy's work on the construction of antebellum and postbellum black masculinity is useful here, as Judy argues that in contrast to the aforementioned "bad man" of postbellum folklore and popular culture, the so-called bad nigger of the antebellum period represented a more ominous and politicized figure. According to Judy, "For slaves, *bad nigger* indicated an individual who, in challenging the laws of slavery, refused to be a nigger thing. A bad nigger, then, is an oxymoron: rebellious property. In rebellion, the bad nigger exhibits an autonomous will, which a nigger as commodity-thing is not allowed to exhibit. . . . The bad nigger marks the limits of the law of allowance by transgressing it."[10] I'd like to suggest that in the distinction between the "bad man" and the "bad nigger" there also lies a distinction between the writers' intention for the character of Hawk and Brooks's intention for the character—"bad nigger" as metaphor, perhaps, for Brooks's own relationship with the writers.

The genius of Brooks's performance as Hawk is the collapse of meaningful distinctions (for Brooks and knowledgeable readers) between the "bad man" and the "bad nigger." As Judy writes, the "bad man possesses a knowledge of self. . . . This knowledge is of political significance, in that it is the basis for a type of morality, or self-government, which then forms the basis for community self-determination."[11] I cite the above passage to make the claim —implicit throughout my discussion of *A Man Called Hawk*— that the character of Hawk represented an embodied knowledge that exists beyond simple references to street smarts or in celebration of his ability to seamlessly navigate the challenges of urban terrain. More concretely, I am arguing that despite Hawk's thuggish exterior, the character is representative of a rather sophisticated intellectual sensibility that is motivated by the historical difficulties faced by black men desiring to remain politically and culturally relevant—legible—to the black communities that produced them while openly confronting their limited and limiting legibility outside those communities.

In that Hawk is a character whose very power is derived from the perception that he is marginal to everyday mainstream life, the writers were also charged to define Hawk's vocation, beyond the obvious Robin Hood / vigilante quality of his interactions with community members and law enforcement. Speaking directly to the issue of legibility that challenged the writers and producers of the series, virtually all thirteen episodes of the series feature a moment where characters publicly question Hawk's identity, often to witty acerbic retorts from Hawk. As a narrative device, the scenes allowed the writers to build upon Hawk's backstory and coalesce disparate identity traits for a figure who lacked depth of character in earlier incarnations. In an early episode, "A Time and Place," in which Hawk is mistakenly accused of murdering a police officer, the officer investigating the case delves into Hawk's past and notes his regular shuttle flights between Washington, DC, and Boston (where *Spenser for Hire* was set) and his legal possession of a gun, to which Hawk responds, "so I carry a big gun, fly on airplanes," dismissing the line of questioning as irrelevant to the flimsy charges he was being held on. In this instance, Hawk arouses suspicion because of his mobility —his cosmopolitanism, if you will. As a black man who travels regularly and carries a weapon, he must be engaged in nefarious and illicit criminal activity.

The exchange with the investigator, perfectly pitched to ongoing anxieties that Hawk exists beyond the law and thus beyond logic, is one of many such narrative exchanges calculated to force audiences to think beyond the standard tropes of the character, including the perception that since he is an enforcer/protector for hire, many of Hawk's activities are motivated by financial gain, as evidenced by his luxury car and expensive wardrobe. The episode "Poison" directly addresses the perception of Hawk's "for-hire" status, as the character investigates the drug overdose of an African diplomat's daughter. Attending a diplomatic gathering with a friend, Hawk is asked, "What do you do, Mr. Hawk?" to which he responds, "I don't." The comment was a dismissive response to a character whose initial query was intended to comment on the supposed oddness of Hawk's presence at a high-level diplomatic event, but also underscores the perception that Hawk's attendance at the event is predicated by his for-hire status, as a bodyguard, perhaps. Later in the episode, when the diplomat assures Hawk that should he investigate the death of the diplomat's daughter, he will be paid handsomely, Hawk responds, "Money is never a problem for me." In the episode "Life after Death," in which Hawk assists a young black girl portrayed by Tatiana Ali, Hawk rejects the girl's attempts to pay him for his services (she offered about thirty dollars), admitting, "I did this for someone I was too late to help. Sometimes we're asked to heal others and we end up healing ourselves." Hawk's responses are critically important to the core values of the character, because they undermine perceptions that exceptional black men are largely motivated by the financial gain attached to their labor as opposed to some sense of loyalty, the pleasure derived from such labor, or the duty associated with those who labor at the behest of those who often can't help themselves. Registering in a much lower frequency in Hawk's responses is the connection between his own humanity and the historical association of black laborers as commodities, especially when black laborers derive little, if any, of the financial benefits from their labor, as was the case during chattel slavery and the sharecropping era. Recalling the theorist Judy again, Hawk refuses to be a "nigger-thing."

Though audiences never see Hawk's place of residence, he is often shown in public settings that suggest his connection to a community. Frequently throughout the series Hawk visits Mr. Henry's, a local jazz club where Hawk enjoys performances, meets with a notable black civil rights attorney, and even composes a song with the jazz guitarist Jean-Paul Bourelly. Located in the Capitol Hill district, Mr. Henry's has its own significant cultural history in that it was the place where the musician Roberta Flack got her start as a professional performer, as did her longtime collaborator, the late Donny Hathaway. In line with its role as a pub, Mr. Henry's is another iteration of the black public sphere and highlights Hawk's fluidity among many publics. In various episodes of the series, notably "Never My Love" (episode 9) and "Beautiful Are the Stars" (episode 12), Hawk is directly engaged in work at the behest of community members, many of whom have known the character since his youth. In the episode "Choice of Chance," in which Hawk is drawn into the lives of a family left unprotected by a failed witness protection program, Hawk responds to the query "Who you supposed to be?" with the quip "I never 'spose, I am." The simple exchange is just a reminder of the integrity that Avery Brooks intended for the character, a character who was ethical and principled. Illuminating these investments, Brooks told *Essence Magazine*, "I grew up in the context of a Black community where ideas such as dignity and integrity and proper behavior still existed. I thought that this was the way the whole world was, and I will insist that, ultimately, that's the way it still is."[12]

The link between Hawk and the community is a character simply known as the Old Man. Portrayed by the late Moses Gunn, the Old Man serves as a mentor to Hawk as well as an interlocutor of sorts; virtually all of Hawk's interactions with the Old Man are cerebral in nature, with the duo playing chess and debating various philosophical tenets. The interactions between Hawk and the Old Man often take place in a study or personal library, filled with various African and African American artifacts. According to Brooks, the relationship between Hawk and the Old Man was intended to be read as part of Hawk's subconscious, though writers scoffed at the idea. "You can't talk about African people without talking about the spiritual dimension," Brooks told the journalist David Mills, adding, "And this place that Hawk went—because you never saw a building or anything —he was just in this place." Producers eventually created scenes where Hawk and the Old Man are seen in public venues like a bookstore and art museum, though Brooks protested, "That's not the idea, baby! . . . We're talking about mythology, contemporary mythology. Just like Superboy, the Lone Ranger, all of that see?"[13] Nevertheless, the Old Man clearly exists as an extension of Hawk's intellectual and spiritual identity—community members, for instance, usually can contact Hawk only through the Old Man, and Hawk frequently works on behalf of those who have long-established ties with the Old Man. In addition, the Old Man often informs Hawk of impending danger, providing counsel ("You are the hunter, not the hunted—the hawk, not the sparrow").[14] In one telling scene, Hawk is disturbed that the Old Man doesn't seem to know what is bothering him (as if part of his own subconscious had been separated from him), to which the Old Man responds, "You give me too much credit."[15]

Throughout the series Hawk's interactions with children humanize his character, highlighting his tenderness, compassion, and patience. Such is the case with the episode "The Divided Child," in which Hawk comes into the lives of a businessman and his family who are being targeted by South American militia. As the narrative unfolds, audiences are made privy to the fact that the businessman established communications links for a South American government during the midst of a brutal civil war. Before leaving the country, the man and his wife adopted a young boy whose parents had purportedly been killed in the civil war. Hawk is hired by the family, primarily to provide safe haven for the child. Hawk's use of Spanish and other gestures to communicate with the child creates yet another vantage point from which to read the complexity of Hawk. Accordingly, it is also in the context of Hawk's employment with the child's family that the character further establishes his level of commitment beyond the lucrative nature of his relationship with them. In a telling exchange with the boy's father, where he admits to Hawk that the boy was essentially taken without confirmed knowledge of his parents' demise, the father questions Hawk's continued interest. Hawk responds by elucidating on the transatlantic slave trade and the regular occurrence of children being separated from their parents. As suggested above, what often animated Brooks's performance as Hawk is his (and Hawk's) deep sense of history, coupled with improvisational sensibilities related to fluid performances of black masculinity.

One example of this fluidity is the deployment of the tropes of the "bad (black) man" and the "good (black) man"—tropes that often reduce black masculinity to mutually exclusive, unassailable, and ultimately false poles. As Bryant Keith Alexander writes in his book *Performing Black Masculinity: Race, Culture, and Queer Identity*, "the expectations and possibilities of being a Black man are conflated into a limited series of performative displays—you are and you are not—as if performative displays somehow transcend physical beings." As such Alexander complicates the performances by suggesting that they are "often embedded in a culturally linguistic transconfiguring move in which bad becomes good and good becomes bad." For Alexander, this means that on those occasions where his performance as "good black man"—mild-mannered and cerebral—renders him invisible, he "symbolically darken(s) [his] face" as an "acknowledgement of racial stereotypes and my use of those stereotypes as a means to an end": legibility. Alexander continues, "my conscious performance of 'Bad Man' becomes a display of an often unnoticed, socially invalidated, and collectively demonized form of intelligence in many black men—that is the ability to read a situation and respond." Alexander suggests that this particular skill set is the by-product of the black male body existing as a site "where there was an attempt to erase an original cultural inscription and replace it with another." Here we can think of the "good black man" as the end game of civil rights–era rehabilitations of the images of black men, but as Alexander emphatically states, "the body always remembers."[16]

Alexander's notion that the "body always remembers" is useful to bear in mind when we think about yet another way that Brooks's performance of Hawk articulates the embodied knowledge of the so-called thug: Brooks often brilliantly conveys myriad meanings at the level of gesture. Grunts, sighs, head nods, and stares become lexicons unto themselves in the context of Hawk's rather economical use of language, particularly in relation to peers and adversaries associated with his past intelligence activities. There's a brilliant exchange, for example, in the episode "Vendetta," where Hawk is reminiscing (with some suspicion) with a former adversary, portrayed by Delroy Lindo. In response to Lindo's character's admission that he is "getting old," Hawk says, "A lotta shooters don't live long enough to say that—you've been blessed," to which Lindo's character offers, "Uh, I was good." Hawk responds to this assertion with a simple "hmmm," which articulates not only a deep respect for his peer, but also the reality of the risk associated with their line of work, where the adage "Real bad boys move in silence" takes on a special relevance. What are those things that black masculinity can't articulate with words, that only the body can acknowledge?

Hawk's gestures take on more significance when considered

in the context of Brooks's stated view of the character as existing "deep down, way down in the culture. Big feet in the African continuum.... So I'm quoting the culture, in every single moment."[17] This idea that Hawk has a "foot deep in the culture" is perhaps best illuminated in the episodes "Beautiful Are the Stars," which references the Harlem Renaissance period of the 1920s, and "If Memory Serves," which examines West African Vodun religious practices. In the former episode, Hawk reaches out to a family of women, led by the veteran actress Frances Foster. With the help of the Old Man, Hawk helps the women save their home, a historic black landmark. The home was once owned by the poet and writer Georgia Douglas Johnson, who from her base in Washington, DC, facilitated a literary salon that was critical to the development of the New Negro Movement. As the literary scholar Gloria T. Hull writes of Johnson's literary salon, "In the years of its flourishing, many black writers, both established and fledgling, partook of the comfort and conversation of [Johnson's] bay windowed living room in northwest D.C."[18] According to Hull, among the figures who frequented the salon were Jean Toomer, Langston Hughes, Countee Cullen, Jessie Fauset, Wallace Thurman, James Weldon Johnson, Alain Locke, W. E. B. Du Bois, Bruce Nugent, A. Philip Randolph, and Alice Dunbar Nelson.

The episode was emblematic of Brooks's desire to illuminate the history of black Washington, DC, as well as aspects of the black literary tradition. Very early in the episode, Hawk presents the Old Man with a signed collection of Langston Hughes's poetry, which leads to a recitation of one of Hughes best-known poems, "A Negro Speaks of Rivers." At the end of the episode, Hawk re-creates Johnson's salon with a performance of her poem "The Heart of a Woman." The juxtaposing of Hughes with Johnson is not without meaning, as in the context of "If Memory Serves" the episode sheds some light on the difficulties faced by women artists, particularly in maintaining a proper artistic legacy and their intellectual property. As Hull suggests of Johnson, "despite her multi-genred prolificness—which approximates that of Langston Hughes—her female life and responsibilities precluded any possibility of Hughes's kind of literary entrepreneurship."[19]

Though efforts to present audiences with a deeper understanding of black culture could at times seem heavy-handed, as the literary scholar E. Ethelbert Miller suggested at the time, one would be hard pressed to think of another occasion when the work of a relatively obscure literary figure like Georgia Douglas Johnson would be featured in mainstream television fare.[20]

The stakes were decidedly more challenging when *A Man Called Hawk* tried to address Vodun culture in the episode "If Memory Serves," which featured the veteran stage actor Paul Butler (who was featured in *The Spook Who Sat by the Door*) as the owner of a bookstore called Time Portal Books. Butler's character, who immigrated from Haiti, served as a griot—a keeper of institutional history—for figures close to the deposed Duvalier family. The episode attempted to present an African American spin on global events—Jean-Claude Duvalier ("Baby Doc") was overthrown three years earlier in February 1986—as well as make more legible the value of Vodun culture, or so-called voodoo. Early in the episode, for example, Hawk and the Old Man share a moment in Time Portal Books, where they come across a copy of Howard Thurman's *Disciplines of the Spirit* as the Old Man comments that "not many are aware of him." One of the twenty-something books by Thurman, a philosopher, theologian, and the first black dean at Boston University's Marsh Chapel, *Disciplines of the Spirit* specifically deals with the five major dimensions of a spiritual life. The scene was an indication of Brooks's desire to elevate forms of Vodun to the same spiritual level as other forms of religious expression, including Christianity. It is beyond the scope of this work to discuss how effective the episode was in that regard, but I'd like to suggest that the metaphor of the "time portal" was so critical to the episode that it offers a useful vantage to think more broadly about *A Man Called Hawk*'s "footprint."

Where No (Black) Man Has Gone Before: Imagining Black Masculinity's Future

The notion of a time portal has long been associated with concepts of time travel, particularly in science fiction or speculative fiction. The latter term has become popular among African American literary critics and theorists trying to recover a history of black writers who have engaged in forms of writing that did not mirror the realism that has informed much of the African American literary tradition in the twentieth century. In recent years, the term "Afrofuturism" has been utilized to contextualize twentieth-century black expression that, according to Mark Dery, "treats African-American themes and addresses African-American concerns in the context of 20th-century technoculture —and, more generally, African-American signification that appropriates images of technology and a prosthetically enhanced future."[21] In the introduction to a special issue of the journal *Social Text* devoted to Afrofuturism, the issue editor, Alondra Nelson, suggests that Afrofuturistic texts "excavate and create original narratives of identity, technology, and the future and offer critiques of the promises of prevailing theories of technoculture."[22] Though urban realism grounded much of *A Man Called Hawk*, in Hawk's relationship with the Old Man—what Brooks earlier refers to as "contemporary mythology"—the series might be said to have engaged in nascent forms of Afrofuturism.

In the predigital era, *A Man Called Hawk*'s reference to Time Portal Books locates the African American literary tradition— black speculative fiction, more specifically—as the site for Afrofuturistic concerns. When *A Man Called Hawk* went off the air in the spring of 1989 after broadcasting thirteen episodes, there was little infrastructure in mainstream popular culture to support the Afrofuturism that the show hinted at, let alone a belief that there was an audience for such programming, as evidenced by the less than stellar ratings that *A Man Called Hawk* generated. The cultural terrain had seemingly changed when Brooks was cast as Starfleet commander Benjamin Sisko on the *Star Trek* spin-off *Deep Space Nine*, which debuted to much fanfare as a syndicated series in January 1993. Brooks's emergence as the commander of a space station was hailed as a groundbreaking moment in the history of the highly profitable *Star Trek* franchise, which at the time of *Deep Space Nine*'s initial episode included two television series and several feature films, all of which featured white male actors

—William Shatner and Patrick Stewart—as the faces of the franchise. As one commentator suggested at the time, "In the real world, the appointment of a Colin Powell to the nation's highest military post produces nary a groan. But in television, where no viewer must be alienated, handing over such a venerable franchise's leading role to a black actor seems revolutionary."[23]

Given the realism intended for the character of Hawk, *Deep Space Nine* on the surface seems an odd choice for Brooks, particularly in comparison to Shatner's kitschy, overwrought performance as James T. Kirk and Patrick Stewart's nuanced cosmopolitan interpretation of Jean-Luc Picard. There is also the issue of *Star Trek*'s famously fanatical fan base, which has been the subject of numerous parodies. Despite the at times cartoonish violence and stunted writing of *A Man Called Hawk,* the work of *Star Trek* seems "beneath" the classically trained Brooks, who at the time of *Deep Space Nine*'s debut also served as the artistic director of the National Black Arts Festival. Instead, what attracted Brooks to the role was the character's humanity as well as the symbolic impact of seeing an African American man in a leadership role. It's important "that this character has to defend the human species," Brooks told *USA Today* shortly before the series debut, and that there's a "chance for some children playing somewhere on the planet to see 400 years hence, that the man in charge is brown."[24]

The futuristic universe imagined by *Star Trek*'s creator, Gene Roddenberry, was premised on the conflicts and confrontations of intergalactic species. In that context, the issue of "race," at least as experienced in the United States in the mid-1960s, was largely an afterthought. Created during the height of the Cold War, the space race, and the civil rights movement, the original *Star Trek* (1966) paid little attention to the racial diversity of its cast, though Roddenberry privately waged battles with network executives over his desire to cast the black actress Nichelle Nichols as Lieutenant Uhura. *Deep Space Nine* was well into the planning stages when Roddenberry died in 1991, but true to Roddenberry's sensibilities and those of Richard Berman, who managed the franchise for Paramount Studios, *Deep Space Nine* attempted to downplay Benjamin Sisko's racial heritage in the context of the show, though Sisko's status as the "first black commander" was clearly part of the show's marketing package. In that Brooks represented a distinct archetype of black masculinity, as most visibly represented by the legibility of Hawk, *Deep Space Nine*'s producers sought to distance Sisko from Hawk and to a certain degree, distance Sisko from a legible black masculinity. For example, Brooks appears in the first two seasons of *Deep Space Nine* with short hair (rather than bald) and without his signature beard, in what was rumored to be a contractual obligation. According to Brooks, the show's "producers wanted an entirely different look," one that had the impact of softening Sisko's image, presenting a character with far more visible vulnerabilities.[25] Additionally, Sisko is a single parent, raising his teenage son alone after the death of his wife. Despite the producer's intentions, broadly considered, these developments had the effect of expanding the range of black masculinity as it existed on mainstream television in the early 1990s.

As such, I'd like to argue that the initial episode of *Deep Space Nine*, "The Emissary," actually marks Benjamin Sisko as a highly legible black man, by situating his existence in the context of trauma and mourning. The series opens three years earlier in Sisko's life with an attack on his previous ship, the USS *Saratoga*. In the midst of the attack, Sisko's wife, Jennifer, is killed. Sisko's histrionic and mournful response to not being able to save his wife or remove her dead body from the ship, which is being evacuated, establishes the character as the embodiment of trauma and mourning. More to the point, it is the reality of Sisko's inability to release himself from trauma's hold that frames the narrative of the initial episode, including Sisko's desire to give up his commission because of concerns for raising his son as a single parent —a reality that also marks his son as a legible black male in the context of widespread cultural and political anxieties about black children being raised in single-parent homes.[26] *Deep Space Nine* is premised on the end of a long war between a "race" known as the Cardassians and another known as the Bajorans, the latter of which was dominated by the former. With the end of the war,

Deep Space Nine is given to the Federation, the alliance to which all of the signature *Star Trek* vessels belong, for administration, while the planet Bajor awaits entrance into the Federation. The Bajorans are a deeply spiritual people, who seek guidance from a race of prophets. Sisko's appearance at the space station is read by Bajor's spiritual leaders as evidence that a long awaited "emissary" between the Bajorans and the prophets has arrived in the form of Sisko.

Time and context don't permit a full examination of the intricacies of the series. The initial episode provides the first occasion for the prophets to communicate with Sisko. It is the traumatic circumstances of Sisko's life that become the focal point of his first confrontation with the prophets, who exist beyond the physical plane, and immediately respond to the "corporeal" nature of Sisko's existence, lamenting that "corporeal" beings "annihilate" them. In an attempt to get the prophets to understand that he presents no danger to them, Sisko engages in a long discussion about human existence as the prophets use Sisko's own memories as metaphors to communicate back with him. The discussion leads to a full philosophical debate about time or, more specifically, human reliance on linear time as a means of ordering their lives. Sisko uses baseball, a sport that is currently of little interest to young African Americans, to get the prophets to better understand the function of linear time. And though Sisko stakes an intellectual claim that he exists in a linear context, the prophets find that spiritually, mentally, and emotionally, Sisko has never left the site of his defining trauma, his wife's death on the *Saratoga*. After Sisko grudgingly admits that he still is tethered to that particular moment, the prophets admonish, "it is not linear—you choose to exist here."

Given the earlier focus on the "corporeal" nature of Sisko's presence and the fact that he is clearly "raced" in a way that is quite legible to audiences, if not so clearly in the context of the show's narrative, it is difficult not to read the prophets' admonishment "it is not linear—you choose to exist here" as a broader commentary on contemporary race relations. Sisko's "raced" corporeal body is wedded to a historical moment of trauma and loss that can be easily interpreted as a critique of the inability of African Americans to distance themselves from the trauma of the transatlantic slave trade as well as the experience of chattel slavery in the United States and Jim Crow segregation. It is important to remember that "The Emissary" was produced in an era when black men such as Michael Jordan and Michael Jackson were global icons and black men such as the aforementioned Colin Powell and the late Ron Brown, the first African American to serve as secretary of commerce, were making political inroads. This was also an era when the United States was recovering from the violence that erupted in the aftermath of the acquittal of four police officers accused of police brutality against an African American man, the motorist Rodney King, in 1991. The violence was largely interpreted as the product of decades of anger and resentment built up among African Americans and other non-white ethnic groups over issues of police brutality and political disenfranchisement.

On the surface, Sisko's reluctance to "let go of the past" seems a commentary on many of the aforementioned political realities. Yet in the context of Sisko's eventual role as emissary between the Bajorans and the prophets, there is also an indication that Sisko's ongoing grappling with a past of trauma and loss may be exactly what the prophets value in him. Sisko's ability to remember a difficult past and use that knowledge to chart a future path for himself professionally and personally eventually prove useful to the Bajorans as they chart their own future in the Federation without forgetting the violence and trauma of Cardassian occupation and their spiritual groundings. As such, Sisko's "raced" corporeality references the long circulated ideal, perhaps best represented by the activism of the civil rights movement, that African Americans serve as moral guides to the nation because of their history of enslavement and disenfranchisement.

Throughout *Deep Space Nine*'s seven seasons, the writers and producers found few occasions to acknowledge Benjamin Sisko's African American heritage. Some of the more consistent efforts included the recurring character of Joseph Sisko, Benjamin Sisko's father, who appeared in six episodes between 1996 and 1998.

The elder Sisko, portrayed by the late actor Brock Peters, was a New Orleans–based restaurateur whose presence in the series allowed for a deeper exploration of the relationship between three generations of Sisko men. Joseph Sisko was prominently featured in the episode "Far beyond the Stars," which featured *Deep Space Nine*'s only direct engagement with race relations in the United States and the social and political conditions of African Americans. Originally broadcast in February 1998 (a likely commercial nod to Black History Month) and based on a story written by Marc Scott Zicree, "Far beyond the Stars" is set in the early 1950s in New York City. The episode revolves around a science fiction writer named Benny Russell who writes for a magazine called *Incredible Tales*, whose readership is unaware that Russell is African American. The magazine's staff also includes a woman writer, K. C. Hunter, whose identity as a woman is also disguised, based on the perception that the magazine's presumed white male audience would be unwilling to read stories written by a woman or an African American.

Benny Russell is in fact part of a series of visions that the prophets present to Benjamin Sisko in an effort to communicate with him, particularly when Sisko begins to doubt his role as emissary and his future as a Starfleet officer. During this particular episode, Sisko is transported back to the 1950s as Benny Russell. In a fit of frustration over limits placed on his creativity as a science fiction writer, Russell creates "Benjamin Sisko," an African American commander of a space station in the far-off future called "Deep Space Nine." In terms of black science fiction writers, Benny Russell anticipates the careers of Samuel Delany, Nalo Hopkinson, and the late Octavia Butler, and brings into greater focus some of the experimental fiction of early-twentieth-century writers such as W. E. B. Du Bois, whose short story "The Comet" was published in 1920, and George Schuyler, whose 1930 novel *Black No More* centers on a scientist who is capable of turning black people white.[27]

Russell specifically conceives of "Benjamin Sisko" after the publisher of *Incredible Tales* decides to run photos of the magazine's contributors without pictures of Russell and his female colleague. Empathizing with the plight of Russell and Hunter, a fellow male writer quips, "Oh yes, the world is not ready for a woman writer; imagine what would happen if it learned about a Negro with a typewriter." Russell, who by this point is bordering on anger, asks rhetorically, "What about W. E. B. Du Bois, Zora Neale Hurston, Langston Hughes, Ralph Ellison, Richard Wright—did you ever hear of *Native Son*?" to which the managing editor responds, "That's literature for liberals and intellectuals. The average reader is not gonna spend his hard-earned cash on stories written by Negroes." Russell's confrontation with the magazine's managing editor is shortly followed by an incident of police harassment, as two officers question him about an illustration of "Deep Space Nine" he is carrying, that serves as direct inspiration for "Benjamin Sisko."

In another example of the ongoing tension about legibility associated with Avery Brooks's characters, the police officers who question Benny Russell specifically focus on his style of dress: "Nice suit. Where'd you get it? . . . What are you, a janitor? Awfully well dressed for a janitor." The confrontation with the police highlights the "sartorial politics" of the era and the historical figure of the black dandy. In his book *Cutting a Figure: Fashioning Black Portraiture*, the art historian Richard J. Powell writes of the black dandy's emergence in the mid-nineteenth century, "In a society that sought comfort in clearly defined social roles and a spatially predictable landscape, the black dandy's audacious appearance on American streets upset the white majority's assumption of racial homogeneity and cultural superiority."[28] The black dandy was troubling, in part, because he could not be easily discerned, hence the police officers' suspicions that Benny Russell was up to something. Powell notes that the black dandy was interpreted as "carnal and irrational, yet also ruthless and corrupt," making the figure potentially more problematic than many of the other widely circulated stereotypes of black men. Indeed, as Powell further observes, the image of the black dandy emerged during the era when prominent African American spokesmen, Fredrick Douglass among them, "dressed in what would have been considered 'white gentleman's clothing'—formal suits, vests, dress suits, and cravats—and thus challenged audiences even before uttering a word."[29] Given these contexts, Russell's creation of "Benjamin Sisko" falls firmly in line with the black protest fiction of the era, perhaps best exemplified in the early 1950s by the work of Richard Wright.

Russell is enthusiastic about his first "Deep Space Nine" story, but his excitement is dampened by the responses of his girlfriend, who thinks he should simply take a job as a reporter at a black newspaper, and the managing editor of the science fiction magazine, who while admitting the story was "very good," rejects the notion of a "Negro" hero. More to the point, the managing editor asserts, "People won't accept it, it's not believable. . . . I'm a magazine editor, I'm not a crusader, I'm not here to change the world," later adding that such a story might cause a "race riot." Rather than accept rejection, Russell writes several more "Deep Space Nine" stories, attracting the ire of the managing editor. But with the support of his fellow writers, Russell is able to convince the managing editor to publish the story by reshaping the narrative as the "dream" of a young black boy. Amidst the excitement of getting the cover story of *Incredible Stories*, Russell again confronts the police officers from earlier in the episode. When Russell tries to intercede on behalf of a young friend, he is badly beaten by the officers.

Russell returns to the magazine offices several weeks later on the day that the new issue is supposed to arrive, only to find out that the issue has been pulped because the publisher thinks the writing doesn't "live up to [its] usual high standards." To add insult to injury, the managing editor also informs Russell that he has been fired. Enraged, Russell argues, "You can deny me, but you can't deny Ben Sisko exists. That future, that space station, all those people in *here*, in my mind, I created it. . . . You can pulp a story, but you can't destroy an idea. . . . That's ancient knowledge; you cannot destroy an idea. That's culture, I created it and it's real." Brooks' performance here has particular resonance in the context of black expressive culture and the creative and physical constraints associated with the history of enslaved Africans in the United States. This is a point that the late poet

Sekou Sundiata makes in his piece "Urban Music" where he suggests that enslaved Africans would "climb into their heads and be free."[30] The theorist Fred Moten makes a finer point about what he calls "freedom in constraint."[31] Comparing the Dutch painter Piet Mondrian's late and unfinished work *Victory Boogie Woogie* (1942–1944) with the example of Harriet Jacobs, author of *Incidents in the Life of a Slave Girl* (1861), Moten writes that *Victory Boogie Woogie* is the "unfinished accomplishment of a victory that finished accomplishment takes away. Mondrian's victory is Harriet Jacob's—it occurs in a cramped, capacious room, a crawl space defined by interdicted, impossible, but existent seeing and overhearing."[32] Moten's argument here, as applied to the case of Benny Russell, is that the real power of what Russell "created" —the future in which Deep Space Nine exists—comes from the physical and creative limits placed on him in the context of Jim Crow segregation. Lacking those constraints, Russell could never imagine "freedom," which is likely the larger point that the prophets hoped to impress upon an increasingly frustrated Benjamin Sisko.

With Benjamin Sisko and Hawk, Avery Brooks brought into existence two compelling black male characters who consistently undermined the most popular and well circulated stereotypes of black males. Brooks invested those performances with historical and cultural resonances that would have been virtually impossible had they not been presented in the very stereotypical disguises that Brooks sought to challenge. As Brooks admitted back in 1989, "People have written letters complaining that Hawk has negative images: the slick clothes, the guns. Unfortunately, many of us in this country are trapped in these superficial definitions of ourselves." Brooks added that he "made [Hawk] part of an African continuum. But when you really look at what the character says and what he does, he's not to justify himself. He's a hero."[33]

2

"My Passport Says Shawn"

Toward a Hip-Hop Cosmopolitanism

Like I would love to have a sister circle where we pray for
Jay-Z. Jay-Z being one of the most intelligent, one of the most
influential, one of the most powerful. And he's one of those
who has the capacity to come with it, and he doesn't share it.
And so what is it about him, [that] he lacks the courage to
actually step outside of his comfort zone and really come with
who he is as a man.
    Toni Blackman

You got rappers afraid to be themselves.
    Jay-Z, *Fade to Black* (2004)

Can a nigga be cosmopolitan? Such a question might have been
unthinkable two decades ago, even as hip-hop itself—the cultural phenomenon largely responsible for circulating the idea of
the "nigga" as a trope of contemporary transnational blackness
—was largely premised on the innovations and contributions of
a wide range of diasporic bodies. Manthia Diawara made such
an observation in his essay "Homeboy Cosmopolitan," in which
he constructs a cosmopolitanism for hip-hop that is an "expression of poor people's desire for the good life," noting that the
"search for the good life is not only in keeping with the nationalist struggle for citizenship and belonging, but also reveals the
need to go beyond such struggles and celebrate the redemption of the black individual through tradition."[1] As Ekow Eshun
writes more than a decade after Diawara's observation, "Success
in the music industry has allowed young black people to breach
the furthest territories of white exclusivity. As with Jack Johnson, . . . who enraged white America with his diamond rings and

expensive cars, their flaunting of wealth is intended as provocation against a society that has striven to confine the aspirations of black people."[2] And while I'd be remiss not to mention that the homeboy cosmopolitanism that Diawara constructs is rife with a nostalgia for the so-called glory days of hip-hop (and hip-hop scholarship, for that matter), I'd very much like to endorse his observations about contemporary hip-hop's unfettered pursuit of leisure, wealth, capital, and movement.

It is in this context that I'd like to posit my own notion of a hip-hop cosmopolitanism, marked in part by a symbolic homelessness from notions of mainstream American morality, political relevancy, and cultural gravitas. I am evoking a cosmopolitanism that finds resonance in the concept of the "Katrina generation," those black bodies deemed little more than "refugees" by corporate media, reinforcing the presumed inhumanity and *foreignness* of this population. In the early moments of the Hurricane Katrina disaster, the evoking of "refugees" also cast a pall of illegitimacy on those so-called refugees who viewed themselves as national subjects deserving of relief at a moment of national crisis *and* citizenship in whatever locale they chose—or were forced—to relocate to. In other words, media depictions of "refugees" cast aspersions on the desires of the "Katrina generation" to see themselves as cosmopolitan. Ifeoma Kiddoe Nwankwo suggests that such aspersions are historically related to the fear among whites of blacks who view themselves as cosmopolitan subjects. Writing about the Haitian Revolution, Nwankwo argues that "the denial of access for people of African descent to cosmopolitan subjectivity coexisted with a denial of access for that same population to both national subjectivity and human subjectivity, and, perhaps most significantly, . . . effectively determining the possible parameters of identity for people of African descent."[3]

Nwankwo's notion that the collapsing of cosmopolitan possibilities is related to efforts to limit the breadth and diversity of black identity is particularly compelling in an era when hip-hop identities are intensely wedded to racial truisms that are often legitimized by some of the most visible (and highly compensated) hip-hop artists, but are often out of sync with those who might otherwise reference their hip-hop identities within a broad range of civic, political, cultural, spiritual, economic, and intellectual activities. As Jayna Brown reminds us, "there is much at stake in suppressing the ways African American expressive practices and cultural and political forms are constituted out of the geo-histories of movement. To acknowledge black people in voluntary transit runs the risk of affirming black people as historical agents, rather than as a timeless people inextricably tied to the land and to a timeless past."[4] In this regard, a hip-hop cosmopolitanism is undergirded by desires for physical, social, and economic mobility, including, for my own purposes, a mobility from or even within the essential tropes—playa, pimp, hustler, thug, and nigga—that define contemporary mainstream hip-hop masculinities.

The possibilities that cosmopolitanism affords hip-hop at this moment can be summarized by Dereka Rushbrook, who argues that "As identity is constituted through consumption, these practices allow for the creation of multiple, shifting identities, of lifestyles that can be tried on, discarded and reformulated."[5] However problematic the idea that one can construct identities via consumption, especially for those preoccupied with more "authentic" experiences, in the world of mainstream hip-hop that desire for the "authentic" is even more palpable. Indeed, those who embrace the kinds of "multiple, shifting identities" that Rushbrook cites are easily marginalized and even queered in the discourses of hip-hop, as "authenticity" is often gendered and sexualized. Thus it is perhaps the defining irony of contemporary commercial hip-hop that as the culture itself becomes more cosmopolitan—a legitimate global culture—hip-hop artists remain wedded to concepts of realness or authenticity that are decidedly local.

In his book *Real Black: Adventures in Racial Sincerity*, John L. Jackson Jr. notes that "Hip-Hop's preoccupation with realness is predicated upon deep-seated doubts about what usually passes for *real*, skepticism toward social performances/presentations offered up as indexical links to realness."[6] Jackson's analysis partly explains the anxieties produced in response to the increasingly cosmopolitan nature of commercial hip-hop in the United States. Jasbir Kaur Puar goes a step further, observing the presumed links between cosmopolitanism, the pursuit of leisure travel and queerness. Citing data from Community Marketing Inc., a company involved in marketing gay and lesbian travel, Puar notes that in the gay tourism market, 89 percent of the travelers held a valid passport a decade ago—nearly triple the national average in the United States. As Puar adds, "Cosmopolitan queerness is thus indebted, in part, to its mobility. What signals as transgressive is not just the right to sexual expression but the right to mobility through that sexual expression."[7] It is in the spirit of these observations that I'd like to suggest that hip-hop cosmopolitanism represents a fertile location to challenge the larger society's desire to impose constraints on how hip-hop constituencies choose to embody themselves, as well as a site to challenge stridently parochial notions of masculine identity (and gender) in hip-hop, particularly those solely rooted in the local. Indeed, I'd like to argue that the constraints placed on hip-hop–infused identities are analogous to the historical difficulties experienced by those blacks desiring to be read as cosmopolitan—legitimate citizens of the world.

The title of the chapter refers to a highly publicized Hewlett Packard ad campaign that featured the hip-hop icon Jay-Z (Shawn Carter). With individual wealth rumored to exceed $300 million, ownership stake in a professional basketball team, a résumé that includes presidencies of a major recording label and clothing line, a groundbreaking recording and concert deal worth $150 million, and a reputation as one of the handful of legitimate arbiters of highbrow urban style, Jay-Z is the very embodiment of "homeboy cosmopolitanism." As Jay-Z once told the activist and writer Bakari Kitwana, "People don't say anything about all of these White people that own Fortune 500 companies [who] take private jets. . . . It seems like Black people ain't deserving of some of the same things."[8] Jay-Z's cognizance of the value of cosmopolitanism to his own masculine identity can be heard in the lyrics of "30 Something," where he disparages his younger peers with the quip, "You ain't got enough stamps in your passport to fuck with young H-O, international, show you young boys how to do this thing."[9] In his artistic memoir, *Decoded*, Jay-Z recalls his first trip abroad: "Up until that point my life could be mapped with a triangle: Brooklyn, Washington Heights, Trenton. So everything about the trip to London—going to Rockefeller Center to get my passport, packing for a month-long trip, preparing for a trans-Atlantic flight—was new to me. It was a surreal, disorienting experience."[10] Jay-Z's regular referencing of his working-class Brooklyn roots, though, is reflective of his ongoing concerns for the local. In this regard Jay-Z is akin to the characters of Blake and Placido in Martin Delany's nineteenth-century novel *Blake*. In her reading of the novel, Nwankwo notes that the two characters are "exceptional individuals (the race men) because they are both cosmopolitan and locally grounded." She further suggests that "cosmopolitanism and the ability to be a citizen of both the world and a specific place are at once valued and gendered," adding that it is not accidental that Delany's "protagonist and the most 'manly' figure in the novel, is also the most cosmopolitan character."[11]

As such, I'd like to argue that Jay-Z / Shawn Carter serves as an entry point to examine more concretely how black bodies (as constructed via the discourses of mainstream American hip-hop) travel through the world, but also how the world travels through those bodies. I am particularly concerned with the productive value of having the theoretical worlds of black feminist and queer theory—rendered as discursive interventions—travel through the body of a highly visible and influential masculine icon of hip-hop, as an alternative iteration of diaspora.[12] I am swayed here by the work of the political scientist Richard Iton, who argues for a decoupling of diaspora from notions of national citizenship and hardwired geography so that "we might conceive of diaspora as an alternative culture of location and identification to the state, which would encourage a de-emphasis on the circulation and primacy of national blackness and suggest different and dissident maps and geographies."[13] In other words, a diaspora that you could carry with you. For the purposes of this work, the geographical terrain is theoretical.

Trafficking in Monikers

Around 1977, the poet Audre Lorde began to introduce herself at poetry readings as a "black, lesbian, feminist, mother poet warrior." According to Alexis De Veaux in *Warrior Poet*, her biography of Lorde, her fellow poet June Jordan was disturbed, in particular, by Lorde's need to articulate her lesbian identity, because "she felt distanced from Lorde's complex definitions as more than black."[14] Lorde's choice of a complex identity rooted in her blackness is something she began to grapple with in her youth in relation to her Caribbean roots. De Veaux suggests that "Lorde was to become 'a living philosopher' whose social consciousness was articulated through constant intellectual shape-shifting as she came to view herself as representative of multiple oppressed communities—identities that were at once externally static and internally fluid" and perhaps even embodied in identities as seemingly disparate as "nigger" and "lesbian."[15]

Lorde's conceptualization of a complex black identity was fully articulated in her book *Zami: A New Spelling of My Name*. According to De Veaux, *Zami* "originated a new discursive space for more complex renderings of black women's lives. . . . With this reframed identity at its center . . . *Zami* posed Lorde's identity and sexuality as fluid aspects of her transnational blackness, rooted both in migration between 'there' and 'here' and in the 'there.'"[16] *Zami*, both as concept and as biomythography, was, as De Veaux asserts, a "response to an absence or negation of black lesbian narratives. It became a testament to her own life, to loving, to the women who'd nourished her essential ways."[17] At the center of *Zami* was the figure of Afrekete, who Lorde describes in the book's epilogue as the "mischievous linguist, trickster, best beloved, whom we must all become."[18]

Nearly twenty years after the publication of *Zami*, Jay-Z taped a performance eventually broadcast as part of MTV's *Unplugged* series. Sitting on a stool, wearing a Che Guevara t-shirt and jokingly referring to the session as "Jay-Z's poetry reading," Jay-Z begins his performance stating that "I go by a couple of names. . . . Sometimes they call me Jay-Z, sometimes they call me Jigga, sometimes they call me young hov' [Iceberg], tonight I'm 'H to the Izzo, V to the Izza' [sung by vocalist Jaguar Wright]." Here Jay-Z articulates what has been a time-tested practice in hip-hop: the multiple personas. But whereas most hip-hop artists simply adopt alternative personas, often referencing underground drug lords or fictional Mafia figures, Jay-Z created a complex "hip-hop" identity that speaks to concepts such as fluidity, mobility, and social capital. Christopher Holmes Smith suggests that among so-called hip-hop moguls, including Jay-Z, a "major aspect of the mogul's utopian sense of freedom is one of identity shifting, or at the least, identity layering." Smith adds that "while hip-hop moguls can never be said to deny their racial and ethnic heritage, they are encouraged to use the material aspects of gangster social formations . . . to expand the options for social performativity normally afforded blacks or Latinos."[19] Smith's point is reinforced by journalists who are often enamored by the ease with which hip-hop moguls negotiate their commercial personas and their real identities. As Lorraine Ali observed of Jay-Z, "he even raps in his own natural speaking voice—unlike almost any rapper you can think of. It's not that there's no distinction between the star and the man—it's that he navigates between them so gracefully."[20] This collapsing of stage(d) personas and "real" identities by some hip-hop figures plays into the desires of audiences concerned with notions of authenticity: "Are these cats for real?"

The theorist Ronald A. T. Judy defines authenticity in hip-hop as "adaptation to the force of commodification." Notions of "adaptability" and "fungibility" are economically expressed in hip-hop discourse via a term like "flow," which references not only a technical proficiency at reciting lyrics but also the global circulation of hip-hop culture. In a telling and at times bizarre profile of Jay-Z on an episode of *60 Minutes II* broadcast in November 2002, the interviewer, Bob Simon, says to the rapper, "Now people have told me that in the business, you've got the best flow. My problem is, I don't know what that means." Jay-Z responds, "Here's the melody [hums]. Me I'll rhyme like [making rhyming sounds]. So I'm in sync with the beat, like when the music's going [hums] I'm going [making rhyming sounds], with words though. See?" What Jay-Z has articulated to his somewhat befuddled interviewer is the concept of "flow" as a metaphor for adaptability.[21] Jay-Z's very career as a rapper is largely premised on his ability to adapt. The artist's earliest recorded tracks, "The Originators" (1990), with his mentor Jaz-O, and "Can I Get Open" (1993) which he recorded with the group Original Flavor, are instructive. On the tracks, Jay-Z features a rapid-fire delivery originally associated with Big Daddy Kane (with whom Jay-Z served as a roadie in the early 1990s) and later refined by acts like Leaders of the New School (featuring a young Busta Rhymes) and Das EFX. By the time Original Flavor released "Can I Get Open," the rapid-fire style was passé as hip-hop fell under the sway of West Coast G-funk. When Jay-Z reemerges in 1996 with *Reasonable Doubt*, his delivery is more subdued —some have called it lazy—but more in sync with the flow of artists like Nas and the Notorious B.I.G., who were at the forefront of the national resurgence of the New York City rap scene in the mid-1990s. As the critic Kelefa Sanneh describes it, Jay-Z's "words pour out so effortlessly that rhyme and rhythm seem almost like an afterthought."[22] Jay-Z alludes to his switch-over on the track "My 1st Song" on his recording *The Black Album*, by mimicking his rapid-fire delivery from "Can I Get Open" and "The Originators."

In the Jay-Z oeuvre, songs like "Can't Knock the Hustle," "Rap Game / Crack Game," "Hard Knock Life," "Dope Man," "Heart of the City (Ain't No Love)," and "All around the World" are legendary examples of the relationship between rhetorical and social flow. A great example of Jay-Z's flow is found in the remix to his popular hit "Girls, Girls, Girls." With the lyric "but for now I get Around / like the late Makiavelli or Perelli twenty inches / or Caine and O-dog stick up tape from menace," Jay-Z metaphorically captures his fluidity by first linking his flow to "I Get Around," a popular song by the late Tupac Shakur (who changed his name to Makiavelli toward the end of his life) that celebrated Tupac's social capital as a sexual icon in hip-hop. Second, Jay-Z links his flow to the literal rotation of a brand of automobile tires held in high regard among ghetto taste makers at the time of the recording. Finally, Jay-Z's flow references a fictional videotape that circulated in the Hughes brothers' groundbreaking ghetto-centric film *Menace II Society*. The film begins with the characters Caine and O-Dog's involvement in a shooting of a Korean store owner. After shooting the store owner, O-Dog took the videotape that captured the shooting. Throughout the film, O-Dog shows the video to others as a way to validate his supposed hard-core reputation. Thus Caine and O-Dog's social capital is directly linked to the circulation of the videotape—it was indeed their calling card. By linking his own social capital to the most celebrated icon in hip-hop, a material possession that conveys a sense of ghetto chic, and what has become a seminal cinematic example of how to build social capital in ghettocentric publics (both real and imagined), Jay-Z offers a compelling example of how "flow" functions in the context of hip-hop culture.

In addition to the identities that Jay-Z articulates at the opening of his *Unplugged* performance, he has also been known by his birth name, Shawn Carter, and S. Carter. Each moniker that Jay-Z references serves distinct purposes related to his ability to exhibit social capital and remain fluid in the various publics in which he has influence, be it the upper echelons of the recording industry, the mainstream pop charts, Madison Avenue taste makers, or of course the "hood." For example, Jigga relates to his identity as the "ghetto everyman." "Hova"—as in Jehovah, the "savior" of hip-hop—represents a moniker that has value to hard-core hip-hop fans who desire the most "authentic" product, the hard-core ghetto thug. "S. Carter" initially represented Jay-Z's song publishing identity, the name that shows up in the songwriting credits of his recordings and those for whom he ghost writes. Given the history of black musicians—early blues musicians and hip-hop artists in particular—who sold off their potential publishing royalties for paltry advances, "S. Carter" is evidence of Jay-Z's savvy in the recording industry. "S. Carter" also adorned his signature athletic shoe line (in partnership with Reebok), which was one of the best-selling signature shoe lines not named for a professional athlete.[23] Of course, the moniker

Jay-Z is the quintessential hip-hop commodity that is at the root of the rapper's social fluidity. In addition, there are Roc-A-Fella and Rocawear, the urban entertainment and clothing companies that Jay-Z founded with Kareem "Biggs" Burke and Damon Dash. The names of the companies are an obvious play on the Rockefeller family wealth and New York state's Rockefeller drug laws. What these examples make clear is the extent to which Jay-Z's various monikers represent distinct *brands*.

Much of Jay-Z's music is rooted in his own "biomythography": the world of "Shawn Carter the hustler," the drug dealer from Brooklyn's Marcy Projects. It is "Shawn Carter" who embodies the rapper's hustling instincts ("More than a hustler, I'm the definition of it. . . . I'm a hustler's hope, I'm not his pipedreams"), instincts that have helped translate his street wit into a rap career of some distinction.[24] In the guise of the hustler, Shawn Carter embodies the improvisational aspects of both his persona and his vocation. In this regard it should not be surprising that Jay-Z urged journalists and others to refer to him only as "Shawn Carter" when he made the transition from best-selling artist to the new "hustle" as president of the Island Def Jam recording label. According to his "biomythography," Jay-Z's initial investment in Roc-A-Fella came from his profits from the crack cocaine trade. Jay-Z's past exploits embody what Houston Baker Jr. identifies as that "subcultural region in which a dominant white culture's representations are squeezed to zero volume," hence mainstream culture's voyeuristic interests in genres of rap music easily given to visual representations.[25] This is a history that Jay-Z shares with many rappers; what has made Jay-Z significant is that he has, as successfully as any of his contemporaries, mainstreamed his "thug-nigga" persona over an extended period of time without losing social capital in the "ghetto-hoods" that helped produce him and continue to inform his musical narratives.

Jay-Z's social capital among ghetto denizens (including those who are socially constructed as such) is best articulated by the fact that he is one of the most bootlegged artists in rap music but has also consistently topped the pop charts for his opening-week sales. Whereas bootlegging represents the outright theft of his music, given its location in the "hood" it is also evidence of his viability as an authentic "thug-nigga." His first-week sales figures —the more traditional and legal consumption of his music—are emblematic of his popularity as a mainstream pop artist. The best example of such popularity was the first-week sales of his recording *The Blueprint*, which sold nearly 500,000 copies and was released on September 11, 2001. In the midst of one of the largest domestic crises in US history, 493,000 people bought copies of Jay-Z's CD during the week of the attack.[26]

I'd like to suggest that Jay-Z embraces a "post-nigga" identity that coyly destabilizes constructions of the essential "nigga" that remains at the root of hip-hop's circulation across the globe. I hesitate, though, to read Jay-Z's efforts in the "queer" context in which Lorde articulated the notion of *Zami*, however enticing the possibility of such a read. Instead, I find Fred Moten's conceptualizations of queerness and discontinuity useful. As Moten writes, "Perhaps political upheaval is in the nonlocatability of discontinuity. Art tries to fictionalize and/or redeploy such location among other things. . . . What one begins to consider, as a function of the nonlocalizable nature or status of discontinuity, is a special universalization of discontinuity, where discontinuity could be figured as ubiquitous minority, omnipresent queerness."[27] Thus in the context of hip-hop, flow still retains its utility in the service of adaptability, but this notion of adaptability is less about fluidity and more about managing discontinuity, or in this particular case, managing Jay-Z's queerness (per Moten's use of the term).

And it is the marketplace that is the all-too-willing compatriot in Jay-Z's attempt to manage his monikers. For example, in May 2006 Hewlett Packard unveiled the first in a series of commercials featured in its ad campaign "The Computer Is Personal Again." The initial commercial in the campaign featured the Olympic snowboarding champion Shaun White. The second commercial, featuring Jay-Z, was initially broadcast during the National Basketball Association championships in June 2006. In the latter commercial a disembodied Jay-Z—only his torso, attired in a business suit, appears in the commercial—states, "My whole life is on this thing," referring to his Hewlett Packard laptop computer. Produced by the San Francisco firm Goodby, Silverstein and Partners, the sixty-second television ad elaborates on the branding of Jay-Z as the artist discusses his many endeavors as then president of Island Def Jam, CEO of Rocawear ("New Rocawear campaign—shot it in Aspen. Think it's kinda cool"), co-owner of the NBA's New Jersey (Brooklyn) Nets ("New Frank Gehry plans for my team in Brooklyn"), and of course an internationally known recording artist embarking on a world tour ("trying to be a rock star and a role model"). The commercial also gives some inkling of Jay-Z's personal life via references to his investment portfolio ("I'm retired, right?"), vacation pictures, and his love of online chess ("Game over. I wonder if he knows"—the latter quip a veiled reference to any number of detractors).

The website for the ad campaign features a simulated desktop of Jay-Z's HP Pavilion dv8000t Entertainment Notebook.[28] Among the things that appear on Jay-Z's desktop is a folder simply titled "Nicknames," which includes many of the aforementioned monikers. The "personal" nature of the Hewlett Packard campaign—the idea that its notebooks hark back to the personal empowerment that the term "personal computer" originally suggested—only heightens the sense that Jay-Z closely manages and maintains his monikers. The full power of those monikers is evidenced throughout the "Computer Is Personal Again" commercial by the clear recognition of who Jay-Z is despite the fact that his face never appears in the commercial. Though admittedly some audiences might have recognized Jay-Z's voice, the point of the commercial was that Jay-Z and his monikers are synonymous with a highbrow brand of hip-hop culture that those very monikers have helped to circulate. The ad exemplifies a particular brand of commercial cosmopolitanism—"I'm not a 'businessman', I'm a *business*, man"—which Jay-Z has come to embody.[29] In this regard I am cognizant of Judith Halberstam's observation that "bodily flexibility has become both a commodity (in the case of cosmetic surgeries for example) and a form of commodification." Well taken is Halberstam's point that "promoting flexibility at the level of identity and personal may sound like . . . a queer program for social change. But it easily describes the advertising strategies like the Gap, who sell their products by casting their consumers as simultaneously all the same and all different."[30] And yet I remain committed to fully exploring the very gestures that Jay-Z makes toward a more progressive and even radical conceptualization of black masculine identity in hip-hop, even as his skill at manipulating and exploiting those very gestures in the name of branding is quite apparent.

"Take This Beat, I Don't Mind / Got Plenty Others . . ."

In the song "Moment of Clarity" from *The Black Album* (2003), Jay-Z asserts that "hustlers and boosters embrace me and the music I be makin' / I dumbed down for my audience to double my dollars. . . . if skills sold, truth be told, I'd probably be Talib Kweli / Truthfully I wanna rhyme like Common Sense / But I did Five Mil—I ain't been rhymin' like Common since." At the time of its release, the lyric was Jay-Z's most public acknowledgment that many of his core hip-hop identities were little more than constructions aimed at keeping his music relevant in an industry that by definition reduces black identity to the most simplistic terms. As Imani Perry observes in her book *Prophets of the Hood*, thug narrators are "especially vulnerable to being understood in terms of prescribed racial narratives, regardless of the more nuanced levels on which they communicate or aspire to communicate."[31] As the quality of music video production improved for hip-hop artists (a measure of how important the genre had become for the recording industry), music videos became valuable forums for artists to further complicate their commercial and personal identities. With regard to Jay-Z's career, I am particularly interested in the music videos for the songs "Girls, Girls, Girls" (2001) and " '03 Bonnie and Clyde" with Beyoncé Knowles (2002). The two music videos give the earliest indication of a budding hip-hop cosmopolitanism in Jay-Z's work, highlighting his flow (in the broadest sense), while undermining the essential character of the "nigga" that he naturally embodies in the context of the marketplace.

The original version of Jay-Z's "Girls, Girls, Girls," like the remix, is largely a celebration of Jay-Z's heterosexual masculine flow within what could only be described as a transnational femininity. The first verse of "Girls, Girls, Girls" begins with Jay-Z listing the kinds of women he dates: a Spanish chick, a black chick, a French chick, and a woman who, while referred to as an "Indian Squaw," is clearly East Indian. By linking these women to various ethnic food products like fried chicken, curry chicken, arroz con pollo (chicken and rice), and crepes, Jay-Z articulates a well circulated belief in hip-hop that women are little more than consumables. In the song's second verse a second group of women is identified—a young chick, a project chick, a model chick, and a stewardess chick, but instead of these women embodying Jay-Z's appetite, if you will, they are emblematic of the various publics in which his "product" resonates—the neophyte hip-hop fan, the hard-core ghetto, the fashion industry, and international hip-hop audiences. The rather problematic gender politics aside, the video serves as an indicator of Jay-Z's emerging cosmopolitan taste.

In the third verse Jay-Z highlights his relationships with a wider range of women, including a narcoleptic and a "weed-head chick." His reference to an "African chick with Eddie Murphy on her skull" reads as most problematic, however, as Jay-Z alludes to a particularly misogynist and homophobic rant from Eddie Murphy's concert film *Raw*.[32] Though the video for "Girls, Girls, Girls" seems to reinforce common perceptions of hip-hop's proclivity for sexist and misogynistic sensibilities, the video's narrative ultimately unravels as little more than a literal video set—a stage. Thus Jay-Z performs the song's last chorus while walking off the set, in the process giving handshakes and nods to many of the women who appeared in the video. Tellingly, Jay-Z removes his shirt—his uniform, if you will—and walks off the set by himself. While I hesitate to give Jay-Z any credit for anything close to feminist vision in this context, I will suggest that the video creates a significant distance between the essential "nigga" who embodies his music (including the notion that he is promiscuous) and "Shawn Carter."[33] The video's closing frame, which focuses on a sign that says "Girls, Girls, Girls—Closed Set," leaves open the possibility that Jay-Z is nothing more than a constructed persona; this gesture is a radical move in a commercial subculture largely premised on highly contrived essentialist notions of black masculinity.[34]

"'03 Bonnie and Clyde" was released in the fall of 2002, amid rumors that romantically linked Jay-Z and Destiny Child's lead singer Beyoncé Knowles. Knowles's performance on the song and appearance in the video were the first public acknowledgment that the pair had a relationship, professional or otherwise. "'03 Bonnie and Clyde" is essentially a remake of Tupac Shakur's "Me and My Girlfriend," which was an ode, not to a woman, but to Tupac's gun. The title of the Jay-Z and Knowles remake highlights their status as "outlaws," though in the context of the lyric that asserted that they were the "new Bobby and Whitney"—a reference to the scandal-filled marriage between Bobby Brown and the late Whitney Houston—their presumed outlaw status may simply be the product of what might be perceived as an unusual union, between a former drug dealer and a mainstream pop princess. When Brown married Houston in 1992, she was at the height of her popularity and very much viewed as the reigning African American princess, a status that seemed to be threatened by a renowned "bad boy" like Brown, whose proclivity for dreadful personal choices is legendary. Such a perception was easily applied to the relationship between Jay-Z and Knowles, given his constructed commercial personas and Knowles's reputation as the leading black pop princess of this generation. It is also important to remember that there were long-standing rumors suggesting that Houston was a lesbian; thus some viewed her marriage to Brown in 1992 as little more than a marriage of convenience aimed at protecting her value as a commercial artist. In this regard, Jay-Z and Beyoncé's invocation of "Bobby and Whitney" takes on a different meaning, one that I suggest is less about constructing a sexual façade than evoking sexual fluidity —role shifting—in the contexts of their personal and professional relationships.

The narrative for the "'03 Bonnie and Clyde" music video is premised on the couple trying to escape law enforcement, led by an officer portrayed by the actor Lance Reddick, most widely known in his role as Lieutenant Cedric Daniels in the critically acclaimed HBO series *The Wire*. The series, set in West Baltimore, often presented "queered" visions of urban blackness that consistently challenged essentialized notions of black sexuality and black masculinity. I use the term "queer" here deliberately, referencing not just sexuality but also modes of blackness that are often seen as out of sync and at odds with acceptable notions of who black people are and what black culture is supposed to be. Shanté Paradigm Smalls's distinctions about what marks a body as "queer" are useful here:

> There are bodies marked, that is to say, interpolated as queer (i.e., varying from the normative white standard), the bodies that nominate themselves as queer (homosexual, pervert, invert, gender queer, transgender, bisexual, polyamorous, heteroflexible, metrosexual, odd, pierced, tattooed), and the bodies that repossess or queer—disrupt—their own images.[35]

In his role on *The Wire* Reddick supervises "queer" bodies, such as Shakima Greggs, an out lesbian detective, and several officers who are referred to as "natural police"—queered because they possess critical intellects amidst legions of career-minded bureaucrats. Reddick's character also polices "queer" bodies such as Omar (Michael K. Williams), mainstream television's first recurring "homo-thug" character. In other words, I'd like to suggest that Reddick's appearance at the beginning of the "'03 Bonnie and Clyde" video is an indication of the "queerness" to come.[36]

"'03 Bonnie and Clyde" was produced by Kanye West, who along with Just Blaze (Justin Smith) was the primary producer of Jay-Z's recording *The Blueprint* and its follow-up *The Blueprint 2*.

The two producers are well known for mining obscure soul recordings from the 1960s and 1970s and changing the pitch of the voices they sample from those records. This technique has given Jay-Z's music a distinct soulfulness, particularly on tracks like the West-produced "Izzo (H.O.V.A.)," which samples the Jackson Five's "I Want You Back," or "Never Change," which samples David Ruffin's "Common Man." According to one critic, West's production style creates a context where "men sound like women and women sound like chipmunks."[37] This style of production presents yet another vantage point from which to interpret the queering of Jay-Z's music. West suggests as much when he recalls his first production efforts with Jay-Z on the track "This Can't Be Life" (2000): "Man, I really wanted more like of the simple type Jay-Z, I ain't want like the, the more introspective, complicated rhyme."[38] The point here is that Jay-Z was working in a narrative framework that could be perceived as queer in the context of traditional hip-hop narratives and his earlier body of work.

The "queerness" of Jay-Z and Knowles's relationship is also conveyed musically, notably in the bridge to "'03 Bonnie and Clyde," where Knowles sings a hook appropriated from Prince's 1987 recording "If I Was Your Girlfriend." The song was originally recorded by Prince as a side project for an artist named Camille (Prince's vocals sped up to sound like a "female" voice). Though the Camille project was scrapped, "If I Was Your Girlfriend," with the cross-gendered vocals intact, was included on Prince's career-defining recording *Sign o' the Times*. The literary critic C. Liegh McInnis Jr. writes that the song "builds on this notion of finding happiness and inner peace by breaking the walls of prescribed normality that regulate our romantic relationships, which are the building blocks for society."[39] Prince deliberately heightens the sexual ambiguity of "Camille" with lyrics like "if I was your girlfriend? / Would you remember to tell me all of the things you forgot when I was your man?" Thus when Prince (credited as Camille in the liner notes) sang "If I Was Your Girlfriend," the song could alternately be read as a woman addressing a woman, a woman addressing a man, or even the possibility, since Prince is in fact a man, of a man addressing another man.[40] Though Knowles is clearly a woman who is addressing Jay-Z, her invocation of Prince through "If I Was Your Girlfriend" suggests a sexual fluidity between them that can't be easily articulated in the context of a music genre easily given to homophobic posturing at the time. The video's decidedly "queer" references heighten the sense of flow associated with Jay-Z, as such references earn him a hearing in yet another disparate public. Not surprisingly, in the context of the video's main narrative, Jay-Z and Knowles are able to escape the police by switching identities with two Mexican men.[41]

Of particular interest to me here is the importing of Prince into the texts of a mainstream hip-hop artist. For example, there is a subtle reference to Prince on the track "My 1st Song," where Jay-Z suggests that his so-called retirement was his "second major break-up / my first was with a pay truck and a hooptie, a cook pot and the game / This one's with the stu, with the stage, the fortune," only to quickly assert "naw, maybe not the fortune."[42] Jay-Z's cadence, delivery, and intent here directly mirror a line from Prince's ballad "Adore," where he claims to his lover that he would do anything for her, including burn up his clothes and "smash up my ride," only to quickly recant, "well, maybe not the ride." The complexity of Prince as an artist and icon over the course of his thirty-year career is beyond the scope of this project, but it is not terribly difficult to suggest that Prince's construction of his own masculine persona was often at odds with the masculinities that have historically circulated in hip-hop. In the mid-1980s, for example, the images of Run-DMC, LL Cool J, and Chuck D of Public Enemy seemed direct responses to the performances of popular black male R&B artists during that era, such as Prince, Michael Jackson, Rick James, and Luther Vandross, who often trafficked in androgyny or, in the case of Vandross, a decidedly "sentimental" performance of masculinity.[43] The tensions between these versions of black masculinity are perfectly captured by the rapper KRS-One's homophobic quip "Are there any straight singers in R&B?"[44] Given the intensification of hypermasculine performance in hip-hop since the mid-1980s,

Jay-Z's identification with the music of Prince, however clever and nuanced, strikes me as potentially undermining his "authenticity" among the genre's core constituencies.

Jay-Z's *Black Album* shares a title with a Prince recording from the late 1980s, which the latter initially shelved, in large part because of fears that the brooding introspection and darkness of the recording would alienate some of his fans. *The Black Album* highlights Prince's odd commercial choices after the mainstream pop success of the *Purple Rain* (1984) soundtrack —the Beatles-inspired *Around the World in a Day* (1985) being the best example—in which he seemed to want to distance himself from the very commercial success he had cultivated. Some tracks from *The Black Album* appear on *LoveSexy* (1988), notably the ballad "When 2 R in Love," and the album would eventually be released by Warner Brothers in its original form in 1994. The original *Black Album* was recorded at a moment when Prince was anticipating the changing terrain of black pop, including the burgeoning influence of "new jack swing" and hip-hop. According to McInnis, "*The Black Album* expresses a 'no holds barred' feeling toward the industry and the mainstream listeners. . . . The lyrics are driven by Prince's angst over being labeled a soft crossover who has been stripped of his funk card."[45] As such, it's not surprising that Prince's *Black Album* contains his first open criticism of rap music, via the track "Dead On It."[46] McInnis explains, "As songs go, 'Dead On It' is pretty unmemorable except for its public challenge and criticism of rap. The song is parody, spoof and challenge all at once."[47] In the late 1980s Prince would dissolve his band the Revolution, replacing it with the New Power Generation, which incidentally included two rappers. What I am suggesting is that, with Prince's own *Black Album* serving as partial inspiration, Jay-Z's *Black Album* serves the function of allowing the artist to break ranks with the very commercial hip-hop aesthetics that he, in part, helped to define.

The Black Album accentuates a moment in Jay-Z's career when an openness toward—dare I say, a willingness to be penetrated by—influences not in sync with mainstream hip-hop became more pronounced. His subsequent use of Indian Bhangra music on the track "Beware the Boys," his signing of the British-born rapper Lady Sovereign to the Island Def Jam label, and his comical cameo on the remix of the late British musician Amy Winehouse's "Rehab" are all examples of Jay-Z's interests in not simply traveling the world, but also allowing the world to travel through him. Jay-Z recalls hearing "Mundian To Bach Ke" by Panjabi MC in a London club in early 2003, and immediately reaching out to the artist to arrange a remix of the song, admitting that when he first heard the song's "propulsive and familiar bassline" (drawn from the *Knight Rider* theme), he was unaware that the song featured the tumbi, a traditional South Asian instrument: "all I knew is that it was something totally fresh." Though Jay-Z intended the remix, "Beware the Boy," to be just a "party song," he eventually inserted an anti–Iraq War lyric ("We rebellious back home / screamin' leave Iraq alone / But all my soldiers in the field / I will wish you safe return) to counter widespread national approval of the Iraqi invasion. As Jay-Z writes in *Decoded*, "I'd been traveling all over the world and knew that there was a different perception [of the war] outside of the United States."[48]

In this period Jay-Z also exhibits a generosity that could easily be read as "weak" in traditional hip-hop circles. When Jay-Z released vocal-only versions of *The Black Album*, he openly courted alternative presentations and interpretations of his musical (commercial) identity. The best-known example of this was the controversial *Grey Album*, by Danger Mouse (Brian Burton), which mashed Jay-Z's vocals from *The Black Album* with the Beatles' *White Album*. The reason Jay-Z would allow such use of his music —virtually all of the remixes of *The Black Album* were made without permission—is evident in the "Grey Video," which mashes his "Encore" with the Beatles' "Glass Onion" and "Savoy Truffle." The video, which features footage of the Beatles performing in *A Hard Day's Night* (1964), intersperses images of Jay-Z performing "Encore" and those of hip-hop fans encroaching on the lily-white audiences who were the core of Beatlemania. The video, directed by Laurent Faucherè and Antoine Tinguely (known as the Swiss directing team Ramon and Pedro), offers a digital complement to the cut-and-paste aesthetics that frame Danger Mouse's *Grey*

Album, but also makes an explicit claim that contemporary hip-hop—as embodied by Jay-Z—is the source of a similar mania among contemporary American youth. Additionally the video suggests that "blackness" was an always/already subtext to the so-called British invasion, given the inspiration that the Beatles took from African American blues and rock-and-roll artists and the private spheres in which American youth consumed black music, in contrast to the culturally sanctioned performances of "blackness" that were consumed via mainstream media, like *The Ed Sullivan Show*. Jay-Z's music, rendered in such a classic context, asserts the classic status of hip-hop, again as embodied by Jay-Z.

Similar liberties were taken with Jay-Z's work on Jean Grae's *Bootleg of the Bootleg EP*, where she uses beats from Jay-Z's "Breathe Easy" and "U Don't Know" (both from *The Blueprint*) and "Excuse Me Miss" (*The Blueprint 2*) to offer distinctly classed and gendered revisions of Jay-Z's narrative. As Smalls notes, "Grae, through her performances, resists the bondage of hetero-normativity." Grae, she adds, " 'shows the show' of performing Black heteronormativity, and exposing it as a show, a performative posture [that] allows one to engage with the critical possibilities of alternative or 'queered' formations to heteronormativity."[49] Grae's decision to signify on the music of Jay-Z might have simply been governed by the rapper's popularity, but perhaps also by her sense that Jay-Z might have gestured toward counter-heteronormativity in his own work.

As Danger Mouse's unauthorized use of the Beatles' *White Album* and Grae's *Bootleg of the Bootleg EP* suggest, both artists clearly understood the illicit dynamics associated with their work. Notably, it was EMI Records that issued a cease-and-desist order to Danger Mouse.[50] The former Beatle Paul McCartney gave tacit support of the project when he performed a mash of "Yesterday" with Jay-Z and Linkin Park during the Grammy Awards show in 2006. In contrast to EMI, Jay-Z admitted that "work like Danger's [Danger Mouse] is what I had in mind when I was in the studio doing *Black*. . . . I did that a capella version just to see what DJs would do with it."[51] Of course Jay-Z's comments about DJs begs the question as to whether or not his generosity extends to cultural theorists taking liberties with his commercially constructed personas.

Change Clothes and Go

However interesting the issues of fluidity and hybridity in the context of the core masculinities of commercial hip-hop culture, it is important to remember that "niggas" largely circulate in transnational commercial culture as flattened images, images that are a projection of historic fears of black masculinity in the United States, the desires of young white men (and others) to consume the supposed visceral pleasures and dangers associated with black masculinity, and the willingness of young black men (and others) to make those images available for consumption. Not surprisingly, it would be in the arena of fashion that "niggas" would arguably be most accessible. In this regard the desire of young hip-hop fans to consume the uniform of the "nigga" —as produced by companies like FUBU, Phat Farm, Sean John, or Rocawear—has helped hip-hop transition from subculture to mega-brand.[52] In other words, the wearing of the uniform of the "nigga" conveys an authenticity to the act of consuming said "nigga" that simply listening to *his* music would never convey.

Though there are examples of hip-hop fashion that are seemingly accoutrements to young black criminality—real and imagined—hip-hop has for some time laid claim to the world of haute couture. In the mid-1980s, the images of shell-top Adidas, velour running suits, gold chains, and Kangol caps, as displayed by the group Run-DMC, were synonymous with hip-hop culture, but as hip-hop moved into different commercial and discursive markets, hip-hop fashion has become more diverse. The examples of Tommy Hilfiger (purportedly the first major designer to take notice of hip-hop's potential to sell fashion) and the black designer Karl Kani are regularly cited as critical to a shift in hip-hop fashion where "trends were specifically created for hip-hop markets."[53] In her book *Troubling Vision: Performance, Visuality, and Blackness,* Nicole Fleetwood notes that "Central to the evolution of hip-hop fashion and its transformation into an industry is the fixity of the black male icon of hip-hop. Examining the significance of urban male fashion and the iconic, racialized, adorned male body of hip-hop's material and visual culture offers insight into the relationship among materiality, representation and consumption within black popular culture."[54]

Fleetwood also cautions, though, that contemporary hip-hop fashion is often fraught with ambivalence and anxiety. "Embedded in representation of the fashioned black male body of hip-hop is the interplay between a highly stylized and reproducible racial alterity, nationalism, and hypermasculinity," Fleetwood writes, adding that the "black male body signifies within and outside of black communities a form of coolness through racialized and masculine difference and diaphanous 'outlawness.' "[55] The result of these tensions is an ambivalence that, according to Fleetwood, is "central to the success of hip-hop fashion marketing campaigns."[56]

The ambivalences that Fleetwood references are easily correlated with some of the anxieties associated with contemporary hip-hop culture in general. Fleetwood suggests that these anxieties are in part related to the fears of artists and other representational figures in hip-hop of being marginalized as "ethnic" or some other identity construction that marks them as non-American at a moment when hip-hop's stake in Americana is so pronounced. Among elite cultural producers and consumers, anxieties related to belonging are further amplified given general societal apprehensions about citizenship in the aftermath of the September 11 attacks, the ratcheting up of anti-immigration discourse, and questions about the citizenship of the first black president, Barack Obama. This partly explains the move by hip-hop's elite fashion producers from so-called urban fashion to what could be described as upscale or even metrosexual in the case of male fashion. For elite hip-hop icons like Russell Simmons, Sean Combs, and Jay-Z, the shift from urban to upscale mirrors their own ascendance to the higher echelons of American celebrity culture.[57] This shift is initially evident in the work of Jay-Z in the music video for "Excuse Me Miss" (2002). The video's primary labor is to articulate the branding power of Jay-Z, but it also provides a transitory landscape on which to read the emotional and existential complexities that mainstream rap music largely and, I would suggest, deliberately obscures.

Tweaking the accepted uniform of the "nigga," Jay-Z and other artists signed to the Roc-A-Fella label appear in the video for "Excuse Me Miss" donning business suits. With Jay-Z uttering phrases like "this is for the grown and sexy" and "Can I get my grown man on?" throughout, the video anticipates the emergence of the hip-hop metrosexual as exemplified by artists like Kanye West, Andre 3000, Pharrell Williams, and later Drake and Kid Cudi. In the context of hip-hop, these men are not quite the "mirror men" that the journalist Mark Simpson talks about, but rather men whose consumption habits—particularly in the realm of fashion—are akin to those that mainstream American society generally assigns to women.[58] The attention to highbrow style throughout the video, directed by Little X, is an attempt to identify Jay-Z and the other members of the Roc-A-Fella clique as exceptional men, among the clichéd archetypes of black masculinity that have historically circulated in hip-hop culture. The video also links the Roc-A-Fella brand to an earlier, more "classic" moment in hip-hop, when it wasn't unusual to see hip-hop artists such as Dr. Jeckyll and Mr. Hyde, Whodini, or the Sugarhill Gang wearing dress suits. In the context of establishing Rocawear as the brand of exceptional men, Jay-Z is of course established as the most exceptional of exceptional men.

In his book *Constructing the Black Masculine: Identity and Ideality in African-American Men's Literature and Culture, 1775–1995,* the literary scholar Maurice Wallace discusses the importance of portraiture as related to the well-known black freemasons Prince Hall and Martin R. Delany. According to Wallace, the portraits were representative of an exceptional model of black masculinity, but with the introduction of a more economical and expedient method of reproducing such portraits, they "came to portray not an exceptional man, but a typical one, general and reproducible."[59] The reproduction of portraits of Hall and Delany largely served the interests of those desiring respectable images of black masculinity in the late nineteenth and early twentieth centuries. In comparison, the exceptionalism of a figure like Jay-Z, as re-produced by the video for "Excuse Me Miss," translates not only as typical and general, as was the case with Hall and Delany, but also and more importantly as infinitely consumable. This is not to suggest that the portraits of Hall and Delany were not com-modities in the traditional sense, but their consumption as com-modities was not the primary motivation for their availability in the marketplace. In other words, if Hall and Delany were men who were branded as exceptional, then Jay-Z's exceptionalism is branded as just that: a consumable brand.

The song and video for "Excuse Me Miss" are rife with product placements, with references to "S. Dots" (the S. Carter sneaker collection), Armadale (a Scottish-produced vodka that was briefly distributed in the United States by Roc-A-Fella), and Zino Platinum Crowns, upscale cigars targeted to hip-hop-generation consumers. What links these products was Jay-Z's relationship with Peter Arnell, the chief creative officer of the Arnell Group, which specializes in "product creation" and "brand invention," and Steve Stoute, a longtime music industry executive, who with Arnell formed PASS, an agency dedicated to linking high-end producers with hip-hop consumers. The S. Carter Collection is Arnell and Stoute's most visible success, with the Reebok prod-uct generating more than $100 million in sales. Jay-Z's profes-sional relationship with Stoute began when the latter encour-aged the artist to name-drop Motorola in one of his songs. As his fellow hip-hop artist Xzibit noted at the time, "You listen to a Jay-Z record and it's damn near a commercial. . . . He talks about every brand of alcohol and every kind of clothes. There's noth-ing wrong with that. But I'm not gonna be a fucking billboard for corporate America."[60] Underlying Xzibit's critique is also the implication that figures like Jay-Z and others are blindly ap-propriating the totems of mainstream culture at the expense of "authentic" hip-hop. In her book *Modern Blackness*, the cultural anthropologist Deborah Thomas cautions that "if we approached a more complex understanding of the politics of popular culture, we would, for example, reveal the emphasis on consumerism as something more than consciousness and a capitulation to Americanized commodification of desire."[61] Indeed, Jay-Z makes clear that what he traffics in is not simply about products; he tells Bakari Kitwana, "Hip-hop is culture. This is somebody's life and a way of thinking. This isn't like a place to go. . . . There's no culture attached to a raincoat. There's culture attached to hip-hop and it runs deeper that just [vacationing in] St. Barts."[62]

According to Arnell, "We create propriety intellectual capital that is fresh and desirable to the public." While Jay-Z's ability, per Xzibit, to hawk for Arnell and Stoute's clients is obvious here, I'd like to argue that "Excuse Me Miss" helps establish Jay-Z as "proprietary intellectual property." What is being bought and sold in Jay-Z as "proprietary intellectual property"? The branding of Jay-Z as an elite "product"? Yes, of course, but less pronounced is Jay-Z's attempt—a simple gesture, really—to broaden the contours of a commercially viable black masculinity. Notable about Jay-Z's gesture is that he has chosen to do so in the context of branding, thus making claims on a progressive notion of hip-hop masculinity at the level of consumption. Stoute, who founded the advertising agency Translation with financial support from Jay-Z, also partnered with the artist in the creation of "Jay-Z Blue."[63]

The image of hard-core hip-hop acts wearing Armani suits would not normally elicit much comment if the images were not buttressed by the musical narrative of "Excuse Me Miss," created by Jay-Z and his collaborator Pharrell Williams. "Excuse Me Miss" borrows from the chorus of Luther Vandross's song "Take You Out." With Vandross as a referent here, I'd like to suggest that Pharrell Williams's deliberate use of elements of "Take You Out" creates a narrative that destabilizes the accepted heteromasculine narrative of the song and video. Vandross never responded to queries about his sexuality, but it was widely believed among audiences and industry peers that he was gay. Vandross often appeared opposite women in his music videos, but his record company, perhaps sensing how palpable questions about his sexuality were becoming, blatantly attempted to "heterosexualize" Vandross's image for "Take You Out," the lead single from his 2001 recording *Luther Vandross*. Thus Vandross appeared in the video for "Take You Out" wearing Sean John clothing (a normative, youthful masculinity tailored just for Vandross), while pursuing the actress Garcelle Beauvais. The creation of a romantic narrative between Vandross and Beauvais in the "Take You Out" video and a subsequent video from the album was reminiscent of the relationship "staged" for the former New York City mayor Ed Koch and the former Miss America Bess Myerson, to quell rumors of Koch's homosexuality when he was an emerging national political figure in the mid-1970s. Rather than challenge beliefs about Vandross's sexuality, the video for "Take You Out" became a visual representation of the "down-low" narrative. The incidence of black men being on the "down low," or on the DL, has sensationalized existing anxieties in black communities about homosexuality and rising HIV rates among black populations, particularly women. This particular reading of the song "Take You Out" is reinforced via a club remix that sampled Snoop Dogg's "Lay Low"—a metaphor in and of itself for "laying in the cut"—providing yet another layer to a reading of Vandross's sexuality.

But I'd like to make more of a fine point here regarding notions of being on the "down low" by suggesting that in the context of hip-hop's hypermasculinity, notions of a homosexual body—any homosexual body—"laying in the cut" is an all-too-obvious reductive reading. Taking license with hip-hop's own genealogy with "the cut"—the creative tensions that produced the innovations of Grandmaster Flash and Grand Wizard Theodore, in the process transforming Kool Herc's sound system aesthetic into a legitimate art form—I'd like to read Pharrell Williams's use of "Take You Out" as evidence of the levels of complexity that almost always reside in the crevices of mainstream popular culture, that is, if one is willing to submit to the illegibility of it all. Again Fred Moten is useful here, as I take the liberty of remixing Moten's "Cecil Taylor" with my own "Jay-Z": "What is the sound of a certain misogynistically and hyper-heterosexually politicized black manhood . . . ? Here can we think [Jay-Z] as the site of an ambivalence regarding not only the complexities

of individual sexuality or the sexuality or procreativity of an aesthetics, but regarding the question concerning the revolutionary
potency or impotency of a highly, if impossibly, gendered and
heterosexualized black politics."[64]

Rather than read "Excuse Me Miss" as simply a celebration of
the "bling" that Jay-Z's celebrity and branding power affords, I'd
like to suggest that there is a performative labor associated with
bling, beyond its ability to provide access to the radio, video, and
clothing outlets that mainstream rappers find absolutely necessary for crossover success. In other words, I'd like to argue that
in line with bling's singular attribute, it literally blinds audiences
(and critical readers) to the complexities that "lay in the cut"
and in fact, this blindness is more than a residual effect of artists
trying to provide nuanced and progressive performances in the
full glare of mainstream popular culture, in that it is concretely
related to attempts by artists and critics to make a progressive
politics "illegible" in an era when anxieties about the legibility of
such politics are heightened.

Set in a club, "Excuse Me Miss" opens with Jay-Z and his
entourage being greeted by the gaze of virtually every woman
—all conveniently scantily clad—in the club. The club setting
establishes one of the defining clichés of rap music at the time
as expressed in the track "Do It Again (Put Your Hands Up)"
from Jay-Z's 1999 recording *Volume Three . . . The Life and Times
of S. Carter*. On the track Jay-Z and his label mate Beanie Sigel,
who also appears in the video for "Excuse Me Miss," make explicit references to the kinds of sexual favors they receive from
women at clubs, all ostensibly related to the celebrity and social capital that even second-rate rappers are thought to possess.
Additionally, an earlier collaboration between Jay-Z and Pharrell (The Neptunes), "I Just Want to Love," explicitly celebrated
Jay-Z's inability to commit to a single woman. In comparison to
those narratives, the video for "Excuse Me Miss" features Jay-Z
and others simply engaging in casual conversation with some of
the women in the club.

The critical action, though, in the "Excuse Me Miss" video
occurs in an elevator, where Jay-Z is rendered speechless (he

literally bites his lip) by an attractive woman—the embodiment of bling—who enters the elevator. As such I would also like to argue that there is some significance to the fact that Jay-Z's fantasy occurs in the proverbial closeted space—an elevator. Rather than use Jay-Z's heterosexual gaze to construct another cliché of male objectification of black female sexuality, the director, Little X, employs Jay-Z's gaze to fuel a romantic fantasy in which the rapper imagines that this woman is "the one," the love of his life. The scenes of Jay-Z romancing the woman are not particularly extraordinary, except when juxtaposed with some of the rapper's previous musings about women—"The only time you love them is when your dick's hard."[65] Here the director has established a broader context—beyond the bling—to catch a "glimpse of Shawn." Jay-Z's fantasy—in part simply a longing to just be "Shawn"—ends when the rapper utters the line, "I'm about to give you all the keys and the security codes, . . . but before I jump out the window, what's your name?" In the narrative of the video, Jay-Z wakes from his fantasy, still speechless, as he and the woman exit the elevator. Referencing Moten again, I'd like to argue that Jay-Z's query "What's your name?" is the invocation of the lack of language available to represent the politics and poetics of a cosmopolitan masculinity in contemporary rap music.[66]

Marlon Ross suggests that the "closet has become ground zero in the project of articulating an 'epistemology' of sexuality," adding that the closet has also become "a philosophical concept grounding both lesbian-gay history and queer theory by joining them at the hips as a legitimate academic discipline"[67] To this point, Maurice Wallace adds, "If what we imagine as the closeted body . . . may be racialized to the indifference of sexual speculations, the singularly gay character of the closet no longer holds."[68] I cite Ross and Wallace here to make the collateral point that the "closet" is also a site for the production of knowledge, particularly in consideration of Jay-Z as a "proprietary intellectual property." If the closet has become the most visible metaphor for those identities beyond the legibility of a vastly heteronormative, homophobic, and patriarchal society, I want to claim the elevator as yet another metaphor for closeted identities. But whereas the space of the closet remains largely static, the elevator is mobile (if only hierarchically); in other words, the elevator renders the spatial logic of the closet as cosmopolitan when one considers issues of mobility and the fact that bodies are often in flux—the literal comings and goings—in the space of an elevator.

The potential for reading Jay-Z through the parameters of the cosmopolitan closet was further buttressed by his interest in the comic book hero Superman. *Kingdom Come* (2006) was the aptly named "comeback" recording for Jay-Z after his so-called retirement following the release of *The Black Album* (2003). *Kingdom Come* is also the title of a graphic novel based on Superman, written by Mark Waid and illustrated by Alex Ross, in which the mythical comic figure returns from his own retirement. *Kingdom Come* details Superman's disillusionment with humanity after Magog, a rival superhero or "god" (as human characters in the novel refer to the class of "metahumans)," is acquitted in the blatant murder of the Joker. When Magog challenges Superman to a battle as a means of "passing the torch," Superman chooses to retire in exile to a computer-generated version of the Kansas farm he grew up on as Clark Kent (in part mourning the deaths of his parents and his life partner, Lois Lane), rather than giving in to the vigilante spirit that empowered figures like Magog among humans. Superman's retirement inspires many of his generation to do the same, creating a context where a new generation of largely metahuman vigilantes emerges. When the recklessness of Magog and his Justice Battalion leads to the death of a million innocent people in Kansas—a measure of the distance that had developed between humanity and the race of "gods"—Superman is forced out of retirement to exert a leadership that he had previously been unwilling to assume.

Jay-Z was reportedly introduced to *Kingdom Come* by a studio hand, and it became a useful metaphor to frame his own disillusionment with the recording industry. The rhetorical gauntlet that Magog throws down to Superman paralleled the challenges that Jay-Z faced as an artist as figures such as 50 Cent (Curtis Jackson) and Lil Wayne (Dwayne Carter) emerged as viable commercial, if not fully artistic, competitors. When Superman returns and tells a group of reporters, "In our absence a new breed of metahumans has arisen, . . . a vast phalanx of self-styled 'Heroes' unwilling to preserve life or defend the defenseless," it could have easily been Jay-Z or his longtime nemesis Nas (Nasir Jones) lamenting the lack of artistic integrity found in contemporary hip-hop.[69] Indeed, as part of his new leadership role in hip-hop (buttressed by references to President Carter), Jay-Z "squashed" his so-called beef with Nas, signing the artist to the Island Def Jam label, as the latter recorded one of his career-defining projects, *Hip-hop Is Dead*, on which the two men performed together on the track "Black Republican." The "unification" of Jay-Z and Nas—the two also appear on "Success" from Jay-Z's second post-retirement recording, *American Gangster* (2007)—mirrors the coming together of Superman and Bruce Wayne (Batman) in the context of *Kingdom Come*.

On *Kingdom Come*'s title track, Jay-Z makes explicit claims on the Superman legacy: "Up in the office you may know him as Clark / Just when you thought the whole world fell apart / I take off the blazer, loosen up the tie / *Step inside the booth*, Superman is alive" (my emphasis). Of particular interest here is Jay-Z's deployment of the space of the "booth." In the traditional narrative, Clark Kent usually changes into Superman in a phone booth. A closeted space in its own right, the phone booth is representative of a site of both transformation and communication, but in the era of cell phones, the phone booth is more of an antiquated trinket from a bygone era. Of course the "booth" is also a reference to the location in a recording studio where performers lay down or record their vocal tracks. Jay-Z's invitation to "step inside the booth" retains the phone booth's original metaphoric value as a site of transformation and communication, while transferring the function of the phone booth to the recording studio. In the context of *Kingdom Come,* the recording booth functions as a closeted, cosmopolitan space writ large for public consumption.

In the cases of "Excuse Me Miss" and "Kingdom Come," the closeted cosmopolitan space renders Jay-Z's embodied queerness palpable in the context of mainstream hypermasculine hip-hop, where he can be queered only in the most idiosyncratic ways. Such was the case when Jay-Z encountered his longtime business partner Damon Dash in an *elevator*, shortly after the two had dissolved their professional relationship and Jay-Z became the president of Island Def Jam. According to Dash, "[Jay] was coming from whatever he was doin' at Def Jam . . . and he had on a suit with shoes and a trench coat. And I had on my State Property [clothing line] and my hat to the side. *It was ill.* Our conversation was brief, wasn't no malice, but he was not the same person I had met. *I would never expect him to wear a trench coat and shoes*" (my emphasis).[70] In the context of Dash's description, simple apparel like a pair of shoes and a trench coat were enough evidence that somehow Jay-Z had changed. The implication here was that Jay-Z was no longer "real" in the sense that mainstream hip-hop traffics in the "real" as emblematic of the overwrought caricatures of black masculinity that have become one of hip-hop's most treasured commodities. Festering beneath Dash's somewhat benign comments was the fact that as part of Jay-Z's negotiations to take over Island Def Jam he accepted part ownership of the Roc-A-Fella label that he founded with Dash and Kareem "Biggs" Burke; the three men had sold the label to the Universal Music Group (Island Def Jam's parent company) only the year before. Dash was later divested of his interest in the Rocawear clothing line for more than $20 million; Jay-Z later sold the clothing line for more than $200 million, while retaining creative control. After the initial break Dash admitted some disappointment, acknowledging that "it's business . . . but we were supposed to be about more than business."[71] Dash's hurt was less masked when he appeared in a video for Cam'ron's "You Gotta Love It," where the rapper serves as a mouthpiece for Dash's grievances and attempts a public queering of Jay-Z at the level of footwear.

"How You Gonna Be the King of New York?": The Death of Jay-Z

"How You Gonna Be the King of New York?" was the implication of a simple query directed at Jay-Z by the former Roc-A-Fella artist Cam'ron. In an industry where rappers regularly challenge the status and stature of other rappers, Cam'ron's question is seemingly innocuous. More specifically, though, Cam'ron asked, "How the King of New York rocking sandals with jeans? Open-toe sandals with chancletas with jeans on. How's the King of New York rocking sandals with jeans and he 42-years-old?" and in the process enacted a very public queering of Jay-Z. The stimulus for Cam'ron's attack were grievances, outlined in the spoken introduction, specifically related to the split between Jay-Z and Damon Dash (who was responsible for signing Cam'ron to Roc-A-Fella and later named him a vice president of the label against Jay-Z's wishes) as Cam'ron accuses Jay-Z of stealing Roc-A-Fella, Kanye West (one of the label's best-selling artists), and Rocawear from Dash. The basic premise of Cam'ron's attack is that Jay-Z's choice of *footwear* (homophobia rendered on the level of the conceptual) was not reflective of someone who should lay claim to being the "King of New York"—the best rapper in New York—a title to which legendary rappers like Nas and the late Notorious B.I.G. have also laid claim. The quip about open-toe sandals was in reference to a picture of Jay-Z that appeared in a New York City daily. Cam'ron's query comes toward the end of a spoken introduction to "You Gotta Love It" and follows a more explicit queering of Jay-Z at the song's opening, where Cam'ron refers to Jay-Z as a "bitch nigga," a well circulated pejorative that feminizes Jay-Z on a more literal level.

With his later description of Rocawear as "cock-a-wear," Cam'ron's "You Gotta Love It" functions as little more than a homophobic rant directed at an artist who, because of his public heterosexual persona, can only be queered figuratively on the basis that he was not "keeping it real" enough.[72] In his work on authenticity in hip-hop, the rapper and cultural critic Tim'm West suggests that slogans like "keep it real" and others that index some notion of authenticity in hip-hop are related to the anxieties produced by the increased presence of women and non-black male rappers in mainstream contemporary hip-hop. "But is the real ever really 'real'?" West facetiously asks, noting that the "real must be perpetually managed and kept in check by those who want to secure hip-hop's connection to 'straight' black and Latino men who started hip-hop. But the straightness of the men in early hip-hop is questionable—though those vested with the authority to control hip-hop's image would prefer that none of us believe this."[73] While the term "questionable" suggests a familiarity with a generation of men with whom I believe we are really not all that familiar, West's point is well taken. One's identity and thus sexuality are always up for negotiation, but given the ongoing conflation of hip-hop (most pronounced in commercial rap music) and hypermasculinity, there are many who presume that the men who have become the public face of hip-hop's origins would have to be "straight." This line of thinking is buttressed by the rarely disturbed assumption that the foundational generation of hip-hoppers would of course be responsible for the most "authentic"—purest—forms of hip-hop.

The very questioning of the stability of hypermasculinity in hip-hop manifests an anxiety that demands the presence of a queer figure, in order to continually reconstitute the hypermasculine figure that is at the mythical center of hip-hop discourse. The sheer volume and quickness with which many make claims on hip-hop authenticity in the contemporary moment—southern rappers, feminists, queers, spoken-word artists, journalists, academics, so-called back-packers, to name a few—explain the vigor with which the hypermasculine/queer dichotomy is maintained in hip-hop. The point here is that in hip-hop discourse, "queer" is an open signifier that is deployed whenever and wherever (the pages of a mainstream tabloid) the myth of hypermasculinity in hip-hop is challenged. The rapper Beanie Sigel's comments in the film *Beef IV* are exemplary in this regard. Asked about figures like Kanye West and Pharrell Williams, artists with whom he has worked in the past, Sigel responds, "Them dudes is not cool; that's not cool to be in the hood. They whole image, who would wanna be that? You wearing [Louis] Vuitton driving shoes, who dresses like that?" and tauntingly encourages them to "come all the way out the closet homeboy."[74] Here, Sigel jettisons the metaphoric power of the closet by producing, in his mind at least, the bodies ensconced within them. Thus even Sigel's homophobia adheres to a "keep it real" mantra, as he questions the masculinity—manhood—of those who might be closeted (on the basis that they are closeted), while undermining their authenticity in the event they might come out.

For those who refuse to yield to the hypermasculine dictates of contemporary rap music, there is literally no place to exist in an industry that seemingly demands their silencing and removal. Tim'm West observes that as "hip-hop culture has been compelled to shift in order to give expression to women and non-blacks, . . . the homosexual becomes a figure indicating the proverbial death of hip-hop."[75] In the context of Cam'ron's rant, "The King of New York" with his open-toe sandals is evidence of the death of hip-hop. Cam'ron's comments are also clearly intended to facilitate the "social death" of Jay-Z, in the context of a culture in which literal death—particularly at the hands of gun violence—takes on mythical proportions. Michael Eric Dyson observes that many black youth "accept the bleak inevitability of death's imminent swoop—which, in truth, is a rejection of the arbitrariness we all face, since death to these youth is viewed as the condition, not the culmination, of their existence."[76] In the context of Dyson's observations, I'd like to suggest that Jay-Z was cognizant of the inevitability of his "social death" and thus used the video for the track "99 Problems" (purportedly his last at the time) as the vehicle in which he ultimately gains control of his legacy in hip-hop, by rendering his own social death.[77]

With Brooklyn, New York, as a partial backdrop, the black and white video for "99 Problems" features a cavalcade of disparate images of New York City and its residents—ski-masked kids, a group of bikers, a fraternity step team, frontally nude black male prisoners being hosed down, the actor Vincent Gallo, a gospel choir, pit bulls, a Hasidic Jew, a man in a coffin, the Def Jam founder Rick Rubin, and of course, Jay-Z, who is depicted walking through a record shop, performing in a dimly lit space, sitting in the living room, presumably, of the Marcy Project apartment where he once lived (a wedding picture of a Hispanic couple adorns the wall behind him), and being stopped by the cops in a car he is driving with Rubin. Jay-Z's movement throughout embodies the very notions of flow that his vocal delivery has been celebrated for. The critic Armond White writes that the video is a "strong, strangely beautiful fiction that subverts hip hop cliché."[78] In contrast to the totems of black urban life that have consistently circulated in rap music videos, the director, Mark Romanek, presents an urban landscape that is decidedly cosmopolitan. As White describes it, Romanek's "structure shifts from borough to borough, playground to jailhouse—a series of interlocking actions from a crazy-quilt travelogue of New York City"—that is all too comfortably navigated by Jay-Z. In the context of the song and video, it's not surprising that Jay-Z would thus embrace a cosmopolitan—"Afropolitan"—subjectivity ("half a mil for bail, 'cause I'm African").[79] Notably, Jay-Z's use of the term "African" is framed in the context of a politicized subjectivity, produced in response to the realities of the criminal justice system; Jay-Z's confrontation with a police officer earlier in the video is another example of this ("well my glove compartment is locked, so is the trunk in the back, so you gonna need a warrant for that"). Jay-Z's gestures here are concessions to a larger gesture. "In '99 Problems' images and words become a wrecking ball against the familiar edifice of ghetto-fabulous determinism," as White argues.[80] To which I would add that Jay-Z is the embodiment of that wrecking ball.[81]

In his book on the late rapper Tupac Shakur, Dyson takes note of the ways young black gang members meet with funeral directors to plan for their own funerals. Given the presumed inevitability of their deaths, a premium is placed on portraying their "dead bodies with a style which may defeat their being forgotten" and distinguishes "them from the next corpse."[82] Nevertheless, these young men can't realistically predict their own deaths; thus the planning of their own funeral, with all the excesses one might expect, grants them some agency. In contrast, as a highly successful commercial artist functioning in an industry in which "reality" is largely constructed for mass consumption, Jay-Z possesses an agency that working-class and impoverished black youth can only imagine; nevertheless, Jay-Z goes to great lengths to stylize his own murder in the video for "99 Problems." In the closing moments of the video, Jay-Z is depicted being shot multiple times by an unknown assailant—the gunshots themselves punctuate the very rhythm track that Jay-Z performs over, and thus highlight the stylized nature of the depiction. The shooting occurs in front of a gated church—Jay-Z perhaps attempting to repent on behalf of his vocation and his masculine privilege, hence the need to murder him at this point. This is clearly a performance, but one that consciously trades in some of the major discursive concerns of contemporary hip-hop, particularly the hip-hop elite.

For example, the rappers Christopher "Notorious B.I.G." Wallace (a mentor to Jay-Z) and Tupac Shakur were immortalized in the aftermath of their murders, to the extent that the two are often viewed as the pinnacle of the hip-hop elite. It is a commonly held belief among hip-hop purists that all that has gone wrong (hyper-commercialization, materialistic lyrics, etc.) with commercial hip-hop can be traced to the still unsolved murders of the two men. In fact, a major conceit of *The Black Album* was that Jay-Z had finally surpassed Wallace as the best rapper from New York ("I'm not a biter, I'm a writer for myself and others / I say a Big verse, I'm only bigging up my brother, bigging-up my borough / I'm big enough to do it, I'm that thorough").[83] In addition, at the time that Jay-Z recorded *The Black Album*, Curtis "50 Cent" Jackson had established himself as a best-selling artist, ultimately selling ten million copies of his debut recording, *Get Rich or Die Tryin'* (2003). A major factor in Jackson's success was his backstory, which included surviving an attempted murder: he was shot nine times. Thus the image of Jay-Z being shot multiple times in the video for "99 Problems" was clearly intended to make a claim on his legacy in relationship to Shakur, Wallace, and Jackson. But I'd like to suggest that Jay-Z is after more than simply establishing his legacy among hip-hop's elite. On his 1999 track "There's Been a Murder," Jay-Z details aspects of his creative process, with a particular emphasis on his hustling instincts. Creatively it was "Shawn Carter" who fueled the imagination of Jay-Z ("I gotta do Shawn, cause even when Jay-Z was lukewarm / I was getting' my loot on") and, as the rapper admits, he metaphorically murders his commercial persona to get his mind right, if you will ("back to Shawn Carter the hustler, Jay-Z is dead").

Much of the early press surrounding the release of Jay-Z's "retirement" disc suggested that *The Black Album* was an attempt to recapture the energy of his first recording, *Reasonable Doubt*, when the artist was "doing what came naturally."[84] Kanye West, who contributed production to *The Black Album*, told Elizabeth Méndez Berry that Jay-Z wanted to "take it back [to] before he was in the industry, to the drug game, to make it how *Reasonable Doubt* was."[85] Indeed, in response to his violent ending in the video for "99 Problems," Jay-Z told MTV's censors that the violence was symbolic of "the death of Jay-Z . . . and the rebirth of Shawn Carter."[86] But whereas many of these comments are framed as Jay-Z looking back, I am arguing that the grandiose way that Jay-Z presents his murder—with striking finality—is about the future of Shawn Carter, not his past. The symbolic death of Jay-Z allows for what the scholar Greg Dimitriadis calls a discursive rebirth. Writing about reactions to the death of Tupac Shakur, Dimitriadis explains that "when Tupac was shot and killed, . . . he was discursively reborn, his life and music becoming fodder for a range of myths from the mundane to the implausible, performed and reperformed in unpredictable ways."[87] With the "death" of Jay-Z in the video for "99 Problems," I am arguing, Jay-Z and Shawn Carter (used interchangeably according to how each resonates in distinct markets) are discursively reborn and thus open to forms of critical exegesis that progressively challenge the status quo in commercial hip-hop and black masculinity. In other words, it is the discursively rendered Jay-Z that can make hip-hop cosmopolitanism plausible.

"Watch the Throne?": A Postscript

Kingdom Come (2006), Jay-Z's first full-length post-retirement recording, represents the possibilities that critically resonate in his discursive rebirth. In a revealing profile of Jay-Z in the December

2006 edition of *GQ*, Mark Healy observes that with previous re-cordings, the artist often sequestered himself from the world, but as if he was cognizant of the myriad meanings that could be attached to his discursive body, Jay-Z chose a different strategy. According to Healy, "For *Kingdom Come*, [Jay-Z] hasn't kept the world at bay but rather exposed himself to it—burning through Europe, Africa and the Middle East."[88] Jay-Z's travels included a much-celebrated trip to the African continent on behalf of the United Nations and its efforts to address the fresh water crisis across the continent.[89] Though not the focus of Healy's profile —Jay-Z was named one of *GQ*'s "Men of the Year"—it illumi-nates that as Jay-Z travels the world, embodying the notion of a hip-hop cosmopolitanism, the "world" inevitably travels through him. One of the by-products of Jay-Z's evolved persona is what Samuel Delany calls a "discursive collision," where the "Jay-Z" that first emerged in the mid-1990s is always going to be at odds with the "Jay-Z" that is discursively reproduced in the context of a hip-hop cosmopolitanism. Thus the "signature hubris" that the journalist kris ex observes often undermines the figure that admits on *Kingdom Come*'s title track, "And there's much bigger issues in the world I know, but I first had to take care of the world *I know*."[90] I would further argue that these discursive collisions are often exploited by those unwilling or unable to grant hip-hop culture at large the gravitas it demands, particularly in the political realm.

In her acclaimed profile of Jay-Z, the journalist Elizabeth Mén-dez Berry describes him as a "confidence artist"—a con man—and it's a fair criticism, given the efficiency with which Jay-Z has trafficked in such disparate markets and publics.[91] Thus it's not surprising that a figure like the noted hip-hop critic and activ-ist Jeff Chang would take such a cynical view of *Kingdom Come*, as he did in the pages of the *Nation*. Commenting on the afore-mentioned *GQ* profile, Chang writes, "Jay-Z threw up a black power fist while dressed in a Club Monaco cardigan, a Purple Label button-down and his own Rocawear sweats," adding that Jay-Z had "repackaged hip-hop's rebellion into a symbol of the postmulticulturalist good life." Chang then juxtaposes this image of Jay-Z with that of founding hip-hop fathers like DJ Kool Herc, Grandmaster Flash, and Afrika Bambaataa and the "black radical ideologies" that inspired them in the late 1960s and 1970s.[92] And again, this is a valid critique of Jay-Z, but when such imagery is interpreted in a broader discursive context, the image of Jay-Z in *GQ* can be read as a critical revision of the often problematic masculinities that undergirded some of the radical and black nationalist politics of the 1960s. Chang's commentary on Jay-Z anticipates one of the most enduring critiques of him, namely, that Jay-Z's fixation with the accumulation of wealth sits uncomfortably with many, including those who have some amount of faith in his discursive possibilities.

The wealth that Jay-Z and figures like Russell Simmons and Sean Combs have amassed is in many ways unprecedented, particularly given their ages; all were under forty when they achieved their wealth. Their financial success has created anxieties among traditional black political leadership and various activist communities, particularly among those located on the political left. Given the ways that poverty and frugality have been romanticized, even fetishized, on the political left—particularly in relation to one's commitment to "struggle"—it's understandable that it is difficult to think of Jay-Z and his reported $400 million net worth in progressive political terms. Indeed, a Black Power fist or Che Guevara t-shirt is not a substitute for concrete political activity, but the wealth of individuals like Jay-Z and Simmons can be leveraged on behalf of their particular social and political passions in ways that conservative figures like the Koch brothers have done rather effectively. Even some so-called conscious rappers have admitted that the accumulation of wealth and the subsequent pursuit of the "good life" are not antithetical to the pursuit of social justice. For example, on his track "It's Your World (part 1 and 2)," the Chicago-based rapper Common asserts that "My generation never understood workin' for the man / And, of bein' broke I ain't a fan."[93] His fellow "political" rapper Talib Kweli takes the critique a step further, holding black political organizations accountable for their failure to consider the importance of finances: "You join an organization that know black history / But ask them how they plan to make money and it's a mystery."[94]

Many of these issues came to the forefront when Jay-Z and Kanye West collaborated on the project *Watch the Throne* (2011). Few artists in the prime of their careers have ever decided to come together in the ways that Jay-Z and West do on *Watch the Throne*, which begs the question, what was in it for each? For example, when Jay-Z and R. Kelly collaborated on the popular club hit "Fiesta," from the latter's *TP-2.com* (2000) and then followed up with two underwhelming studio albums, *Best of Both Worlds* (2002) and *Unfinished Business* (2004), the projects were viewed as little more than cynical money grabs. Indeed, when word of *Watch the Throne* began to surface—the project took over a year to complete—some fans and critics reacted with cynicism, despite that fact that Jay-Z and West often expressed real affection and respect for each other—the big brother and the petulant little brother—and have generally produced memorable tracks when they have collaborated, such as "Diamonds from Sierra Leone" (2005), "Never Let Me Down" (2003), "Run This Town" with Rihanna (2009), "Monster" with Rick Ross and Nicki Minaj (2010), and of course West's production on *The Dynasty Roc la Familia* (2000), *The Blueprint* (2001), *The Blueprint 2* (2002), and *The Black Album* (2003).

Such cynicism was likely the product of collective fears that Jay-Z and West's pairing would not only *not* produce great art, but would confirm their unwillingness—or, more troubling, their inability—to say anything of consequence at a moment when many desire mainstream pop artists to index their secular and spiritual concerns. Yet part of what possibly made *Watch the Throne* attractive for Carter and West is the fact that they were all too aware of their disconnect from the working-class worlds that produced them, and the unique and isolated positions that each holds at the pinnacle of his craft and celebrity, as well as the relative power, or lack of power, associated with those positions.

Their ambivalence is evidenced in the oh-so-casual way that the recording was rolled out, minus the usual shock and awe that one would expect from artists of their stature.

As such, *Watch the Throne* serves as a meditation on Black Power, not in the sense of the social movement that challenged America in the 1960s and beyond to live up to its radical democratic tenets, but rather in the will of so many generations of black folk to imagine the highest quality of life for themselves. In line with Diawara's earlier point about the desire to live "the good life," what has often made hip-hop matter to the working-class communities that produced it, even in the days of "party and bullshit," is its ability to be aspirational. This is a point that the branding expert Steve Stoute argues in his book *The Tanning of America: How Hip-Hop Created a Culture That Rewrote the Rules of the New Economy*, where he writes that the "force of aspiration" is the "power that turns nothing into something, that creates worlds and paves destinies, and changes the have-nots into the have-somes and occasionally have-it-alls."[95]

In a country marked by the richness of immigrant cultures, black Americans may represent some of the most aspirational of peoples—willing themselves off of plantations and into some semblance of a still unrealized full citizenship—long before Shawn Carter and Kanye West ever walked into a recording studio. Black aspiration is Black Power, dating to the time, per the late poet Sekou Sundiata, when some "slave" dreamed of a freedom that she would never fully experience.[96] Yet even this long tradition of aspirational power falls flat at a moment when there exists an unprecedented wealth gap between the poor and the so-called super-rich, and the United States is faced with a double-dip recession. To be sure, this is not the first recession that black America has borne the brunt of, yet it might be the first in which black artists were increasingly burdened with an expectation to speak to its palpable presence in the lives of their fans and supporters, in the absence of the kinds of social and political movements that informed the politicized art of previous generations of black artists. In the midst of a recession in the mid-1970s, when New York City was on the brink of defaulting on its loans and

President Gerald Ford threatened to veto any legislation aimed at bailing out the municipality, William DeVaughn wistfully sang about the "diamond in the back / sun-roof top / digging the scene with the gangster lean," on his aspirational classic "Be Thankful for What You Got."[97] The song was as much a cautionary tale about the trappings of materialism (as black flight was becoming a reality) as it was a reminder that the culture already embodied a sense of wealth, where a gangsta-lean—yet another precursor to ghetto fabulousness—was a hard-earned commodity, as valuable as the pimp car rolling down the avenue.

Hip-hop's genius move from the outset was to make the trinkets of everyday life the stuff of hyperconsumption—a story at least as old as Pig Feet Mary selling chitlins', hog maws, and of course pig feet out of a baby carriage in Harlem in the early twentieth century and later becoming a real estate tycoon, or the Fisk Jubilee Singers traveling around the globe providing European audiences with a taste of those good old Negro spirituals in the late nineteenth century, or Henry Box Brown re-creating his escape act for European audiences years before the Emancipation Proclamation.[98] Perhaps no commodity was as valuable to hip-hop as the conceit of the lyrical boast, itself intimately related to the traditions of black expressive culture, whether expressed by school kids playing the dozens, the dandy on Chicago's Stroll in the 1920s, or Nikki Giovanni's 1969 poem "Ego Tripping," a direct precursor to rap music.

When the late Notorious B.I.G. opined, "Fuck a dollar and a dream"—putting into context the way that hood-controlled numbers running had been appropriated by the state—he did so knowing that he was of a generation of young blacks who were part of a commercial culture that no longer simply had to dream.[99] There's no denying that rap music has changed over the years; the conceits that were once simply metaphors—yes, the dreams of Black Power—are now quantifiable assets. *Watch the Throne* is compelling because it allows working-class audiences to eavesdrop on what a particular segment of the black elite thinks. The trafficking in the toys of the hip-hop elite is a given—count the references to Maybachs, but also Basquiats—and the gratuitous flaunting of Jay-Z and West's possessions and status is downright offensive, particularly in the moment they were recorded in—but arguably significantly less so than a "political industrial complex" that funnels billions of dollars into a political process that only a minuscule percentage of the population (which controls a large majority of the nation's wealth) truly benefits from. Give hip-hop credit: it has built its wealth well beyond and despite the forces of the state. As the cultural theorist Vijay Prashad describes this latter point, hip-hop "recognizes that the state is repressive and not responsive. And it has a different understanding of the state than Civil Rights organizations that continue to operate under the assumption that we have a responsive state to whom we can make a plea."[100]

Carter, West, and a host of other hip-hop–generation black elites were not products of blue vein enclaves, summers at Oak Bluffs, Jack and Jill programs, and Boule meetings. This is a point that Bakari Kitwana makes in his essay "Zen and the Art of Transcending the Status Quo," where he notes, "Jay-Z is reshaping the idea of black bourgeois culture . . . [and] is making sexy the notion of elite class blacks who identify more with the black masses," adding that Carter is a "bridge between the black poor and black elite in a way that current activists in the tradition of Malcolm X can never realize, in a way that the current crop of black elected officials, the political descendents of Adam Clayton Powell, can never realize in today's political landscape."[101] Carter and West are two of the most accomplished trickster figures—shape-shifters—working in contemporary culture, and their seemingly thoughtless celebration of their wealth and status must also be read as potentially signifying on the very elite culture(s) that still deny them full access. The portraits of Jay-Z and West that accompany *Watch the Throne*'s digital booklet (in collaboration with Givenchy's Riccardo Tisci), reveal that the two men—West in particular—are all too aware of how they are perceived in mainstream American culture; they are still relatively young black men whose success—if not their aspiration —is framed by the realities of their race and gender.

In line with my earlier comments regarding the metaphoric

value of "bling," Jay-Z and West's video for the song "Otis" offers yet another example of the layered discourses within which their art functions. Produced by West, "Otis" deconstructs Otis Redding's classic recording "Try a Little Tenderness," but in a way that leaves Redding's signature vocal style, replete with grunts, hisses, and screams, at the forefront (hence the title). "Try a Little Tenderness," written by the British songwriting team of Jimmy Campbell and Reg Connelly (often credited as Irving King), was initially recorded by the Ray Noble orchestra in 1932 and was subsequently recorded by the likes of Bing Crosby and Jimmy Durante. A popular Tin Pan Alley tune, the song became popular with black vocalists in the 1960s, when Aretha Franklin, Nina Simone, Sam Cooke, and Nancy Wilson all recorded versions of the song that were relatively faithful (Simone's version notwithstanding) to the original composition. Redding's 1966 version of the song, with arrangements by Isaac Hayes, reconfigured the song in the context of southern soul and his own singular vocal style. Redding's is the best-known version of the song, having been covered in his style by Three Dog Night, Etta James, and Amber Riley of the *Glee* cast. The musical soundtrack to "Otis" had a seismic impact on hip-hop, inspiring many artists to quickly record tracks using the West produced beat, including the Pittsburgh-based political rapper Jasiri X, whose "Bomb the Throne" offered a critique of the presidential administrations of George Herbert Bush and George Walker Bush.

Not surprisingly, Carter and West tapped the director Spike Jonze to shoot a conceptual video in support of "Otis." Jonze had collaborated with West on the video for "Flashing Lights" from his 2007 recording *Graduation*. In the past Jonze had also shot conceptual videos for artists such as the Pharcyde ("Drop") and Fatboy Slim, where the actor Christopher Walken dances throughout the video for "Weapons of Choice," recalling his dance steps in the film *King of New York* as well as theatrical films like the recent *Where the Wild Things Are*, an adaptation of Maurice Sendak's 1963 children's book of the same title.

The "Otis" video opens with a view of a Maybach 57 in the distance, while West and Jay-Z walk into the frame toward the

luxury car carrying a cold saw and blow-torch. With an unadul-
terated version of Redding's "Try a Little Tenderness" serving as
the soundtrack of the video's opening, the scene juxtaposes notions of material wealth (the Maybach) and cultural wealth (soul
music): for example, Jay-Z begins his verse with the lyric "So
soulful, isn't it?" The power tools that Jay-Z and West carry are
an indication of their intent to customize the car, but they also
serve as a broad metaphor for the ways that various ethnic and
racial groups have "customized" wealth, often to the dismay of
those who are traditionally associated with wealth in American
society, the proverbial White Anglo-Saxon Protestant (WASP).
The German-made Maybach line dates back to the early twentieth century, but after some years of dormancy, the line was
reintroduced in 1997 (initially as a concept car) with the intent
of establishing the renewed brand as a high-end competitor for
Rolls Royce and Bentley. Though the brand has received acclaim
from automobile critics, its sales have diminished since the line
became available in 2002, in no small part due to the collapse of
the global economy and the company's willingness to reach out
to celebrities and the so-called nouveau riche to serve as brand
spokespersons; the brand is tainted by its association to "young
money," of which hip-hop entrepreneurs like Jay-Z and Sean
Combs are prominently featured. Simply put, Maybach's association with hip-hop can be read as diminishing the brand's value,
an argument that has been made about many high-end brands,
including, most famously, Timberland.

At the time that the video was shot, the Maybach 57 had a
base list price of more than $370,000, and the brand's parent
company, Daimler AG, considered closing down the line in light
of its inability to find an audience among high-end consumers.
Thus Jay-Z and West's decision to customize the car seems a direct commentary on the state of the brand. Recalling the work of
Robin D. G. Kelley, where he details the political implications of
the pursuit of leisure among working-class African Americans,
the car is transformed into a source of pleasure, replete with spoil-
ers often associated with working-class and ethnic car cultures,
where luxury and sports cars are fitted with the idiosyncrasies of

drivers and their ethnic communities.[102] It is no small observation that Jay-Z appears in the video like a child in a playground; the regular expressions of joy on his face throughout the video stand in stark contrast to the mean-mugging that most hip-hop artists, including Jay-Z, feel compelled to perform. Though the video can at once be read as a celebration of Jay-Z and West's wealth, at the close of the video, viewers are informed that "the vehicle used in this visual will be offered up for auction. Proceeds will be donated towards the East African drought disaster." Like the message conveyed in the "Girls, Girls, Girls" video, the message tacked on to the end here might have been missed by casual viewers.

Additionally, like much of Jay-Z's most recent work, the message at the end is a gesture toward something beyond the purview of the music video itself. Both Jay-Z and West suggest as much when they individually shift the camera's angles at the opening and closing of the video, as if they were changing or correcting popular perceptions of them or their work. Yet the auctioning of the car is no small gesture, as Jay-Z, West, and Jonze's ability to transform the former Maybach 57 into an objet d'art likely generates a higher price in auction than if a "simple" Maybach 57 had been auctioned. Thus the video offers some insight into Jay-Z's own branding power, his and West's (and by extension hip-hop's) ability to confer value on products and brands traditionally associated with so-called racial and economic elites, and the willingness of hip-hop artists to engage in conceptual art forms.

Jay-Z's video for "On to the Next One" (*The Blueprint 3*, 2009) is an instructive antecedent to the artistic theme of "Otis." Directed by Sam Brown, the video traffics in Jay-Z's taste in high art, notably the work of Damien Hirst; "On to the Next One" features a replica of Hirst's "For the Love of God," a diamond-encrusted skull (cast in platinum) that was sold in 2007 for $100 million to a group of investors that includes the artist himself. The critic Jonah Weiner observes that Jay-Z has regularly cited —visually and lyrically—the work of Basquiat, Hirst, and Takashi Murakami, noting that the latter two artists "make art that is largely about the markets they exist in and the wealth they generate."[98] More specifically, Weiner says that "For the Love of God" is "largely about its own value, both before and after its art-world debut; the question of how much it cost to buy the stones, and how much of a markup Hirst's imprimatur can sustain, is part of the narrative of the piece."[103] Similarly, the video for "Otis" has raised questions about the cost of the video's raw materials, for example, that Maybach 57. Underpinning the work of Hirst and Jay-Z is the simple notion that one must have wealth to generate more wealth, though in contrast to Hirst, at least in the "Otis" video, Jay-Z is producing wealth for social good. Jay-Z's interest in high art frames one of the regular obsessions of his career in recent years, namely, how to build and sustain wealth, or, to appropriate a more vernacular description, how to go from being "nigger rich" to truly wealthy.[104] In a world where even luxury automobiles depreciate in value, Jay-Z is building wealth by investing in appreciable assets such as fine art—and in the case of work by black artists such as Jean-Michel Basquiat, increasing the value of black artistic expression.

While framed in the trappings of wealth and privilege, the video for "Otis" also gestures to more concrete political messages. In one of the more popular lyrics from *Watch the Throne*, West describes the project as "luxury rap"—cited often by detractors as evidence of how out of touch West and Jay-Z were—yet the lyric is followed by a lyric that describes West as the "Hermes of verses." Hermes is, of course, one of the important messengers in Greek mythology and often described as a guide to the underworld. West's juxtaposing of the lyrics was likely just a means of recognizing his ability to speak to both highbrow and lowbrow audiences, a notion seemingly confirmed with the following lyric, "sophisticated ignorance." Later, though, Jay-Z picks up on the theme of the underworld or underground, referencing Fidel Castro's Cuba (saluting the Cuban dictator while standing in front of a customized American flag in the song's video) and economic success among Spanish-speaking immigrant communities, before adding, "not bad, huh, for some immigrants? / Build your fences, we diggin' tunnels / Can't you see we gettin' money up under you?" Here Jay-Z uses the metaphors

of American immigration policy and the underground econo-
mies to construct political and economic affinity with immigrant
communities. Even Jay-Z's gesture to Castro suggests more an
acknowledgment of his ability to stay in political power while
facing down American efforts to destabilize the Cuban government in the region for more than fifty years.

Indeed, the huge replica of an American flag, which serves
as the video's backdrop, is not an endorsement of America's domestic and foreign policies, but reference to the fact that figures
like Jay-Z, West, and others were created in the United States,
despite the challenges. The flag was designed by House of Givenchy's Riccardo Tisci, whose designs are known for their neo-
gothic features and who also designed the cover art for *Watch the
Throne*. Notable among the illustrations that accompany *Watch
the Throne*, including the aforementioned American flag, are
portraits of Jay-Z and West as both human and animal, building
on the themes that West establishes in the video for "Monster"
from *My Beautiful Dark Twisted Fantasy* (2010), which visually
addresses perceptions of the artists as monsters. A statement
from the French clothing company says of Tisci's contribution
to *Watch the Throne* that "the artwork's bold colours and angular
lines are symbols of masculinity for two of the most iconic rap
figures of our time. Riccardo Tisci naturally incorporates references to his long time signature codes, from meticulously engi-
neered prints to blurred religious images."[105] According to Tisci,
who also collaborated with West on the latter's women's clothing
line, "when it came to the artwork, it was really important to me
to represent the pure genius inside of them, and in some ways,
go back to the roots—the real rap, which has been more experimental in the last few years. I also wanted to showcase how proud
they are to be Americans."[106]

Many of those who dismiss Jay-Z's potential—discursive or
otherwise—do so because they disregard the so-called subaltern
consciousness that is palpable throughout his music and informs
some of his choices as a corporate taste maker. Jay-Z and West's
seemingly throwaway lines about their Mercedes Benzes and paparazzi ("They ain't seen me cause I pulled up in my other Benz /

Last week I was in my other other Benz. . . . Photoshoot fresh, lookin' like wealth / I'm 'bout to call the paparazzi on myself') are as much about the modes of surveillance that are often associated with celebrity, a space that both men share with many other black men in American society. In another example, when Jay-Z was asked about his interest in purchasing a London-based soccer club—the presumed coming together of hip-hop and "soccer hooligans"—Jay-Z quipped, "There's a ghetto everywhere," highlighting again Nwankwo's notion of a cosmopolitanism that is both local and global.[107] That Jay-Z's music doesn't concretely address the poverty and misery that exist among the black poor (and what *music* has?) and his wealth does not allow him (and hip-hop, for that matter) to speak back to the state in the ways that might more directly address subaltern concerns, does not detract from that fact that his wealth does allow him to speak back to *corporate* power. Jay-Z's lyric "Just sent a million dollars through a hands-free / that's big money talk can you answer me" from *Kingdom Come*'s "Prelude" is not just a simple boast when read alongside his widely reported admonishment of Frederic Rouzaud, president of Champaign Louis Roederer (producer of the hip-hop elite's champagne of choice, Cristal), for comments that Jay-Z deemed racist.[108] More importantly, with the conflation of the state and the corporate sphere—of which the privatization of the state is but one example—Jay-Z's wealth, and that of the hip-hop generation, is not a minor conceit.

Perhaps a more compelling example of Jay-Z's subaltern sensibilities can be found on the track "Minority Report," which also appeared on *Kingdom Come*. Written in the aftermath of Hurricane Katrina's destruction of the Gulf Coast, "Minority Report" represents Jay-Z at his most politically lucid, as he holds the state accountable for failing to deliver goods and services to its citizens. Jay-Z's critique then goes a step further as he also admonishes his peers with the observation "Silly rappers, 'cause we got a couple Porsches / MTV stopped by to film our fortresses / We forget the unfortunate." But rather than revel in his own propensity for giving—Jay-Z and Sean Combs donated $1 million of their own money to relief efforts—Jay-Z holds a mirror up to himself: "Sure I ponied up a mil' but I didn't give my time / So in reality I didn't give a dime or a damn / I just put my monies in the hands of the same people that left my people stranded. . . . Damn, money we gave was just a band-aid."[109] The lyrics are revealing because Jay-Z is willing to be self-critical as he grapples with the limits of his capacity to directly address the conditions of the Gulf Coast and the recognition that, at the time, there was not an infrastructure in place that could better serve the needs of those in the region.[110]

The larger point that I'm making here is that the popularity and influence of hip-hop demand that we develop the language to better address the seeming contradictions between the pursuit of the "good life" and all of its material accoutrements. "Modern blackness," a concept employed by the cultural anthropologist Deborah A. Thomas to discuss contemporary cultural practices in Jamaica, provides some critical perspective here. According to Thomas, modern blackness "requires that we abandon the binaries of hegemony and resistance, global and local, and instead try to understand the range of cultural formations among . . . African descended people throughout the diaspora."[111] For Thomas, modern blackness is "unapologetically presentist and decidedly mobile. It challenges the past-tenseness of 'folk' blackness and African heritage as well as the notion of an evolving future based on creole nationalists' modernist visions."[112]

3

The Block Is Hot

Legibility and Loci in The Wire

Thirteen years after the thirteen episodes of *A Man Called Hawk* aired on ABC, *The Wire* debuted on the cable television network HBO. By then, HBO had established itself as the premier cable network, largely on the strength of groundbreaking hour-long dramas like the cerebral Mafioso series *The Sopranos*; *Six Feet Under,* which focused on a family-owned funeral home in Los Angeles; and the prison drama *Oz*. Arguably HBO helped redefine the possibilities of the hour-long drama format, in the process carving out a small niche for original African American programming. Exploiting the failure of network television to develop quality and compelling original programming and the tepid support for serious black cinema from Hollywood studios, HBO has produced feature-length films like *The Tuskegee Airmen*, Cheryl Dunye's *Stranger Inside*, *Boycott* (which depicted the events of the Montgomery bus boycott in 1955), and documentaries such as *When the Levees Broke* (directed by Spike Lee) and *Unchained Memories*.

The Wire represents arguably the best that the network had to offer in the realm of original drama that captured the fluid complexities of black life in working-class urban America. At the core of *The Wire* are a cadre of characters who can best be described as outliers to mainstream America, as well as centerpieces of some of the most complex, sophisticated, and potentially progressive readings of black identity in contemporary popular culture. *The Wire* was based on the writings and experiences of David Simon, a Baltimore beat writer, and Edward Burns, a former homicide detective and public school teacher. The duo is also responsible for other critically acclaimed Baltimore-based dramas such as

Homicide and *The Corner*. Simon and Burns initially met when Simon was covering the case of Melvin Williams, a notorious Baltimore drug dealer, who decades later would play the role of a local minister on *The Wire*. Simon and Burns's very first encounter at a Baltimore County library is instructive to understanding the value of "deep" knowledge that their series traffics in. "When I first met Ed," Simon recalls, "he was sitting by the checkout desk, a small pile of books atop the table in front of him. *The Magus*, by Fowles. Bob Woodward's *Veil*. A collection of essays by Hannah Arendt." He said to Burns, "You're not really a cop, are you?"[1] The very crisis of legibility that framed this initial encounter became a hallmark of the series. I am particularly interested in issues of legibility/illegibility in the series, as related to location and urban spatiality. In other words, what happens to the legibility and illegibility of black masculinity in the world of *The Wire* when some of the characters, notably Russell "Stringer" Bell (Idris Elba), transgress the boundaries of the urban landscape both literally and metaphorically? What happens when black drug dealers are no longer simply drug dealers?

In that cops and robbers—good guys and bad guys—serve as a lingua franca for television drama, the American viewing public has regularly viewed heroic characterizations of law enforcement that often reinforce notions of American men as mavericks. Series as varied as *Hill Street Blues, Law and Order*, the *CSI* franchise, and *Miami Vice* have offered compelling and complex views of law enforcement; very rarely has that complexity been extended to the bad guys. It was the "intricate bureaucracy" of drug crews, which Simon and Burns encountered in the Williams case, that the two men, with the show's writers, reproduced in *The Wire*.[2] This was not an empty gesture or gimmick on their part; as Simon told the *New Yorker*, "*The Wire* is dissent. . . . It is perhaps the only storytelling on television that overtly suggests that our political and economic and social constructs are no longer viable."[3] Nevertheless, *The Wire*, like *A Man Called Hawk* before it, needed to navigate the whims of corporate executives. As Simon describes the show's relationship to the HBO network and its parent company, Time Warner, "Our 35mm misadventure

in Baltimore—for all its self-professed iconoclasm—is nevertheless sponsored by a massive media conglomerate with an ab-
solute interest in selling to consumers. And yet on the conglomerate's premium cable channel, the only product being sold is the
programming itself."[4]

Reading Simon's comments in another light, one could argue
that what was being sold to consumers via *The Wire* was a view of
black complexity that even in the relatively progressive world of
HBO programming was destined to be misconstrued, misread,
and dismissed as little more than standard "ghetto shit." For all
the critical acclaim that the series has received from critics, *The
Wire* has received very little recognition from industry peers—it
received just one Emmy nomination for writing. There are likely
myriad reasons for the show's lack of recognition, including its
rather paltry audience compared to HBO's standard bearers. I'd
like to argue, though, that for many television industry gatekeep-
ers and for many audiences, the series had a "believability" issue.
For some, the show's characters were simply unbelievable, while
for others the characters were all too believable—again, everyday "ghetto shit"—and thus the labor of the show's actors was
devalued in the process.

The Wire draws its name from the federal wiretap employed
by the Baltimore police in the 1980s as part of their surveillance
of Melvin Williams. Baltimore detectives cloned the pagers—
the proverbial beepers of the 1980s—used by Williams's operation and eventually decoded the system of communication by
which dealers sent information to each other via an elaborate
number code that entailed crossing over the 5 on the keypads of
pay phones. Burns was in awe of the crew's ingenuity: "Isn't this
brilliant. . . . Figuring it out was one thing, but creating it was a
stroke of genius."[5] The point was echoed in *The Wire* by Detective Jimmy McNulty (loosely based on Burns), who in the very
first episode describes the Barksdale crew—the target of *The
Wire*'s wiretap—as "good, deep, organized." As the late journalist Earl Byrd wrote about his childhood friend Melvin Williams
in 2003, the "organizational skills and leadership qualities it took
to build such a drug organization could have made him a captain

of industry, instead of staying up all night using money count-
ing machines to sort a million in small bills."[6] Such brilliance
—criminal or not—is rarely associated with black characters on
network or cable television and explains why *The Wire*'s biggest
fans are critics and those who most identified with the show's
characters. For those audiences familiar with the stories of Melvin Williams or legendary New York City drug lords like Frank
Lucas, Pappy Mason, or Leroy "Nicky" Barnes, the believability
of *The Wire*'s Avon Barksdale, Stringer Bell, or Marlo Stanfield is
not a stretch.

The Wire's producers and writers seemed to revel in the potential illegibility of its characters—the series is filled with moments where crises of legibility are front and center. For example,
Detective Shakima "Kima" Greggs—an out lesbian—portrayed
by Sonja Sohn, says to her partner McNulty at one point in the
initial season, "I know I look like someone who could go either
way," making light of the fact that her sartorial choices challenge
the stereotype of the "butch" lesbian. Sohn, who appeared opposite Saul Williams in Marc Levin's film *Slam* (1998) and earned
her first film role playing a lesbian in the Rachel Reichman film
Work (1998), says of her character, "I have to be female. That's
what they call me. But I feel that there's a duality in everybody
in every way and shape possible. I've never felt completely one
way or the other."[7] Throughout the five seasons of *The Wire*, a
significant portion of the character's storyline revolves around
the domestic tension between Kima and her live-in lover, Cheryl,
portrayed by Melanie Nicholls-King, who as the dutiful police
wife would rather Kima attend to her night law school studies.
In many regards Kima is the most domesticated character on the
series, a fact that allows audiences a view into the humanity of
lesbian relations, as opposed to simply portraying Kima's relationship as a spectacle. This point is made humorously during
the second season when Greggs and her supervisor, Lieutenant
Cedric Daniels (Lance Reddick), compare notes about "wives"
who are not supportive of their careers as law enforcement officers. These tensions are brought to a head toward the end of
the first season when Greggs is shot and police brass are unsure

of the protocol regarding notifying closest kin in the context of a same-sex relationship.

If Sohn's character might elicit minor curiosity along the axis of gendered sexuality, the character of Snoop, a contract killer from the Stanfield crew portrayed by Felicia "Snoop" Pearson, raises the ante by openly performing what some scholars refer to as "female masculinity." Specifically, Snoop represents what might be described as a "butch." In the book *Female Masculinity*, J. "Jack" Halberstam notes that butch images of blacks and Latinas "represent a particularly complicated location. . . . The image of the Black and Latina butch may all too easily resonate with racial stereotypes in which white forms of femininity occupy a cultural norm and nonwhite femininities are measured as excessive or inadequate in relation to that norm."[8] Though white women characters are featured in *The Wire*, notably the officer Beatrice Russell (Amy Ryan) and the state's attorney Rhonda Pearlman (Deirdre Lovejoy), who in later seasons is romantically linked to Cedric Daniels, they remain on the periphery of the urban terrain where Snoop exists. Halberstam suggests that a butch-like character like Snoop really offers commentary on masculinity as opposed to stereotypical notions of white femininity. Writing about the character Cleo (Queen Latifah / Dana Owens), an earlier cinematic iteration of the black butch from the film *Set It Off* (1996), Halberstam argues that the "black female masculinity that Latifah portrays is convincing precisely because it is infused with racial and class dynamics that render the masculinity part and parcel of a particular form of abjected female identity."[9] Halberstam adds, "Cleo's masculinity is as much a product of her life in the hood as it is about her lesbianism; it is a masculinity learned in poverty, . . . a survival skill as well as a liability."[10] Assuming that Snoop's ambitions can be tied to her attachment to the drug trade, her female masculinity made her legible to her peers in a decidedly male-centered endeavor.

Snoop is an extension of the actress Felicia Pearson's own life, troubling the boundaries between fact and fiction. Growing up in Baltimore's foster care system and dealing drugs as a tween, Pearson was convicted of second-degree murder at the age of fourteen for the shooting death of Okia Toomer. Though Pearson was not an adult at the time of her conviction, her female masculinity likely affected the perceptions of the grand jury that indicted her as an adult for first-degree murder. Upon her release from prison, at the age of twenty, Pearson returned to life on the block until a chance meeting with the actor Michael K. Williams—The Wire's Omar Little—in a Baltimore club. According to Williams, "I saw her strength and her vulnerability. You look in her eyes and you see things."[11] Williams introduced her to the show's producers; Burns asserts that with her "smoky, husky voice—she's quintessential street."[12] As the journalist Teresa Wiltz describes Pearson's pre-Wire days, she was "the only girl surfing a sea of testosterone."[13] Echoing Avery Brooks's experiences in the early days of his portrayal of Hawk, Pearson's sartorial choices create a crisis of legibility that has real-world implications; Pearson recalls dining at a restaurant and heading for the women's restroom when a waiter informed her that "the men's room is over there."[14]

Michael K. Williams, the man who introduced Pearson to The Wire's producers, portrays a character who was initially intended to be only a minor part. Omar Little easily became one of The Wire's most arresting characters, if not one of the most striking black characters to ever appear in a television drama. As the quintessential "homo-thug"—a character that before The Wire was largely known through the novels of James Earl Hardy and in the underground hip-hop clubs of America's cities, like the Warehouse in the Bronx. As Joel Barraquiel Tan explains, "Brown and Black gay men thrilled to the macho posturing and related to the outlaw nature of gangsta rap, despite its homophobic lyrics. . . . This shift was a survivalist return, a move back into the closet as a response to AIDS, racism, and homophobia."[15] In Guy Trebay's classic Village Voice essay "Homo Thugz Blow Up the Spot," the club-hopper Craig Henderson adds that "there are these myths about faggots being soft and feminine, like you're lacy and wear chiffon and listen to Barbra Streisand. Straight-up homies, niggaz, and thugz can do what they want. You can walk through the projects and be gay. But you can't walk through the projects and be a faggot."[16] Under the terms of Henderson's criteria there is little about Omar that connotes being a "faggot." As such, the homo-thug has come to index anxieties in black communities about DL, or down-low, sexuality. Though men on the so-called DL have historically existed in many communities, the scholar Jason King cautions that "if there's a DL community today, it's the result of . . . brazen marketing."[17]

Though Omar is not the first black gay man regularly featured on television—*Spin City*'s Carter Heywood (Michael Boatman) is perhaps the best known—many of those "out" characters were portrayed as stereotypes of effeminate men. *The Wire*'s writers and producers would have been perfectly within their rights to pursue storylines with Omar that highlighted the spectacle of DL sexuality, particularly given the binary heterosexist logic that pervades the construction of queerness in mainstream media and the stereotypical functions of race in that context. For example, José Esteban Muñoz invokes the term "minstrelsy" when discussing the role of queers of color on the popular series *Queer Eye for the Straight Guy*.[18] To its credit, *The Wire*'s production team went against expectation, creating a character whose homosexuality is matter-of-factly referenced throughout the series without much fanfare. With his homosexuality and hypermasculinity firmly established and not in contest, Omar emerges as the site of multiple projections. It is the excessive meanings placed on Omar's body that ultimately mark him as queer. John Nguyet Erni suggests that queer sexuality "can be defined as a practice of discursive excess that twists normal notions of gender and sexuality"; queer identity, he adds, "has to do with the relation across unfixing and unfixable political and social positioning against 'heteronormativity.'"[19] Omar's identity is as slippery as his character is; slipping in and out of legibility much the way the character literally slips through urban shadows and crevices throughout the five seasons of *The Wire*. As Michael K. Williams suggests, "Omar is who he is."[20]

The character of Omar was inspired by the stickup artists and street robbers that Burns came across while working in the Baltimore police department. "The stickup guys are mavericks," Burns explains, and accordingly Omar is the projection of some of the more daring and creative of those Burns was in contact with.[21] Omar's specialty is stealing drug stashes from various drug crews. In the logic of the standard television drama, Omar might be read as simply a predator—a troubling construct when conflated with his homosexuality. In this instance Omar reproduces the "always already present" sense, particularly in the age of HIV, that queer bodies are little more than self-interested contagion that literally disperses and destroys publics upon appearance, as is often the case with Omar. As much as his character presses the boundaries in which black masculinity has been portrayed on television, there's no denying that Omar is a dangerous psychopath, albeit one who is part of the social fabric of *The Wire*'s Baltimore. Omar's activities are rarely personal—"there are no hidden agendas," Williams says of his character—though they ultimately put him at odds with the Barksdale crew: Avon Barksdale (Wood Harris) places a bounty on the "cock sucker's" head.[22] Unable to capture Omar, Barksdale's street soldiers retaliate by torturing and brutally killing Omar's young lover, Brandon. Omar's identification of his lover's body at the city morgue is one of the most dramatic scenes of *The Wire*'s first season. Omar's arresting howl is a metaphor for the lack of language available for black men in pain or in mourning.[23] Indeed, Omar's mourning instilled the character with an enduring humanity.

In response to Brandon's murder, Omar turns state's evidence, implicating Brandon's killer, Bird (Fredro Starr), in another murder case. Bird's trial, during the second season, allows writers, via Omar's testimony, to establish his legibility in the context of the series. As the court is an extension of the carceral state, it would logically be the site where Omar's identity would be most "imprisoned" by traditional black male legibilities. Accordingly, when Omar enters the courtroom to testify, he is taunted by Stringer Bell and Bird, who refer to him with the well-worn homophobic pejoratives, "faggot!" and "cocksucker." Bird's lawyer, Maurice Levy (Michael Kostroff), continues to inscribe Omar's legibility in the confines of mainstream logic during his cross-examination, when he asks Omar about his profession.

The question begins a rather comical exchange between the two, in which Levy goes on to describe Omar as a "parasite" and a "leech" who feeds "off the violence and the despair of the drug trade." Omar quickly responds, "Just like you, man. . . . . I got the shotgun, you got the briefcase." Here, Omar brings into crisis Levy's own legibility as an upstanding defense attorney, revealing an opportunistic lawyer who generates profit from the spoils of the illicit drug trade; Levy is on retainer to Avon Barksdale. Though Levy and Omar are clearly distinguished by their respective trades, their legibilities are also inscribed by the loci of their activities, in this case the courtroom and law offices, versus the street corner and back alley. Omar can strip Levy of his legible respectability—and become a credible witness for the prosecution —because of his knowledge of Levy's activities in the Baltimore drug underground.

For many of the show's characters, Omar is firmly constructed within the confines of his exploitive trade and his homosexuality, but the writers consistently present a view of Omar that undermines such limits. Case in point: moments before taking the stand, Omar sits in the waiting room with a court officer, who seeks his advice for a crossword puzzle he is working on. The guard is looking for the "Greek god of war," and when Omar responds that Mars is the name of the god of war and a planet, the guard dismisses him ("I know it's a planet"). After a noticeable frown, Omar quickly responds, "Greeks called him Aries —same dude different name," adding that he loved studying Greek mythology in middle school. The scene is simply a short interlude that serves as an introduction to one of the second season's most fascinating episodes, "All Prologue" (besides Omar's testimony, a key character from season 1 is murdered in prison), but it does the labor of providing a glimpse of Omar's complexity. As such, the court officer's initial inability to recognize that Mars and Aries were in fact the same deity becomes a subtle reminder of Omar's own slippery identity. This fact is made clearer during the aforementioned court testimony, when Levy accuses Omar of shooting a man and lying about it to the police and Omar responds, "I ain't never put my gun on no citizen." Omar

is, in fact, offended by the suggestion that he represents a threat
to civil society, reiterating that his targets were only those embroiled in the drug game. Omar's distinction makes him no less
of a dangerous sociopath—there are often collateral damages
associated with his profession—but bespeaks a level of integrity
that is fundamental to understanding the character. According
to Williams, "Omar is a double-edged sword. You look at him
and you see this hard exterior. You see his ruthlessness and at
the same time you see him crying in the morgue over his dead
lover's body."[24]

Omar's integrity vis-à-vis other characters in the drug game
is on display during season 3 when underlings from Barksdale's
organization attempt an ill-conceived and unsuccessful hit on
Omar one Sunday morning, while Omar is accompanying his
grandmother to church. The attack breaks a long-held Sunday-
morning truce between warring drug crews, leading one of Barksdale's lieutenants, Slim Charles (Anwan Glover), to admonish
the underlings for disturbing a "bona fide colored lady" and
"trifling the reputation" of Avon Barksdale. The dressing down
is a reminder that some members of the drug game continue to
see themselves as part of a civil society that demands that their
activities adhere to some of the basic values of the communities
where they exist.[25] In the classic sociological study *Black Metropolis*, a Baptist minister explains to the authors, St. Clair Drake
and Horace Cayton, the dynamic between black civil society and
the organized criminal element: "I was severely criticized for my
contact with [numbers runners]. It was said that I was catering
to racketeers and gamblers . . . [but] they were men of families
—men who could stand for something in the community."[26] The
informant's logic falls in line with what the anthropologist Francis A. J. Ianni observed in his 1974 study *Black Mafia: Ethnic Succession in Organized Crime*: "A successful black organized crime
activist may be respected and even emulated by his neighbors,
provided he isn't involved in something messy . . . and he offers
some form of community service."[27] The lore and mythology
surrounding organized black crime is filled with stories of criminal benefactors who hand out turkeys on Thanksgiving, bankroll

summer basketball tournaments, and support the urban arts, but *The Wire* manages to bring nuance to that reality. Examples include scenes during the series' run where members of Marlo Stanfield's crew engage in target practice with beer and soda bottles. What seems like an aimless activity might be read as an attempt to protect their business interests—and their standing in the community—as the "legitimate" violence in the drug trade brings much less attention from law enforcement than the stray bullets and random violence that kill "citizens." In the case of the Stanfield crew, the practice sessions are an attempt to make sure they always hit the right target.

It is Omar's sense of integrity—his code—and the notion of shared communal values that Detective Bunk Moreland (Wendell Pierce) utilizes at various points in the series to address Omar's violence, particularly after one of Omar's capers goes awry and leads to the death of one of his crew members, Tosha (Edwina Findley).[28] Moreland was less offended by the violence itself than by the fact that the children who witnessed the murder were mimicking Omar while playing on the sidewalk: "calling your name, glorifying your ass." Omar dismissively responds, "Y'all gonna have to call this one of them 'cost of doing business' thing y'all police be talking about all the time. . . . No tax payers, shit the way y'all looking at things, ain't no victim even to speak on." Though Omar legitimately highlights the way only certain bodies matter in the business of big-city policing, Moreland responds angrily ("Bullshit. . . . You don't think this violence ripples out?") by nostalgically invoking the very civil society that Omar upheld in his earlier court testimony. "I know you remember the neighborhood? How it was," Moreland begins a rather dramatic monologue, continuing,

> We had some bad boys for real. Wasn't about guns, so much as knowing what to do with your hands. . . . My father had me on the straight, but like any young man, I wanted to be hard too. So I show up at all the house parties where all the tough guys hung. Shit they know I ain't one of them. . . : 'go home school boy, you don't belong here.' Didn't realize then

what they were doing for me. As rough as that neighborhood could be, *we had a community. Nobody no victim that didn't matter.* Now all we got is victims and predatory muthafuckas like you. (my emphasis)

Drawing on a nostalgia for the beloved community and shared sense of masculinity, rooted in responsibility, Moreland shames Omar for his "moral" lapse; the shame is visible on Omar's face as he sits on the verge of tears while Moreland walks away. Like the grandmother with whom Omar attends Sunday church service (she believes he works at the airport), Moreland functions as a moral authority for Omar. Moreland holds this authority not because of his police badge, but because of Omar's earlier recognition of Moreland's ability to challenge the confines of the legibility that was afforded them as black youth. In the season 1 episode "One Arrest," Omar recalls seeing Moreland play lacrosse as a teen: "You were the first brother I ever seen play that game with the stick." In a later episode, "Duck and Cover" from season 2, Moreland's lacrosse career is a bit of a joke when he walks into a detail wearing his high school lacrosse team sweatshirt, responding to his colleagues' surprise with the quip, "What, a brother can't run with a stick? Jim Brown was an All-American mid-fielder at Syracuse." The larger point here is that Moreland's ability to exist "outside the box" in the face of an implied racism ("those prep school boys, used to piss in their pants") gave him moral standing with Omar—moral standing that was buttressed by Moreland's illegibility beyond the beloved community.

"A Man without a Country": The Boundaries of Legibility, Social Capital, and Cosmopolitan Masculinity

In "Ebb Tide," the first episode from the second season of *The Wire*, Bodie Broadus, a rising lieutenant in the Barksdale crew, travels to Philadelphia on behalf of Stringer Bell, who in the aftermath of the first-season arrest of Avon Barksdale is running the day-to-day operations of the crew. The trip is Bodie's first outside the city of Baltimore, a fact that is comically presented by his confusion when his car radio begins to lose the signal to the radio station he had been listening to. Bodie's confusion speaks to the larger issue of worldview and how the boundaries of the block often limit the worldviews of *The Wire*'s many characters. Indeed, part of the appeal of *The Wire* is that it privileges the worldview of the block, though in the absence of experiences beyond the confines of Baltimore's so-called inner city, the block literally becomes the world—a *country* that must be policed and defended at all cost for far too many of its characters. To speak of concerns beyond the block—a cosmopolitan worldview—is to risk censure from tightly knit hood relations and to raise suspicions about even more tightly held convictions of what constitutes legitimate hood masculinities. Aspersions directed at Omar for his sexual preference aside, even he adhered to the code of the block. In his book *The Minds of Marginalized Black Men: Making Sense of Mobility, Opportunity, and Future Life Chances*, the sociologist Alford A. Young Jr. argues that such a limited view —a social isolation—has adverse effects on the ambitions and life chances of black men relegated to the inner city. Rather than frame his study solely from the standpoint of that isolation, Young observed men whose worldviews and ability to creatively respond to their conditions were enhanced by their mobility beyond the confines of their insular communities. As Young writes of his informants, "the group of men with the greatest awareness of the complexity of the processes of mobility and attainment in American society were those with the most extensive contacts beyond the neighborhood."[29]

If there is one character in the world of *The Wire* who personifies an awareness of the complexities that Young outlines, it is Stringer Bell (Idris Elba), Avon Barksdale's second in command and arguably the most integral figure in Barksdale's operation. Bell played a secondary role during *The Wire*'s initial season, but with the incarceration of Barksdale at the end of that season, Bell became more prominent, ultimately becoming a primary focus of police surveillance. Audiences were further briefed on Bell's complexity during the first season when Detective Jimmy McNulty (Dominic West) follows him around the city after a chance sighting at Baltimore's Northeast Market, eliciting the re-tort "market day for Stringer too" from McNulty's partner Bunk Moreland. That it is McNulty, the character with whom main-stream audiences were seemingly expected to most identify, who provides a real-time glimpse into Bell's movements signals Bell's critical role in *The Wire*'s larger narrative. In a subculture defined by the contradictions of crass materialism (the bling) and un-derstatement (the proverbial white tee), Bell's modest sedan, button-down oxford shirts, and windbreaker easily mark him as illegible in the context of "the block." That Bell was also enrolled in business courses at Baltimore City Community College—"In-troduction to Macroeconomics" the day McNulty follows him ("What the hell?")—only adds to the allure of a character whose worldview is so clearly beyond the realm of the "corners" that Barksdale's empire controls.

Bell's corporate demeanor provides some clue to his motiva-tion for being in the drug game in the first place; despite his evi-dent skill set, intelligence, and discipline, the glass ceilings and doublespeak around issues of diversity in the workforce and on elite college campuses in the pre-Obama era would have likely made it difficult for Bell to function in those institutions at the high level he does in Barksdale's operation. Bell's embrace of the drug trade allows him the ability to make his way on his own terms—literal ownership of the game, if you will, mirroring the rise of the so-called hip-hop mogul. Of *The Wire*'s many charac-ters, Bell is the one who seems most emblematic of the American Dream. It is Bell, for example, who is largely responsible for man-aging Barksdale's holdings, which during the first season include a strip club, a tow truck company, a warehouse, a print shop, and an apartment complex. By season 3, Barksdale's businesses are formally known as B&B Enterprises (presumably for Barksdale and Bell), which has also invested in the business of building luxury condominiums.

Criminal organizations have long used business fronts to launder money and provide a sheen of respectability on their activities, as was likely the case with Barksdale's holdings, but Bell suggests otherwise in an episode from season 1 where he admonishes underlings for not taking their "jobs" in the copy store seriously. Returning to the Copy Cat print shop after class, Bell discovers that some orders hadn't been filled. Directing his displeasure at three workers standing lazily a few feet away, Bell states, "We got work orders here and ain't nothing happening. These jobs were promised yesterday and people gonna be coming in and asking for their work and nothing been done." When one of the workers dismisses Bell's concerns—"Man fuck 'em, let 'em wait"—Bell responds angrily, "No, you not gonna bring that corner bullshit up in here, you hear me? You know what we got here? We got an elastic product. You know what that means? It means that when people can go elsewhere to get their printing and copying done, they gonna do it. You acting like we got an inelastic product and we don't. Now, I want this to run this like a true fucking business—not no front, not no bullshit—you understand me?" Setting aside Bell's obvious concerns, his rant is emblematic of his ability to apply the lessons he has just learned in class, where the teacher lectured about "elastic products," to his on-the-ground concerns running the Barksdale operation. Thus, when he warns the workers about "corner bullshit," he is not just referring to their demeanor, but making clear a distinction between Barksdale's inelastic product—the drugs—and the elasticity of some of his more traditional holdings. With control of the high-rise towers and low-rise apartments (the pit) in the section of Baltimore where he operates, Barksdale has an effective monopoly; customers have little choice but to wait for product.

Bell's corporate-style skill set aside, his character remains a primary cog in what is essentially a murderous crew of drug dealers. Audiences were first introduced to Barksdale because he ordered the murder of a state's witness. Barksdale ostensibly ordered the hit to protect his nephew, D'Angelo Barksdale (Larry Gilliard Jr.), who had been charged with murder. Throughout the first season, until his own murder in the second season, D'Angelo Barksdale functions as the series' moral conscience. The younger Barksdale is eventually convicted on a charge of drug trafficking late in the first season, which also implicates his uncle and

a group of street soldiers. In jail D'Angelo Barksdale only in-
creases his penchant for reflecting on the culture of violence that
he was implicated in as one of his uncle's mid-level managers,
particularly as he comes to terms with his uncle's ordering the
murder of Wallace, a teenager he had mentored in the pit, who
they feared was also going to turn state's witness. In the episode
before his murder, D'Angelo Barksdale turns ghetto-philosopher,
discussing the choices made and not made by F. Scott Fitzger-
ald's Gatsby, noting that "it don't matter that some fool say he
different 'cause the only thing that make you different is what
you really do or what you really go through." The scene represents D'Angelo's symbolic final break from the "game," though
that break becomes the impetus for his murder in the next episode. The architect of D'Angelo's murder is Bell, who, sensing
that D'Angelo is about to turn state's witness himself, reaches
outside Baltimore into neighboring Washington, DC, to stage
the prison murder.

The murder of D'Angelo Barksdale was one of the few instances during season 1 where Bell could be directly implicated
in violence and where he acted unilaterally, without Avon Barksdale, who thinks that his nephew committed suicide. But even
when getting his hands dirty, Bell pulls off the deed with the te-
nacity and aplomb of a seasoned CEO of a Fortune 500 company,
and in many ways his value to Avon Barksdale is much the same.
Bell's effectiveness is premised on his access to various forms of
capital. Referencing the work of Pierre Bourdieu, Alford Young
describes capital as "anything that is a resource for engaging strategic action toward a desired end," adding that for the men in
his study, *The Minds of Marginalized Black Men*, "capital is that
which they accumulated (or did not accumulate) through their
past and present experiences such that they found themselves in
positions near the bottom of the American socioeconomic hier-
archy."[30] Bell notably possesses varying degrees of cultural and
social capital, defined as "the knowledge of how to function in
specific social settings in order to mobilize, generate responses
and affect" and the "degree to which an individual is embedded
in social networks that can bring about the rewards and benefits

that enhance his or her life," allowing him to flow rather easily in disparate spaces.[31]

According to David Simon, though both Avon Barksdale and Stringer Bell were composites of a variety of Baltimore dealers, much of the first season was drawn directly from the aforementioned Williams case. Bell's function in the story was closely related to that of Lamont "Chin" Farmer, Williams's "elusive Stringer Bell–like Lieutenant."[32] Of Idris Elba, the actor chosen to portray Bell, Simon asserts, "Idris was doing stuff that reminded me of how real players would have existed in some of those scenes. It wasn't over-the-top gangster bullshit. . . . It was somebody who was rational, professional and always thinking, and that was the role."[33] Elba suggests, again echoing comments by Avery Brooks fifteen years earlier, "Stringer is one of the characters I've lived with for a long time: . . . this very tailored, ferocious man, a mix between a Black American gangster and an Italian American gangster," specifically citing the characters of Nino Brown, Wesley Snipes's role in *New Jack City* (1991), and Al Pacino's Tony Montana from *Scarface* (1983).[34] Both films were critical to the developing cinematic sensibilities of hip-hop culture in the United States.[35] "When I was freestyling with this character," Elba notes, Brown and Scarface "would be the two characters that brought him to life."[36]

Bell's cosmopolitan sensibilities come naturally for Elba, who grew up in Hackney, a working-class section of London, with a Ghanaian mother and a father from Sierra Leone. The ease with which Elba captures a presumed African American drug dealer from inner-city Baltimore mirrors the ways the character Bell flows in decidedly disparate and often competing spaces;[37] this is clearly a character who has been elsewhere and, as evidenced by the gaze of Detective McNulty in his surveillance of Bell, audiences are encouraged to go elsewhere with Bell, be it a meeting with the drug dealer collective he founds in season 2, negotiations with local architects, or his regular strategy sessions with State Senator Clay Davis. But the gaze into Bell's world is not simply about his cosmopolitan sensibilities; the gaze is also eroticized. Part of what made Bell such a breakout character in the series was his physical attractiveness. As one journalist described it, Bell/Elba's "statuesque, coffee skinned matinee-idol look was primetime eye candy."[38] In a cover feature on Elba in the leading African American magazine *Essence*, the journalist Jeannine Amber says of the actor, "he possesses that mysterious charisma that can catapult an actor from leading man to sex symbol. . . . Physically flawless and emotionally reserved, they convey a dignified sexuality, a breathtaking magnetism that, coupled with their talent, draws us to them like a flame."[39]

In his insightful essay "The Lost Boys of Baltimore: Beauty and Desire in the Hood," James S. Williams takes observations about Elba's physical attractiveness a step further, complicating the aforementioned heterosexist gaze by arguing that *The Wire* offers an "eroticization of the hood." Writing about the " 'to-die-for' black gangsta thugz" that populate *The Wire*, Williams argues that "With their mean poses, impassive stares, and fixed killer smiles, these sad and doomed lost boys constitute in their heightened availability and vulnerability one of the great unavowed pleasures of *The Wire*. What is one person's nightmare is another man's fantasy."[40] Williams notes that audiences are enticed by these characters, in part, because a "homoerotics of style is created by the very way the camera 'takes' its young male figures. . . . We are drawn into rituals of spectatorial desire through the stylized representation and mise-en-scene of the black body."[41] Highlighting my own interest in how cosmopolitanism might literally be "framed" in the context of *The Wire*, Williams notes, "The camera is almost always moving in *The Wire*, ... cutting as it were vertically into a horizontal continuum and, in the process, *queering cinematically* the standard codes of television realism. Only young black male characters receive this degree of visual investment" (my emphasis).[42] Writing about a domestic scene with Bell and Donette—the mother of the late D'Angelo Barksdale's son—Williams notes that "whereas he moves and 'flows,' she is held static within the frame. The same occurs when Stringer encounters his lawyer Levy in his office; while Levy remains fixed in his seat in medium shot, we move slowly and irresistibly towards Stringer in a close-up on the other side of the table."[43] I cite Williams at length here because his work places the conceptual movement of Bell's character in conversation with the philosophical movement on which my own interests in Bell's character pivots.

Bell's worldview serves the needs of Barksdale's empire well until shifts in the drug market occur during season 2. With Barksdale incarcerated, Bell tries to adapt the operation's functions to adhere to the logic of a marketplace that transitions from controlling the project towers, to a sharing of street corners with other drug crews, to finally a wholesale distribution model. The shifts begin with the razing of the project towers, which forces Barksdale's workers to share street corners with rival crews. In addition, Bell is forced to address being cut off from his drug supply in New York City, forcing him to cut a deal, against Barksdale's initial wishes, with a rival cross-town dealer, Proposition Joe (Robert Chew), who gets his supply from mysterious ethnics simply known as "the Greeks." Back on the street corners, Barksdale's workers are in direct competition with the laborers of other crews—notably those of Marlo Stanfield—and it is the violence produced by these new tensions that brings the increased scrutiny of law enforcement. In a telling exchange that portends an increasing rift between Bell and Barksdale in season 3, Bell attempts to assuage Barksdale's concerns about the crew's lack of firepower on the corners by stating, "Every market based business runs in cycles and we going through a down cycle," to which Barksdale quickly retorts, "String, this ain't about your motherfuckin' business class. . . . It ain't that part of it. It's that other thing; the street is street always."

Though Bell and Barksdale grew up together and are ostensibly of the same generation, their differences in opinion about the operation begins to reflect a generational divide regarding the state of illegal drug markets. At the time that Ed Burns and David Simon were "covering" Melvin Williams in the mid-1980s, many urban drug crews followed a model that the researchers Ric Curtis and Travis Wendel describe as "corporate style drug distribution operations," which represented "monolithic enterprises that tightly integrated wholesale, mid-level, and street level markets."[44] According to Curtis and Wendel, beginning in the late 1980s in a period best defined as "buy-and-bust," the corporate model became downsized, in part creating the context for the contemporary prison industrial complex and an inspiration for much that would be called "gangsta rap" in the early 1990s. In this era the corporate model gave way to freelance markets, where holdovers from the corporate era simply franchised the business to local operatives. "In the reconfigured street drug markets of the middle and late 1990s," Curtis and Wendel write, "many of the former employees of corporate-style organizations . . . began their own small drug business, assembling and serving core groups of reliable customers."[45] The Barksdale enterprise in the first season of *The Wire* is a reflection of the terrain that Curtis and Wendel describe above.

As season 3 of *The Wire* begins, Avon Barksdale, who came of age during this period of franchises and the "wave of violence" that was associated with that period, is tethered to that model —"the street is always street." Stringer Bell, in comparison, envisions and embraces a model that Curtis and Wendel describe as the "drug delivery business," where a "booming real estate market"—from which B&B Enterprises also benefits—and "intensive policing made street sales less viable."[46] Additionally, Curtis and Wendel note, "delivery markets are far less likely to be sources of violence or community disorder than fixed location or street based markets, regardless of the social organization of the distributors."[47] Bell, in contrast to Barksdale, fully understands the threat that violence represents to B&B Enterprises, reminding the latter in a conversation before his release from prison that "it's them bodies that got you in here." For Bell, his engagement in the drug trade is apparently a means to an end, as opposed to an end unto itself, as he reminds Barksdale that "we making money straight in our own name." It is in the spirit of Bell's broader worldview that he issues what I'll call "Stringer's Doctrine" at the beginning of *The Wire*'s third season.

The third season begins with the razing of the Franklin Terrace Towers, the real estate that Barksdale and Bell used to establish themselves. In the shadow of the demolition, Bodie Broadus and Poot, two mid-managers in Barksdale's operation, discuss the impact of the towers coming down. While Poot is nostalgic about the human relationships he cultivated in the towers as a youth, Broadus puts their destruction in specific economic terms: "You live in the projects, you ain't shit, but you slang product there? You got the game by the ass. Now these downtown suit wearing ass bitches done snatched up the best territory in the city from ya'll." It is this concern that Broadus later brings to Bell in a meeting that the latter convenes with middle management, using parliamentary procedures via *Robert's Rules of Order*. When Broadus queries him about the lack of available space to operate, Bell responds, "We done worrying about territory, what corner we got, what project. Game ain't about that no more, it's about product. We got the best goddamn project, so we gonna sell no matter where we are, right? . . . We gonna handle this shit like business men, sell the shit, make the profit and later for that gangsta shit." Though Bell makes clear that this new model—Stringer's Doctrine—had thus far translated into the operation selling twice the product, with half the territory, generating an 8-9 percent increase in profit, Poot pushes back over concern about perception: "Do the chair know we gonna look like some punk ass bitches out there?" In a telling response, Bell asserts forcefully, "Ya'll niggas need to start looking at the world in a new fuckin' light? Start thinking about this shit like some grown fuckin' men. Not some niggas off the fuckin corner."

The exchange between Poot and Bell, who accuses the former of being "too ignorant to have the floor," is interesting because it indexes the relationships between space, perception, and masculinity. In the case of Poot, whose response serves as conventional wisdom, his masculinity and presumably that of his peers and rivals are tethered to the control and policing of territory, in this case, the corners. Poot's deployment of the phrase "punk ass bitches," like Broadus's earlier description of politicians as "suit wearing ass bitches," was intended to queer those who don't function on the streets corners in ways that are legible to him. In a broader sense, Poot attempts to queer Bell's "foreign" worldview and by extension, Bell himself. Bell's retort acknowledges Poot's intent, hence his initial response, "Mother-fucker, I will punk your ass for saying some shit," but also offers his own queering function, arguing that "niggas off the fuckin' corner" were in opposition to more legitimate masculinities ("grown fuckin' men"). In this instance, Bell argues that his cosmopolitan worldview represents the most valid iteration of black urban masculinity, one that is in sync with the flow of capital and product. Given the energy that Bell expends to make clear the value of Stringer's Doctrine to his underlings, it was perhaps inevitable that his worldview would tragically contradict that of his "partner," Avon Barksdale.

Nevertheless, Bell is able to convene the New Day Co-op, a collective of Baltimore drug crews, who agree to pool their resources to buy the best product from New York and in the best-case scenario, simply wholesale their product to less established crews still fighting for territory and their reputations on street corners. The only holdout is Marlo Stanfield, who shortly thereafter is embroiled in a war with Avon Barksdale over the very corners that Barksdale has no use for anymore. Stanfield becomes a major concern to Barksdale's operation, especially when Barksdale returns to the fold after spending a year in prison. While Barksdale is still wedded to an antiquated worldview, where territory was directly linked to profit—and perhaps more importantly reputation—Bell attempts to sell him on the brave new world of Baltimore's drug trade. In a sit-down immediately after Barksdale's homecoming party, Bell complains, "I mean, how many corners do we need? How much money can a nigga make? . . . We past that run and gun shit. . . . Nothing but cash, not no corners, no territory, nothin'. . . . Let the younguns worry about retail, where to wholesale, who gives a fuck who standing on what corner if we taking shit off the top, . . . making that shit work for us. You can run more than corners, B." Barksdale's response speaks palpably to his worldview: "I ain't no suit wearing business man like you. I'm just a gangsta, I suppose, and I want my corners," echoing the sentiment expressed by Poot and Bodie Broadus above, albeit minus the distinct queering mechanism. Young notes in *The Minds of Marginalized Black Men* that "social location"—in this instance Barksdale's philosophical and physical tethering to the street corners—"does not merely isolate individuals from better prospects. It also creates a barrier denying them the capacity to interpret that which lies beyond their social milieu."[48]

There are myriad reasons for the difference between Bell and Barksdale's worldviews. The characters themselves suggest that even as kids they fundamentally saw the world differently, as they reminisce during season 3 about a young Bell being "all heavy into that black pride shit, talking about . . . two grocery stores and mak(ing) motherfuckers proud," and conversely a young Barksdale wishing to "go to war" with AK-47s, in the spirit of the film *Scarface*. I can only speculate about the nature of Bell and Barksdale's friendship—*The Wire* doesn't really provide any inkling of the complexity of the relationship—but it seems safe to suggest that Bell found some value in living a life of the mind, whereas Barksdale, as a former boxer who came up through the ranks as a street soldier, was valued for his skill set in that regard. As someone who was essentially a laborer, Barksdale obviously valued what Bell brought to the table as a thinker—in fact, he needed Bell in that regard to act upon the opportunities that presented themselves when the corporate mode of drug trafficking began to collapse. But this also means that Barksdale could only view the world from the standpoint of his role as a laborer. As Young writes, "The narrowness of the men's perspective on potential work opportunities sheds light on another effect of social isolation. The aspect of the world of work that was most desirable to these men was one that was in actuality diminishing as these men came of age."[49]

This is not to suggest that Barksdale and others like him were not thinkers; their ability to function on the block suggests an embodied social awareness that represents a distinct cognitive skill set—the so-called thug knowledges I addressed earlier—that is attuned to the random quality of the urban experience. As one of Young's respondents reflects, "shit can happen anyway."[50] Barksdale's distinct set of knowledges is highlighted during "Game Day" (season 1, episode 9). The episode is notable because it is the first time that Lieutenant Daniels and his officers have a positive physical identification of Barksdale, who was known to them in prior episodes only by a dated photo of the drug lord as a boxer. Adding to the general theme of illegibility, the positive identification occurs at a neighborhood basketball game in which a Barksdale-bankrolled team is pitted against a team funded by his crosstown rival Proposition Joe. After the game, Daniels deploys several of his detectives and officers to follow Barksdale by car, just to get a closer look at the subject of their investigation. Coordinating their own movements in unmarked police cars using their hand radios, Daniels and the others think that they have created an effective visual trap for Barksdale, only to find that they have "lost" him. Suddenly Barksdale emerges from a side street, driving right past Daniels in the opposite direction, waving his finger at him as he passes. On display in these series of events is Barksdale's knowledge of the physical terrain of the neighborhood—highlighting the importance of beat cops in successful policing—and his hyperawareness that he is always/already a subject of surveillance.

It is Barksdale's natural instincts for the block that lead him to try and reclaim the corners he feels were taken from him during his absence and during Bell's reign. It is those instincts that make him aware of his own social capital on the block, despite not sharing Bell's more cosmopolitan view. Indeed, the insular world of the block meant that Barksdale's social capital was even more hard-earned and personally cultivated. While Bell's social and cultural capital are enhanced by a sense of fluidity, Barksdale's is decidedly local and largely buttressed by his effective and strategic deployment of violence.[51] It is this threat to Barksdale's social capital that leads him to attempt an ill-advised attack on Marlo Stanfield. Barksdale is injured with a gunshot wound to the arm and one of his soldiers is killed in the botched attempt to reestablish his authority on the block. Bell, whom Barksdale no longer values with regard to "that part of it," was left out of the loop, and confronts Barksdale in one of the series' most dramatic scenes. Recognizing the threat to the economic empire that he has helped to build, Bell angrily says to Barksdale, "War, man? We past this bullshit." With this comment, Barksdale finally takes aim at Bell's cosmopolitan worldview: "I look at you these days and you know what I see? *A man without a country*. Not hard enough for this right here and maybe not smart enough for that out there. No offense, I don't think you ever were [hard enough]." For Barksdale, Bell's cosmopolitanism is an articulation not just of weakness, particularly given the hypermasculinity that propels identity on the block, but also of indecision—am I a thug or am I a businessman?—that he viewed as a threat to his much-valued social capital.

The literary scholar Walton Muyumba offers some insight here, writing in another context about "cosmopolitan blackness" among African American writers in the post–World War II period. Citing the examples of Ralph Ellison, James Baldwin, and Amiri Baraka, Muyumba writes, "Life outside the U.S. forced each writer to interrogate the meanings of blackness, American identity, and the post–World War II political world in ways that exposed conflicts at the center of his intellectual/literary practices."[52] Muyumba further suggest that it was the concept of jazz improvisation that the three writers effectively utilized as a mechanism to communicate "philosophical attitudes befitting the shifts in American political and social life during the 1950s and '60s."[53] I cite Muyumba here because whereas Ellison, Baldwin, and Baraka could utilize jazz improvisation as a lingua franca for their distinct cosmopolitan experiences, Stringer Bell lacks an available language to articulate his own cosmopolitan worldview. Central to that worldview are the conflicts and contradictions that animate his efforts to move beyond the block, yet to remain wedded to it because it is where his black masculinity is so firmly inscribed and vital. Bell may no longer be of the block, but the block clearly still matters to him, else he would be content with just being another black businessman. Bell thrives on his mobility, but has little available language at his disposal to sing the praises of that mobility in ways that resonate on the block. As such, it's not surprising that Bell falls back on performances of violence, like his public dressing down of Poot, recalling, in response to Barksdale's question of his "hardness," his thus far unknown role in the death of D'Angelo Barksdale.

"Not hard enough because I think, before I snatch a life?" Bell spews before owning up to the life that he snatched and tussling a wounded—both physically and emotionally—Barksdale to the ground, while uttering, "You gotta think what we got in this game for. Was it the rep? Was it so our names could ring out on some fuckin' ghetto street corners? There are games beyond the fuckin' game." Barksdale's faint response, "Let me up," is recognition that Bell is finally speaking back to him in a language that is legible.

Barksdale would have some semblance of a last laugh, when Bell's relationship with state senator Clay Davis sours.[54] The latter accepted payoffs from Bell, but was unable to deliver the kind of municipal services for which Bell had employed him. Bell laughably reaches out to Barksdale to pursue a hit on Davis, but instead Barksdale lectures Bell on the pitfalls of the very violence that Bell had once cautioned him about ("You kill a downtown nigga like that, the whole world gonna stand up and take notice"). Barksdale understands, better than his soon fallen comrade thinks he does, that social capital is a product of location, and the terrain of an elected official is well beyond the scope of life on the block. Bell's desire to bring the culture of the block into the mainstream political and business world was indicative of the frustration he was experiencing at not being able to move the business process forward at the pace that he was regularly accustomed to in Barksdale's criminal enterprises, while also having his legitimacy challenged in Barksdale's operation. Given the disparate worlds that Bell was attempting to navigate, it is not surprising that it was an unlikely alliance between Omar and Brother Mouzone (Michael Potts) that brings about his demise.

Unbeknownst to Avon Barksdale while he is in prison, Bell begins to share real estate with Proposition Joe in order to gain access to his distributor. When word gets back to Barksdale about a beef in the towers with Proposition Joe's dealers, he hires Brother Mouzone, an enforcer from New York City, to provide protection. Mouzone, who usually polices the tower courtyard while reading copies of magazines like *Harper's*, *Atlantic Monthly*, and the *Nation*, is regularly attired in a dark business suit and bow tie, making him most legible as a member of the Nation of Islam, the

Black Muslim and nationalist organization that was founded by
the late Elijah Muhammad and whose most prominent spokespersons include Malcolm X (El-Hajj Malik El-Shabazz) and the
organization's current leader, Minister Louis Farrakhan. Specifically, Mouzone's dexterity with firearms suggests that he might
have been a member of the Nation of Islam's renowned para-
military wing, the Fruit of Islam, which has provided security
at Nation of Islam events and offered protection for prominent
African Americans. The group began to provide private security
in 1988; in the early 1990s it won several contracts to provide security in federally subsidized housing projects in various cities,
including Baltimore.[55] David Simon was coy about Mouzone's
affinity with the Nation of Islam, writing in an online forum, "let
me be clear that Brother Mouzone has not identified himself as a
member of the Nation of Islam. The only thing that even implies
a connection is that he speaks precisely and wears a bowtie."[56]
Given the Nation of Islam's role in protecting housing projects
and its regular presence selling navy bean pies and copies of the
organization's newspaper, the *Final Call*, it is entirely plausible
that Mouzone's attire was simply a clever ruse intended to divert
attention from his true purpose.

Bell, recognizing that Mouzone's presence is threatening his
secret agreement with Proposition Joe, decides to kill the proverbial "two birds" by setting up a meeting with Omar—still prey-
ing on Barksdale's drug stashes—to falsely deliver Mouzone as
the killer and torturer of his lover, Brandon. Respecting Omar's
murderous skill set, Bell banks on the fact that Omar's retribu-
tion against Mouzone would de-escalate tensions with Omar as
well as removing Mouzone's presence in the tower courtyard.
And indeed, Omar successfully moves on Mouzone in a local
motel room, but when the wounded Mouzone denies that he
had anything to do with Brandon's torture and murder—"I'm
at peace with my God, do what you will"—it gives Omar reason
to pause. As Mouzone begins to pray to Allah with the expectation that Omar is about to kill him, Omar relents, sensing that
something is amiss. This initial confrontation between Omar and
Mouzone suggests a bond that the two seemingly share as killers;

the two banter after Mouzone's shooting about the impact of nine-millimeter bullets. Omar decides to spare Mouzone's life, in part because he senses the wounded killer's integrity, deciding to call for medical help for Mouzone before leaving the hotel room with a respectful head nod.

After recovering from his wounds, Mouzone returns to Baltimore during season 3 to seek out Omar, describing his shooter as "homegrown, raised in the streets, skilled, intelligent," and a "nigger." The accuracy with which Mouzone "reads" his shooter suggests that Omar is highly legible to him, and not simply because of the sensibilities that the two share as shooters. When he is given information that Omar likes to "run with a young boy or two," Mouzone begins to send his assistant, Lamar, into black gay haunts, hoping to find Omar's whereabouts. When Lamar resists having to cruise in black gay bars, Mouzone asserts, "You're the perfect bait, Lamar, they'll see you as conflicted, your homophobia is so visceral." What interests me about Mouzone's claim is that it suggests an affinity or intimate knowledge of queer spaces and sensibilities. If Mouzone is to be read here as a loose embodiment of mainstream perceptions of Nation of Islam, an organization whose homophobic views are fairly well known, then Mouzone's critique of Lamar's homophobia suggests that his views might have been contrary to those of the organization. Though Mouzone might have been a product of the organization and its training, he could conceivably have been queered from it because of views—sexual or political—that were outside the realm of the Nation of Islam's core beliefs. Indeed, there are hints of such a read on Mouzone in season 2 shortly before his shooting, when he ask Lamar if the local newsstand has a copy of the new *Harper's* magazine, and Lamar responds in the negative with the remark that the store had "some titty mags . . . if you need." The look of disdain on Mouzone's face at the mention of pornographic materials could easily be read as the product of his devout Muslim faith, but could also be read as a sexual disinterest in women.

What I am suggesting is that the alliance that develops between Omar and Mouzone, after their dramatic alleyway meeting in episode 11 ("Middle Ground") of season 3—described by the episode's writer George Pelecanos as "a faceoff between two mythical figures"—might not have simply been a product of the desire to seek revenge on Stringer Bell, but perhaps a shared sense of queerness that was legible only to each other. Omar's dismissive reduction of Mouzone as "bowtie" encourages readings of Mouzone as a product of the Nation of Islam, though his interactions with him clearly suggest that such reductiveness is off-base. For Omar, it is often deployed as a joke to soften the initial tension between the two. Mouzone later returns the favor, when Omar tells Mouzone that they have to enter in the front of the building in which they will eventually trap Bell, and Mouzone responds, "That's a change for you," offering commentary on both Omar's preferred style of attack and his sexual practices.

When the two men finally confront Bell in an empty building that he is renovating, Bell finds their alliance inconceivable. Bell's subsequent murder at the hands of "the cock sucker" and "the bow tie" speaks volumes, textually, about the inability of characters to fully flourish outside the limited scope in which they are imagined. David Simon has suggested as much, telling the *New York Times* in the aftermath of Bell's murder that "holding on to a character and then twisting the story to serve the character? . . . There's no gratification in that for anyone. We're not doing a soap opera here."[57] Simon's comments suggest the extent to which even the progressive politics found in *The Wire* are ultimately the product of sensibilities that deem black masculinity as little more than a concept that functions in the service of other concerns and narratives, even as said black masculinity is central to the presentation of such concerns and narratives. There's no denying that Stringer Bell was a problematic figure; Elba admits as much in a post-*Wire* interview in the *Guardian*, where he says of Bell's death, "I celebrate the fact that he dies. I have a problem with the glorification of a drug dealer and America is fascinated with that world. We're celebrating the very fucking problem that America has in its hood. But Stringer Bell was no role model."[58] Yet despite Elba's comments, we are left with the memory of the scene in which Detective McNulty enters Bell's apartment in the episode following his death; upon seeing Bell's taste in art and his book collection, which includes a copy of Adam Smith's *Wealth of Nations*, McNulty wonders aloud, "Who the fuck was I chasing?" After surveilling Bell for three years, McNulty found him no more legible than he was on day one. And indeed, I would argue that for David Simon, the series could not serve the character because the character was still illegible, even for the character's creator.

4

R. Kelly's Closet

Shame, Desire, and the Confessions of a (Postmodern) Soul Man

Preface from a Critic Trapped in R. Kelly's Closet

In 2008 the R&B singer Robert Sylvester Kelly was acquitted of over a dozen charges of child pornography. The case centered on a widely circulated and bootlegged video that purported to show Kelly performing sex acts with an underage black female. Kelly's case elicited much discussion about child pornography and rape in black communities, and conversations as well on the role of parenting—or the lack of it—when children become prey to adult sex offenders. According to jurors in the case, they didn't find Kelly's accuser believable as a victim. Such a reading of Kelly's accuser falls in line with historical narratives in which black women are "unrapeable" in the eyes of the law. As Saidiya Hartman, one of the many commentators on the subject of black women and rape, writes in her book *Scenes of Subjection*, "In nineteenth century common law, rape was defined as the forcible carnal knowledge of a female against her will and without her consent. Yet the actual or attempted rape of an enslaved woman was an offense neither recognized nor punished by law."[1] Hartman suggests that the rape of a black woman was "unimaginable" given notions of lasciviousness and immorality that were tethered to black bodies, and black women's bodies in particular, in the minds of many whites.

There has also been a long history in the United States of highly visible and powerful black men publicly humiliated for criminal acts and lapses of judgment. Figures as diverse as the heavyweight boxing champion Jack Johnson, who was punished for flaunting his relationships with white women in the early twentieth century (he was accused of violating the Mann Act —the interstate transport of prostitutes), and the former Washington, DC, mayor Marion Barry, who appeared in an FBI surveillance tape smoking a crack pipe with the FBI informant Rasheeda Moore, have been publicly knocked off their perches. It has often been easier for some in black communities to believe that the disgrace that befell these men was the product of some larger conspiracy to undermine the stature of strong black men, than to admit that these men might have been engaged in behaviors that deserved closer scrutiny or even punishment. Not surprisingly, in the years after the Kelly indictments were announced, he was arguably more popular than at any time in his career. While Kelly owes part of that success to his keen ability to produce music that remains relevant to an audience that is decidedly younger than he is, it also speaks to the extent to which some have sought to protect him or at least not pass judgment on him until he had his day in court.

The fact that so many folks have downloaded footage of the videotape that was at the center of the criminal case against Kelly or have purchased bootlegs of the so-called Kelly sex tape speaks to the extent to which so many of us were already complicit in the crimes that Kelly was accused of. Few who forwarded Internet links of the video to others, for example, seem to be aware that they might be trafficking in child pornography. This is perhaps to be expected in a society that shows little regard for black girls, and among those black folk who don't want to bring further shame to our communities by airing the so-called dirty laundry of pathological and criminal behavior that occurs in our homes. Even those who are critical of R. Kelly as simply a stand-in for the moral failings of the hip-hop generation, often choose to ignore or forget the examples of the former Illinois congressman Mel Reynolds, who maintained criminal sexual relations with a sixteen-year-old campaign worker, or the late rhythm and blues star Jackie Wilson, who attempted to rape Patti LaBelle when she was a young performer with the Bluebelles in the 1960s. The larger point here is that with few exceptions, little of the conversation surrounding the R. Kelly case has dealt with the prevalence of sexual assault and rape of young girls and boys in our society. As such, I'd like to clarify that my critical intervention into the text that is "R. Kelly" is in no way an affirmation of the behavior and criminal activity that Robert Sylvester Kelly and countless others have been accused and convicted of, but an honest critical assessment of the body of work produced by an artist who, despite his—and our—personal and moral failings, demands our attention.

Notes on a Postmodern Soul Man

The title of this chapter is inspired by *Trapped in the Closet*, a twenty-two-chapter episodic music video written and directed by R. Kelly and released in several parts during 2005 and 2007. The first three episodes were initially released as part of the promotion for "Trapped in the Closet," the lead single from Kelly's 2005 release *TP-3: Reloaded*.[2] With Kelly serving as narrator and also as the main character, Sylvester (Kelly's real middle name), *Trapped in the Closet* examines black interpersonal relationships in the age of DL (down-low) sexuality—think *Desperate Housewives* for the ghetto masses, with their attendant fixations on shame, desire, violence, betrayal, and morality. The plot is fairly simple: a woman named Cathy is involved in a onetime sexual tryst with Sylvester and is caught by her husband, Rufus, who finds Sylvester hiding in the closet. This opening sequence serves as a springboard to examine Rufus's own affair with his presumably gay lover, Chuck; Cathy's friendship with Sylvester's wife, Gwen; Gwen's affair with a police officer; and a cavalcade of other questionable relationships between unlikely partners. This was not new terrain for Kelly, who had previously collaborated with the veteran soul singer Ronald Isley on a series of melodramatic music videos that pitted Kelly against an older patriarchal figure simply known as Mr. Biggs (Isley), usually over the control of women who were decidedly younger than Mr. Biggs. "Down Low (Nobody Has to Know)," one of the first recordings in the Kelly/Isley collaborations, helped popularize the term "down low" in the mid-1990s, though it was not initially used to describe married men engaged in same-sex relations.

Trapped in the Closet, as well as the Kelly and Isley videos, is part of a larger tradition of "response" records in soul and R&B music that functioned as serial melodramas. In her book *Blues Legacies and Black Feminism*, Angela Davis places these musical narratives in a broader historical context, particularly in relation to slavery. Writing about the profane and sexually charged blues lyrics from the early twentieth century, Davis writes of the period after emancipation, "For the first time in the history of the African presence in North America, masses of black women and men were in a position to make autonomous decisions regarding the sexual partnerships they entered. Sexuality thus was one of the most tangible domains in which emancipation was acted upon and through which its meanings were expressed."[3] Davis's point is that the lyrics of popular songs take on greater meaning when black communities are unable to more fully explore and articulate the dimensions of their interpersonal relationships in other media.

Davis's arguments could be applied to soul and R&B music in the post–civil rights era, when black communities attempted to locate the best frequency to engage narratives dealing with black sexual relationships as legal segregation began to erode. Among the more well known "response" records from the 1970s is Shirley Brown's 1974 recording "Woman to Woman," where the narrator confronts her husband's lover. In response, Barbara Mason recorded "From His Woman to You," titillating soul audiences with the intricacies of infidelity in the 1970s. In the early 1980s Barbara Mason was again at the center of serial recordings about infidelity, responding to Richard "Dimples" Fields and Betty Wright's popular "She Got Papers" with "She's Got the Papers (I Got the Man)." A few years later Mason added yet another twist to narratives about infidelity when she recorded the club hit "Another Man," which is perhaps the first acknowledgment of DL sexuality in mainstream R&B music. Mason effectively offered a public queering of Richard "Dimples" Fields, whose high-pitched falsetto and decidedly metrosexual sensibilities—two decades before such a term was in fashion—raised questions about the singer's sexuality. Whereas the earlier exchanges between Brown and Mason were intended as little more than entertainment (that largely affirmed black masculine heterosexual desire), Mason's "Another Man" tapped into the burgeoning anxieties in black communities about homosexuality during the early years of the national HIV crisis. Such anxieties are powerfully articulated in the Peggy Scott-Adams recording "Bill" (1997), which treats homosexuality in the black community as a literal virus that undermines the sanctity of the traditional black family.

It is important to situate the work of Kelly, his collaborations with Isley, and *Trapped in the Closet* in the context of ongoing anxieties about black infidelity in the age of AIDS, when casual sexual trysts could easily be fatal. The ongoing presence of violence or potential violence in so many of the Kelly/Isley videos and throughout much of *Trapped in the Closet* is a not-so-subtle reminder of how high the stakes are in this regard. In her book *Private Lives, Proper Relations*, the literary critic Candice Jenkins takes the analysis a step further, suggesting that "violence is a means of expressing frustration with a domestic scene that is 'out of order.'"[4] I would add in response that it is virtually impossible to wade through the politics of gender and sexuality in contemporary black popular culture without a consideration of how the specters of shame, betrayal, and desire function in it. Indeed, *Trapped in the Closet* is unfathomable without such considerations.

Though none of the aforementioned "answer" songs feature particularly progressive notions of gender, they are distinct from the videos for R. Kelly's "Down Low (Nobody Has to Know)" (1995) and the Isley Brothers' "Contagious" (2003) and "Busted" (2005), which share a troubling and at times misogynistic view of black women in the context of contemporary black gender relations. I maintain that the videos initiate a moment in R&B music—so often thought of as an innocuous and romantic alternative to the sexism, misogyny, and homophobia normalized in commercial hip-hop—that sanctions, however subtly, violence against women, be it physical, emotional, rhetorical, or sexual. In the first video of the Kelly/Biggs cycle, "Down Low (Nobody Has to Know)," Mr. Biggs's younger partner is brutally beaten to death in response to her infidelity. The later video for "Contagious" again finds Mr. Biggs confronted by a case of infidelity, again with a younger partner, portrayed by the R&B singer Chanté Moore. Though the video doesn't degenerate into the kind of violence featured in "Down Low (Nobody Has to Know)," there is a sequence of exchanges between Mr. Biggs, Kelly, and Moore's character that gets to the heart of the disturbing forms of patriarchy that the series of videos largely normalizes. When Moore's character tries to intercede in the tiff between the two men, she is told by Mr. Biggs, "Shut up, can't you see two men are talking?" Through Isley, who was in his early sixties at the time the video was produced, Mr. Biggs embraces a particularly potent and regressive gender nostalgia that posits black women as voiceless, inconsequential, and in need of constant surveillance and control—like children.

Rarely disturbed in any of these collaborations is the notion that Mr. Biggs serves as a benevolent patriarch, who brings order to the disorder of contemporary black gender relations and by extension the black family. In such a worldview, the violence that Mr. Biggs enacts in response to betrayals—real and imagined—is thus justified, naturalizing the belief that black women are the source of such disorder. It is not surprising, then, that *Trapped in the Closet* opens with the main character, Sylvester, waking in a strange bed, and viewers are led to believe that he was led into this situation under false pretenses by the character Cathy—she used a fake name, downplayed her knowledge of Sylvester before their tryst, and wore a wig—who thus functions as the root of the dysfunctional drama that follows. Additionally, the connections between *Trapped in the Closet* and the earlier collaborations between Kelly and Isley are critical because of the proclivity of Mr. Biggs to be partnered with women often half his age; Isley himself married one of his backup singers who was in her mid-twenties during this time. Kelly in fact describes Isley as a father figure, noting that conversations between the two "go a lot deeper than music."[5] It goes without saying that many viewed the myriad dramas that unfold in *Trapped in the Closet* as a bold-faced attempt by R. Kelly to distract audiences from his own legal dramas regarding underaged females.

It is perhaps tempting to read the *closet* that *Trapped in the Closet*'s narrator inhabits as somehow linked to the closeted realities that R. Kelly has so deftly obscured while facing criminal charges of child pornography. Equally tempting is a read of *Trapped in the Closet* that can be easily mapped onto those public and legible aspects of R. Kelly's commercial persona and private identity that feed easily into the crimes of which he had been accused, particularly as Kelly shares many of the sensibilities of the primary character, Sylvester. As such, Sylvester, *Trapped in the Closet*'s unnamed narrator, and Kelly can be read as an articulation of the complex identities waging war over good and evil in the body of Robert Sylvester Kelly, placing the artist in the company of many other black male icons, notably Marvin Gaye, who have used such tensions to fuel their art.

But I'd like to first suggest yet another series of closets to exhume, which place Kelly's *Trapped in the Closet* firmly in the musical tradition that he so brilliantly, if not problematically, upholds, as well as in conversation with the broader existential concerns that have framed black life in the post–civil rights era. And this is not to suggest that there isn't critical symmetry between these alternative closets and the criminal charges that Kelly sought to escape. In other words, I'd like to think of Kelly as Fred Moten might, as teetering between fugitivity and incarceration, and *Trapped in the Closet* as ultimately representing the acts of an escape artist, per Daphne Brooks, whose mode of escape is in excavation, because surely such acts will ward off the social death—particularly in the age of AIDS—that is perhaps more palpable than the literal incarceration that criminal acts normally demand.[6]

As troubling as this might seem, I'd like to suggest that R. Kelly's "crime" was not only that he was accused of raping an underaged girl, but that his celebrity and notoriety made aspects of black American dysfunctionality too visibly public—too legible—in an era when many sought continued rehabilitation of the image, if not the idea, of a chaste and respectful black femininity and an equally innocent and even chivalrous notion of a public black masculinity. As Jenkins writes, "the spectacle of 'black bodies in pain'—of black bodies, period—has always had at least some relationship to the spectacle of an assumed black sexual degeneracy." Noting the centrality of R. Kelly and the basketball player Allen Iverson to this reality, Jenkins adds, "the spectacle of degenerative blackness that such figures create by no means excludes black women, particularly in the cases of Kelly and Iverson—in which the sexualized bodies of black females are the subtext of the scandal."[7] In other words, Kelly and his accuser were thought to shame black Americans, though in the context of the normative patriarchy that powerfully functions in many black institutions, it was Kelly's underage accuser and her parents who bore the brunt of early criticism about the case.

The social commentator John Ridley gives some insight into this mode of thinking in his controversial *Esquire* essay "The Manifesto of Ascendancy for the Modern American Nigger." In the piece Ridley rhetorically queries, "If we as a race could win the centuries-long war against institutionalized racism, why is it that so many of us cannot secure the advantage after decades of freedom?" According to Ridley, "that which retards us is the worst of 'us,' those who disdain actual ascendancy gained by way of intellectual expansion and physical toil—who instead value the posture of an 'urban,' a 'street,' a 'real' existence, no matter that such a culture threatens to render them extinct. . . . Them being niggers."[8] Ridley does not mention Kelly in his essay, though he might have; few contemporary figures elicit the level of disdain that Kelly does for embodying what some view as the worst excesses of the so-called hip-hop generation. As such, it's easy to use Kelly as the straw person for a revisionist history of what has gone wrong in black America during Kelly's lifetime. Kelly's defense is his closet, which as C. Riley Snorton argues, "audiovisualizes the manner with which emotion and sexual desire are partially derived from broader structural forces, including economic shifts, migration and negotiations with (urban/public) space."[9] Kelly's defense is, in part, the structural realities of black life in the contemporary black moment. In this context Kelly is not simply emblematic of those structural realities, but a commentator on such realities. Indeed, Kelly's position as the narrator and main character (arguably classed positions) in *Trapped in the Closet* establishes this closet as a privileged site of knowledge and surveillance. Also included in Kelly's closet is his archival knowledge—musical and extra-musical—of the soul men who preceded him.

R. Kelly is, among other things, part of the soul man tradition. Indeed the male soul singer—the proverbial soul man—with his narrative devotion to unrequited love and spiritual redemption, possesses a cultural status that rivals that of his "race man" peer. As I have noted elsewhere, R. Kelly might be the most accomplished aural archivist of his generation, as he is deeply literate in the soul tradition, and resonances of the music of artists such as Jeffrey Osborne, Lenny Williams, Donny Hathaway, Lattimore, Frankie Beverly, Stevie Wonder, Marvin Gaye, Luther Ingram, Sam Cooke, and of course, most famously, Ronald Isley can be discerned throughout his oeuvre.[10] Kelly is likely blessed with the gift of mimicry, honed when his late mother insisted that he faithfully imitate the closing vocal runs on Stevie Wonder's "Master Blaster Jammin'." Yet there is something beyond simple imitation in Kelly's music, something familiar, yes, though wholly immersed in contemporary existential concerns. It is perhaps too easy to suggest that such mimicry extends beyond the realm of the artistic and into the realm of the real.

The soul man can easily be acknowledged as embodying the knowledge produced in the name of a black masculinity firmly planted at the crossroads of desire and fear; the secular and the sacred; blackness and Americanness; deviance and innocence. The soul man icons of the 1960s and 1970s congealed grand narratives of tragedy—shot dead in a motel (Sam Cooke); shot dead by his father (Marvin Gaye); shot dead in a game of Russian roulette (Johnny Ace); killed in an airplane crash (Otis Redding); scorched by a pot of boiling grits (Al Green); forced to leap naked out of an open window (Donny Hathaway)—narratives wedded to even more complicated personal demons:

physical abuse of wives and girlfriends; sexual assault of younger female artists; sex with underage girls; and drug addiction. These dynamics reflect the binary tensions of the foundational narrative of the soul music tradition, namely, that such tragedies were the price these men were damned to pay for offering their godly gifts for sale in the marketplace of the flesh—their relinquishing of the innocent black body kneeling at the altar of spiritual desire in exchange for the deviant black body kneeling at the altar of sexual desire. And yet like Du Bois's notion of double consciousness, such binaries miss the complexities of everyday life, where every decision made, every desire fulfilled, and every pleasure consummated are not manifested at some mythical crossroads of heaven and hell or, more tellingly, some crossroads of slavery and freedom.

Often left unchallenged at these crossroads is a notion of African American innocence, which, Robert Reid-Pharr argues, is dismantled at the moment African Americans become cosmopolitan subjects, not simply as citizens or more likely commodities of the world, but with the acknowledgment that the world lives within African Americans and that African Americans are more than complicit in a state of "impurity." According to Reid-Pharr, African American investment in notions of innocence—and I'm not at all suggesting an investment in victimization—is rooted in attempts to "maintain a rather potent ethical position in this country."[11] I would like to argue that the soul man tradition is no less reflective of this tendency. Thus in an era when Martin Luther King Jr. and others made the claim that African Americans were the moral compass of American society, the soul man becomes the shifting locus for a noble struggle—decidedly secular—between good and evil; blackness and whiteness; military aggression and pacifism; sex and love; and "class and crass," to quote *Dream Girls'* Curtis Taylor, in which the presumed innocence of the soul man serves as little more than a fetish that finds resonance in black communities[12] As these largely symbolic binaries entered into the political and marketplace consciousnesses of mainstream America, distinct limits—fluid as they were—were placed on black male soul singers, depending on which soul man icon found favor in the marketplace at any given time. The career of the legendary Soul singer Bobby Womack is perhaps instructive in this regard.

Though Ray Charles is thought to be the most important creative force in the development of soul music, it was Sam Cooke—Clyde McPhatter notwithstanding—who early on came to define and become, in fact, the template for the soul man. Possessing good looks and a virile and highly sexualized masculinity, Cooke emerged from his apprenticeships as lead vocalist of the gospel groups the Highway QCs and the Soul Stirrers in the mid-1950s very much a sex symbol. It was this particular appeal that helped concretize the foundational myth of the soul man; while Cooke clearly sang of the Lord—often in that fluttering feathery riff that became his signature—he and his audiences clearly desired something more physical and accessible. Cooke's well-known philandering and his murder in 1964, after a decade of bad romantic relationships and near-fatal accidents, were affirmation to many of the "believers" that he was being disciplined for the sin of transitioning from the sacred world to the secular. I'd like to argue that the soul man era—and the mythologies erected in his name—essentially begins with Cooke's death. I am not arguing that soul men didn't exist before Cooke, but that the black public's investment in the palpable power and prestige embodied by the soul man was most pronounced during the height of Cooke's popularity. That Cooke was murdered as he was transitioning from a popular balladeer to a more formal race man—his posthumously released "A Change Is Gonna Come" is seen as a core text among civil rights–era anthems—only heightens the gravitas associated with his vocation.

Before Cooke's murder, Bobby Womack and his brothers were tutored by Cooke about the intricacies of the recording industry. Womack's own recording style was greatly influenced by Cooke, as the latter became a father figure. Womack's instincts in the aftermath of Cooke's death were to offer counsel and comfort to Cooke's widow, Barbara, but three months after Cooke's death and just as Womack turned twenty-one, he and Barbara Cooke wed. "They didn't let his body get cold in the ground" was how the *Pittsburgh Courier* quoted family members in response to Womack and Barbara Cooke's marriage, as Sam Cooke's young charge and his widow were easily cast as deviants in opposition to the fallen race man. Womack became the embodiment of the communal shame produced in the aftermath of Cooke's death, and it ultimately undermined his ability to cultivate a mainstream following such as that which his dead mentor enjoyed. There were, of course, myriad reasons why Womack failed to achieve mainstream appeal, including his own self-destructive behavior, but it is tempting to frame his relative commercial failures—he remains a beloved figure among fans of the soul tradition—with the broader sense of shame that his career animates.

It would be some twenty years after Cooke's death that Womack would musically respond to the drama that unfolded in the months after his mentor's demise. Though Womack didn't write "I Wish He Didn't Trust Me So Much," the story of a man who has fallen in love with his best friend's wife is palpably rendered. By the time the song was released in the summer of 1985, most listeners were not privy to the singer's relationship with Cooke's widow though to complicate matters, Womack's brother Cecil was married to Linda Cooke, the daughter of Sam and Barbara Cooke. During the time that Bobby Womack recorded "I Wish He Didn't Trust Me So Much," Curtis and Linda Womack were popular songwriters and artists in their own right, recording as Womack and Womack and writing and producing tracks like Teddy Pendergrass's hit "Love T.K.O." Bobby Womack had in fact had a brief sexual encounter with Linda Womack when she was a teen, and as he recounts in his memoir, their affair led his wife—her mother and Sam Cooke's widow—to shoot him.[13] I cite the case of Bobby Womack just to highlight that the soul man archive that Kelly and many others have access to is no less absurd than the narrative of *Trapped in the Closet*.

For example, in 1985, the year that "I Wish He Didn't Trust Me So Much" was released, Marvin Gaye had been dead for a year in the aftermath of his shooting death at the hands of his cross-dressing preacher father. The soul man Teddy Pendergrass was on the comeback trail in the aftermath of an automobile accident three years earlier that left him paralyzed from the waist down. Pendergrass's accident aroused suspicions, as the singer was rescued from his car wreck with a transgendered woman, raising questions about the nature of their relationship and the singer's own sexuality. Al Green was a decade into a radical transformation—he turned his back on secular music, favoring gospel recordings instead, in an attempt to reverse the curse of the soul man. Green's transformation occurred in the aftermath of a brutal attack at the hands of a jealous lover wielding a pot of hot grits (some rumors suggested that it was a pot of lye), who moments later killed herself—the scene was partially reenacted in the Tyler Perry film *Madea's Family Reunion*. Finally, Luther Vandross, who had become the standard bearer of the soul man tradition, was a year away from an automobile accident that killed his young white male companion, fueling anxieties about Vandross's own sexuality; the first rumors that Vandross had contracted the HIV virus also circulated at the time. In the context of the lives of many of the aforementioned artists, facts of guilt and innocence are more fluid than standard narratives would have us believe, and perhaps this was one of Kelly's points with the production of *Trapped in the Closet*. When *Trapped in the Closet* is read alongside Kelly's own legal drama, it serves as a not-so-subtle reminder, on Kelly's part, that he is not in isolation from the very communities and traditions that have produced him.

Shame, Desire, and the Confessions of a (Postmodern) Soul Man

Owing much to the groundbreaking work of the late theorist Eve Sedgwick, scholars have found "the closet" a productive site of critical inquiry, in large part because the "closet" resonates in vernacular culture as a common reference to private and secretive behaviors and lifestyles, particularly homosexuality. R. Kelly was likely well aware of these cultural meanings of the "closet" when titling his production, though in the context of *Trapped in the Closet* and Kelly's focus on black and urban domestic spaces, there is a literal quality to his use of the closet—the series begins with a character trapped in an actual closet. It is this literal aspect to Kelly's melodrama that I'd like to highlight, by suggesting that given the closet's utility as a space where things get put away when company comes over—when the public can potentially breach the private—the closet functions throughout Kelly's narrative as a site where the knowledge of domestic clutter, excess, and disarray is contained. Indeed, the role of Sylvester and, later in the series, the narrator (presumably Kelly himself) is to embody an intimate knowledge of that which is contained in the closet.

In the context of episode 1, as Cathy and Sylvester come to terms with the fact that her husband has returned home, it is notable that Sylvester instructs Cathy to "put me in the closet," signaling to audiences his singular role in mediating the messiness of Cathy and Rufus's domestic drama. Sylvester himself signals notions of narrative clutter as audiences are forced to unpack the excessive meanings attached to the character, be it as both the protagonist and narrator of the story, as an extension of Robert Sylvester Kelly and his well-known personal dramas, or, for more discerning audiences, an example of black male performance traditions—preachers, soul singers, comedians, poets, and rappers—in which black male performers are positioned to provide exegesis for the everyday drama of black life. This latter role is one that Kelly himself attempted to fulfill on *Happy People / U Saved Me* (2004), the double-disc recording that immediately preceded *TP-3:Reloaded*. The second disc, *U Saved Me*, features ten original Kelly tracks that range from gospel to inspirational, including "Prayer Changes" and "I Surrender." Though the double disc was met with a relatively tepid response from audiences, the recording highlighted a shift in black cultural spaces, as secular artists increasingly played more significant roles in providing spiritual and moral guidance for their audiences. Indeed, this reality has forced many mainstream black televangelists to recalibrate their ministries, as Jonathan L. Walton argues in his book *Watch This! The Ethics and Aesthetics of Black Televangelism*, to compete with secular artists in the culture industry. Additionally, some gospel artists have been driven to more forthrightly embrace production values that mimic those of popular secular artists.[14] Such a shift is clearly evident in the narrative of *Trapped in the Closet*, in that it is the preacher Rufus's presumed moral failings, at least in the context of mainstream and popular black Christian doctrine, that are at the core of the social deviance that the series puts on display. Where some of these secular figures might differ from their religious peers is their unwillingness—and in the case of Kelly, inability—to pass moral judgment.

In his review of *Trapped in the Closet*, the journalist Chuck Klosterman notes that the series is compelling, in part, because it does resist making judgments. According to Klosterman, in the world of *Trapped in the Closet*, "Is infidelity wrong? Absolutely, . . . but more so if you're a woman. Is homosexuality wrong? Not really, . . . but it is weird and unfathomable. Being a Christian doesn't mean you won't occasionally need to shoot people."[15] For example, the character Rufus—the minister engaged in a down-low same-sex relationship with Chuck—responds to his wife's homophobic taunt "but she's a he" with the quip, "Please, you can't judge me." Though Cathy and Rufus might be dispossessed of moral authority, as Snorton suggests, and Kelly might refuse to offer judgment—recalling the lyric from "I Wish" (2000), "instead of ya'll throwing stones at me, somebody pray for me" —*Trapped in the Closet* does in fact judge, if unintentionally, by placing many of the characters in opposition to a normative Christian and patriarchal worldview.[16] Such a worldview is invoked in episodes 2 and 3, when Rufus offers that the "Christian" in him allows him to give Cathy the "benefit of the doubt" when he suspected that she was engaged in extramarital activities. Additionally, when Cathy initially reveals to Sylvester that Rufus is a minister, he responds that they could handle their drama "Christian like." Though such statements are not overly significant in the story's narrative, they underscore the value of a normative Christian experience for many of the characters, including the so-called sinners. More significant is the way that black Christian discourse is coupled with normative views of patriarchy and the roles of women in the black family, via a discourse of respectability. The stakes here are compelling for the black middle class because, as the historian Kevin Gaines observes, "the requirement of black wives to tend families in the home signified progress for all."[17]

In *Trapped in the Closet*'s narrative, it is clear that the responsibility for the disarray and clutter that mar the lives of the central figures is firmly placed on the female characters, notably Cathy. Indeed, as the drama begins to unfold in episode 3, Rufus openly blames Cathy: "This is all your fault," detailing her betrayal, "behind my back, [in] my bed, [in] my home." The opening sequences of *Trapped in the Closet* firmly establish the household as a patriarchal space, to the point of largely ignoring how Rufus's affair with Chuck might reorder the domestic space. For Rufus the patriarchal domestic space is sacred, a literal extension of the church sanctuary that possesses the sanctity necessary to provide order and the sheen of respectability for black families and communities. As the historian Evelyn Brooks Higginbotham writes, "as the caretaker of the home, ergo caretaker of the race, black mothers were charged with the responsibility of maintaining disciplined and clean homes. The failure to do so, however, left black mothers ultimately responsible for contributing lives to the 'bad' and for 'every discrimination we suffer.'"[18]

Rufus's affair with Chuck is not necessarily factored into this equation, because the action occurs outside the domestic sphere —Chuck openly laments having to sneak around in hotels— whereas Cathy is positioned as more culpable, primarily because her indiscretion occurs in the domestic space. It is Cathy's responsibility to keep such knowledge "in the closet" as it were, to clear away the clutter and maintain order, and she fails to do so. Cathy's cloaked respectability provides cover for Rufus's own indiscretions, while her public displays of infidelity—her club-hopping—can be read as putting the preacher's business out on the street, effectively giving traction to rumors about his own sexuality. This dynamic explains some of the real anger that Rufus directs at Cathy—on a few occasions he refers to her as a "bitch." In her work on middle-class black women, Lisa B. Thompson observes, "the performance of middle-class black womanhood is tied to impossible standards of respectability. . . . To present themselves as ladies, they must either adhere to conservative sexual standards or cloak their sexuality in what Darlene Clark Hine identifies as a culture of dissemblance."[19]

Snorton is correct in asserting that *Trapped in the Closet* "inextricably ties black sexuality to queerness in the popular imagination," as what ultimately queers perceptions of the contemporary black family (particularly and ironically in black communities themselves) is the idea that the black family is out of sync with mainstream American notions of domesticity. In the post–civil rights era, fears that African American family structures were perceived as pathological have taken on the character of a moral panic or media panic. In his book *Notorious H.I.V.: The Media Spectacle of Nushawn Williams*, Thomas Shevory writes that such panics "dredge up feelings of fear and shame as they reveal real or potential social disorder," adding that "even though media panics may constitute fairly brief episodes, their recurrent appearance creates an atmosphere that makes behavioral restrictions and repressions more politically palatable."[20] But as Cathy Cohen suggests, moral and media panics in black communities function differently than those in traditional communities, which are often deemed an irrational response to social, cultural, and political shifts. According to Cohen, "African-American fear and deep concern for what is believed to be the non-normative sexual behaviors of community members is not only a reaction to the internalization of patriarchal heteronormative values about what constitutes proper sexual conduct, it is also . . . a reaction to the knowledge that the idea of black deviant sexuality has been used continuously as a justification for the secondary status of African-Americans."[21]

In this social environment, what marks *Trapped in the Closet*'s narrative as queer is not the same-sex relationship between Chuck and Rufus, but Cathy, who becomes emblematic of the pathological black family in light of her presumed unwillingness or incapacity to fulfill the traditional role of woman and wife. Indeed, throughout *Trapped in the Closet*, women are used to index the narrative's view of normative domestic behavior—and they almost always fail to live up to such norms, unless redeemed by traditional domestic behavior, as is the case with Sylvester's wife, Gwen, who is suspected of infidelity in the action that closes episode 3, but is rehabilitated as she prepares Sylvester's dinner — embodying a traditionally gendered black woman — later in the series.

Klosterman highlights the comic elements in *Trapped in the Closet* (the amount of time spent on an allergy to cherries is instructive here), producing the obvious suggestion that Kelly simply can't be serious — *Trapped in the Closet* must be pure diversionary melodrama that can't be and must not be taken seriously. That Kelly dons drag — a contemporary iteration of blackface minstrelsy that is gendered, classed, and sexed — at various points in *Trapped in the Closet*, notably as Reverend Moseley James Evans and Pimp Lucius, provides the sense that Kelly might have been simply trying to tap into the success of Tyler Perry, who has employed cross-gendered drag and melodrama to become a rather formidable force in the entertainment industry. Writing about the comic appeal of the series to some audiences (not necessarily Kelly's fans), Kelefa Sanneh observes that many "seem to think they're laughing at Mr. Kelly, not with him, as if the whole thing were part of some sort of glorious, terrible mistake."[22] The music critic Jody Rosen suggests that *Trapped in the Closet* remains close to strategies deployed by Kelly throughout his career: "Kelly has managed to breathe life into sex music by embracing sexual farce."[23]

Kelly's genre choice of melodrama and his use of drag, though, suggest that more might be at play than his tapping into the commercial value of such performances. "Melodrama presented blackness as a vehicle of protest and dissent, and minstrelsy made it an embodiment of unmentionable and transgressive pleasure," writes Saidiya Hartman in her study of the performative aspects of terror and captivity in the lives of blacks in the nineteenth century. Hartman adds, "In both instances, the fashioning of blackness aroused pity and fear, desire and revulsion, and terror and pleasure."[24] The film scholar Jane Gaines notes that when African Americans began to direct and finance their own films in the 1920s — the career of Oscar Micheaux looms large here — their genre of choice was the domestic melodrama. As Gaines writes, "these early productions have racial themes that reorganize the world in such a way that black heritage is rewarded over white paternity; they are schematic renunciations of the prevailing order of things in white American society."[25] *Trapped in the Closet* is consumed with remapping the "order of things" in an era marked by distinct disorder, in response to the prevalence of presumed "loose" morals and HIV infections, the transgressive and illicit allure of some black bodies, and the discourses of black respectability that frame and comment on much of public blackness. As the political scientist Cathy Cohen observes, "the reification of the nuclear family, the conformity to institutionally prescribed and informally regulated gender roles and intimate sexual relations are but the tip of the normative moral super structure [that the most vulnerable in black communities] confront daily."[26] In its own way, *Trapped in the Closet* offers responses and challenges to the normative structure that Cohen outlines.

Kelly's use of melodrama is foregrounded throughout *Trapped in the Closet* because musically, the series seems little more than a continuous loop—the repetition throughout forces audiences to pay stark attention to the narrative. There is a mundane quality to *Trapped in the Closet*—in the musical accompaniment, the resignation of the main characters' lives, and even the absurdities, which midway through the twenty-two episodes become normative—that brings greater attention to particularly dramatic moments in Kelly's vocal performance. In the essay "Trapped in the Epistemological Closet," Snorton notes a heightened sense of fluidity in Kelly's vocal performance: "Common vocals strategies in Kelly's storytelling include elision, whereby Kelly begins his next line before finishing out the last, stylistic changes in his ventriloquisms of the numerous gendered, racialized and queered characters, and the use of polyphonic vocal clusters to draw attention to key terms and phrases in the narrative."[27] According to Anne-Lise Francois in her essay on the use of falsetto in 1970s disco and funk music, "as theorists of subversive practices in popular culture, we've all been taught to pay attention to these moments of suspension."[28]

One such case of disruption occurs at the end of episode 7, when Kelly sings with heavy melisma about Rosie the "nosey neighbor," who knocks on Sylvester and Gwen's front door, spatula in hand, after hearing gunshots (Gwen's brother Twan is shot accidently after a scuffle between Sylvester and the police officer James, who is having an affair with Gwen). Rosie might serve as comic relief and is every bit a 1960s-styled caricature of an American housewife, but her presence at the end of the episode, as signaled by Kelly's melismic uttering of her name, is yet another reminder of the normative black femininity that is the ideological focus of *Trapped in the Closet*. Along these lines, it is notable that Rosie arrives equipped with a common kitchen utensil, suggesting that her weapons of choice are always connected to the concerns of an orderly household. She is literally waging war with the (kitchen) tools of respectability.

In another example, in episode 12, Kelly uses a capella to draw attention to an argument between Chuck, Rufus, and Cathy. The scene is notable because it places Cathy's homophobia at the forefront; indeed, Cathy's homophobia, directed most often at Chuck, is arguably the most virulent amongst the characters. After she suggests that Chuck and Rufus's sexual relationship might be the source of a literal contagion ("sneaking in and out of hotel rooms with him, ain't no telling what I got"), the music drops out as Cathy begins a profanity-laced tirade directed at Chuck as she refers to him as a "motherfucker" and feminizes him by calling him a "bitch." Cathy's blatant homophobia is striking, eroding the sheen of respectability that one might expect from a minister's wife—the so called first lady of the black church. For example, when Sylvester is first confronted with Chuck and Rufus's relationship in episode 3, he simply deadpans, "Spare me the details" (albeit with a gun pointed at Chuck), suggesting that his character simply accesses homophobic discourses as an extension of normal competitive interactions between black men as opposed to a real investment in homophobia. In bringing attention to Cathy's blatant and visceral homophobia —the most pronounced in the series—*Trapped in the Closet* also risks indictment of Cathy for her unwillingness to play nurturer and provide empathy in the ways that are expected of respect-able black women. Cathy's performance of homophobia is more likely a recalibration of the betrayal she experiences in response to Rufus's same-sex infidelity, and her homophobic rants are the only way that this betrayal gets a hearing in the narrative and in the broader social universe where *Trapped in the Closet* resonates.

The dis-ruptures that Kelly produces throughout the narra-tive, akin to Fred Moten's theorizations of "in the break," are fer-tile locations to examine the insular meanings of both *Trapped in the Closet* and R. Kelly. I am particularly drawn to the moments in the series when the narrator literally ruptures the frame—often appearing from a closeted space—in effect collapsing distinc-tions between Sylvester and R. Kelly. *Trapped in the Closet* begins with Sylvester reminiscing about his dilemma while standing in the closet that becomes the source of all of the drama that ensues. For virtually all of the first eight episodes, Sylvester largely nar-rates using first-person modes of address. In episode 8, the police officer James returns home after the nonfatal shooting of Twan to find his wife—a plus-sized white woman named Bridget—agi-tated and anxious. James's instincts lead him to believe that there is someone in the house with his wife, and the scene is shot in a way that would suggest that the person might be contained in the pantry. Instead we are introduced to Kelly in the pantry, smoking a cigar, in his role as narrator as he provides commentary ("Little did he know there was someone in his home").

The presence of this second narrator is significant because it decouples Sylvester from Kelly, providing a context to read Kelly as simply the storyteller, but also raises questions about Kelly's motivations for creating such a narrative break. Kelly's intent be-comes somewhat clearer when Kelly the narrator literally breaks into the frame, just as James is about to make a discovery inside a kitchen cupboard. The breaking of the frame is reminiscent of the way Sylvester, then hiding in Cathy and Rufus's closet, also broke into the frame at the close of the first episode. In the context of the narrative, that first rupture helped bring to light a host of "subjugated knowledges," to briefly invoke Foucault, that fuel much of the drama of the first eight episodes. This second

rupture functions much the same way, with Kelly literally freez-
ing the frame—"now pause the movie 'cause what I'm about to
say to y'all is so damn twisted, not only is there a man in this
cabinet, but the man is a midget." Of the discovery of "Big Man,"
the midget-sized black man hiding in the cupboard, Snorton
convincingly argues, "Big Man's cupboard, like Sylvester's earlier closet, serves as a form of protection in its ability to hide
the materiality of indiscretion, although it is never a stable hiding place for long. Rather the cupboard/closet functions for the
black male body as a space of inevitable discovery and escape."[29]
Snorton's observations beg the broader questions: what is to be
discovered about R. Kelly in the cupboard, and what might he be
escaping via these closets and cupboards?

Throughout episodes 9 through 11, audiences are made aware
of Big Man's affair with Bridget, whom he first met at a strip club
where he performs. As the drama unfolds, it is also discovered
that Big Man is the father of Bridget's unborn child (she is three
months pregnant). Upon hearing about his impending father-
hood, Big Man faints (for a second time) as R. Kelly the narrator ruptures the frame a second time, crooning, "The midget's
the baby's daddy." Episodes 9 through 11 are the only ones that
feature Big Man, though the fact that Kelly disturbs the frame at
critical junctures involving Big Man suggests that there is some
greater significance to Big Man and that Kelly himself is tethered
to that significance.

Throughout the episodes that feature Big Man, he is the
object of projections of bodily and sexual perversion. For example, when Big Man faints, there are several references to his
flatulence, with the strong suggestion that he was incontinent.
Additionally, Big Man references how well endowed he is sexually ("I'm Blessed"), juxtaposing his small physical frame with
his apparently large sexual organ. This particular notion of
sexual or physical fitness is undermined by Big Man's asthma
(he reaches for his inhaler as tensions rise). The general narrative suggests that despite Big Man's "gift," he is physically and
emotionally incapable of living up to the expectations associated
with his sexual endowment, particularly given historical myths

about black male sexual prowess and desire.[30] Indeed, Big Man's incontinence suggests childlike qualities, which are buttressed by his physical frame. There are numerous examples in African American vernacular practices of assigning adult masculine attributes to male children, through signifiers such as "big man" or "li'l man," particularly in the cases where black boys might be the only male presence in a household. As such, it is not difficult to imagine reading Big Man, given his performance of naiveté, as simply a little boy. Kelly's signaling of the importance of Big Man suggests some relationship between the perverse sexual behaviors embodied by Big Man and childhood.

One of the more compelling aspects of R. Kelly's music is the consistent perception that, for the artist, sex is perverse. Accordingly, there is perhaps no more vivid example of perverse sex than that of the child pornography and underage sex of which Kelly was accused. Given the public knowledge of the accusations against Kelly and the narrative constructed around Big Man's body, *Trapped in the Closet*'s narrative draws connections between childhood and illicit sexual behavior. Though I do not claim any special access to information regarding Kelly's sexual activities as a child, it is not far-fetched to imagine Robert Sylvester Kelly, as a child, hiding in a closet or cupboard and observing sexual relations—perhaps perverse—among adults or even between children and adults. The tight, spatially restricted domestic spheres of those who live in abject poverty often mean that concepts of privacy become more fluid; it's simply not unusual for children to bear witness to adult sexual behavior. Perhaps more troubling, it is also not difficult to imagine Robert Sylvester Kelly, as a child, being the object of illicit sexual activity and perhaps having to hide in the closet or cupboard as a means of protection from sexual predators. As is clear throughout *Trapped in the Closet*, the closeted space functions as a critical site of surveillance; audiences trust the narrator to present the "truth" of the narrative because of his privileged perch in the closet. What simply is the truth behind the symbolic relationship between R. Kelly as narrator and the "Big Man" hiding in the cupboard?

Hartman offers some insight in her work on the nineteenth-century slave industry in the United States and its relationship to minstrelsy and melodrama. Hartman argues that "minstrelsy and melodrama (re)produced blackness as an essential pained expression of the body's possibilities," and to remix Hartman here, I would suggest that in the context of *Trapped in the Closet*, Big Man is the expression of the *possibilities of pain* (displaced from Sylvester's body) on the closeted or incarcerated (to make a more explicit point) black (male) body. On the surface, Kelly's investment in minstrelsy seems minor, his performances as the church custodian Randolph and his rather comic spins on Pimp Lucious and the Reverend Moseley James Evans notwithstanding. Kelly's performances throughout *Trapped in the Closet*, though, pivot on the authenticity of voice—the characters in the series come alive in the context of Kelly's vocal mimicry, including Bridget, the lone white character. As Louis Chude-Sokei suggests in his study of blackface minstrelsy, successful blackface minstrels had to sound "black." Discussing the legendary Bert Williams in his book *The Last "Darky,"* Chude-Sokei writes, "black dialect was . . . literally a foreign language for Williams since his cultural origins were nowhere near the literal or mythic American South."[31] In his era, Williams had to not only look the part of the "darky," but perhaps more critically, had to sound the part. Not surprisingly, the most recognizable blackface minstrel performances of the twentieth century occurred on Freeman Gosden and Charles Correll's long-running radio broadcast *Amos 'n' Andy*. Gosden and Correll were white comedians, and the "authenticity" of their performances resonated for black and white audiences alike. Thought about in the context of sound and dialect, *Trapped in the Closet* can be read as a blackface minstrel performance.

Again, Hartman is useful here: "the convergences between the bodily politics of minstrelsy and those of melodrama might be said to center on the redemptive and recreational use of violence."[32] Though *Trapped in the Closet* is not particularly violent, characters regularly employ threats of violence, to echo Jenkins's earlier point, to bring order to domestic and narrative disarray.

In this context, threats of violence are often enacted in an effort to summon forms of respectability, prime examples being Ms. Rosie's use of the spatula or Sylvester's threat to "shoot somebody" when presented with evidence of Chuck and Rufus's affair. Notable in the critical episodes 9, 10, and 11, virtually all of the characters are embodied as threats of violence, including Bridget, who eventually brandishes a shotgun to protect Big Man and to bring order to the situation. The only character who does not have access to the potential of violence is Big Man, who seeks protection in the cupboard/closet, in his performance of childhood, and eventually with Bridget's shotgun. In a narrative notably absent of children, Big Man becomes the symbol of a childhood compromised by sexual violence. As to whether this is an admission of guilt on R. Kelly's part, amidst an admittedly convoluted melodrama, or his recognition of the sexual violence to which he—or perhaps his prepubescent body—might have borne witness, or both, seems beyond the point.

Trapped in the Closet ultimately sheds light on the cycles of violence and betrayal that occur in black domestic spheres, where a politics of black respectability is often deemed the only legitimate performance of blackness. For Kelly's part, the grand message of *Trapped in the Closet* might be best captured in the colloquialism "shit happens" and that it behooves black communities to wrap their heads around the ways that the safety of weaker bodies and spirits is regularly compromised under these conditions, including the young woman who stood as Kelly's accuser. If R. Kelly had sex with underage girls, it's shame on him; if R. Kelly was also sexually abused as a child, it's shame on black communities, and the collective silence, adulation, and even protection of R. Kelly (thirty-five years too late) is the by-product of collective desires to render the shame of such abuse in our communities as the personal province of individual demons and victims, but never in the collective essential black body.

At its best, *Trapped in the Closet* mimics the function of the popular telenovelas broadcast on Spanish-speaking networks like Univision and Telemundo. Telenovelas generally run in three- to six-month cycles and, as the scholars Vivian Barrera and Denise

Bielby note, they generally speak across generations—watching telenovelas is a family affair.[33] It was the popularity of such programming that inspired the producer and director Dilsey Davis to create the telenovela *Nuestro Barrio* as part of her work with community advocacy organizations in North Carolina. Davis uses the show to address domestic and social concerns for audiences who don't find their concerns addressed on mainstream television. *Nuestro Barrio* is an example of what the rapper KRS-One termed "edutainment" almost two decades ago. The closing scene of *Trapped in the Closet*, which confirms the likely positive HIV status of several of the characters, literally reproduces the viral-like effect of the disease. In the end audiences might feel as if they sat through a twenty-two-episode public service announcement, and there is precedent to such thinking. As ironic as it might seem, *Trapped in the Closet* might be viewed as R. Kelly's attempt at penance.

5

Fear of a Queer Soul Man

The Legacy of Luther Vandross

Where oh where, are all the real men. . . . You got eyeliner on,
chillin' and maxin' / See you're a man with a spine extraction /
So what I'm askin' is plain to see / Are there any straight
singers in R&B?
> KRS-ONE, "Ya Strugglin'" (1990)

Superman can fly high way up in the sky (cause we believe he
can) / So what we choose to believe can always work out fine /
It's all in the mind.
> LUTHER VANDROSS, "Make Me a Believer" (1984)

Their names ring out like a chorus of singer's singers—Johnny
Mathis, Jimmy Scott, Eddie Kendricks, Al Green, Ronnie Dyson,
Rahsaan Patterson, the fabulous Sylvester, and, perhaps most
spectacularly, Luther Vandross. These men, whose wildly emo-
tive voices summoned both spirits and gods, have also inspired
rumor and innuendo among those who would believe that their
voices—soft, expressive, and feminine—betrayed the strength
and vigor of black masculinity. Luther Vandross, a child of the
post–World War II period, who came of age during the height
of the Black Power movement, was more than aware of the
soul men–turned–race men tradition and the hypermasculinity and hypersexuality that the tradition emboldened and even
demanded. Singers like James Brown, Marvin Gaye, Solomon
Burke, Brook Benton, Wilson Pickett, Bill Withers, Isaac Hayes,
Barry White, and Teddy Pendergrass captured the imagination
of black America during an era when hyperblack, hypermasculine, hypersexual male icons seemed logical retorts to ongoing
ideological threats centered on notions of American masculinity.

Possessing vocal ranges that inhabited the lower registers, some of the aforementioned soul singers were the musical embodiments of popular masculine icons such as El-Hajj Malik El-Shabazz (Malcolm X) and *Soul on Ice* author Eldridge Cleaver.

This was the cultural terrain that Luther Vandross, a heavyset romantic, confronted growing up in Harlem in the 1960s. Born in 1951, Vandross turned to music to salve the pain of the sudden death of his father in 1959. Whereas many of his male peers were modeling themselves after the soul men who so gallantly represented on behalf of the race, Vandross found his inspiration in women vocalists like Dionne Warwick, Diana Ross, Aretha Franklin, Cissy Houston and the Sweet Inspirations, and Patti LaBelle and the Bluebelles. As vocalists these women deftly negotiated the worlds of Chitlin' Circuit soul and supper club pop, providing nuance and range to the whirlwind of emotions that black Americans confronted in the late 1960s and early 1970s. Additionally, many of the prominent black female vocalists of the 1960s were paragons of feminine elegance. Vandross's embrace of these women was not about notions of a diminished or suspect masculinity, but rather a masculinity that challenged the prevailing logic of what the feminist critic Michele Wallace would term in the 1970s the "black macho."[1]

Vandross got his professional start in the music industry in 1969, as part of a youth performance troupe known as Listen Up, Brother. The group was founded in the late 1960s as part of public relations efforts by Harlem's Apollo Theater. As the journalist Craig Seymour explains, the theater was then owned by the Schiffman family, and "at the time neighborhood activists were heatedly raising questions about the large number of white owned businesses in Harlem."[2] Listen Up, Brother was an attempt by the Schiffman family to give back to black Harlem. The group released its first single, "Listen, My Brother," in 1969 and shortly thereafter made its television debut on an experimental television program created by the Children's Television Workshop, *Sesame Street*. Though Listen Up, Brother largely focused on educational uplift—one of their *Sesame Street* appearances featured a soulful rendition of the alphabet—their style of performance was akin to that of the Black Arts Movement, with its attempt to reach youthful audiences via the use of black vernacular and style. Vandross's stint with Listen Up, Brother ended when he enrolled in Western Michigan University in the fall of 1969.

After leaving Western Michigan University after only one year, Vandross returned to New York to continue his musical career and began to write songs. In 1973 he sold two songs to Dolores Hall, then performing in the Broadway musical *Godspell*. Hall, who also appeared in the groundbreaking musical *Hair* (1968), would later win a Tony Award for her performance in *Your Arms Too Short to Box with God* (1976). Vandross's "In This Lovely Hour" and "Who's Gonna Make It Easier for Me" appeared on Hall's *Hall-Mark* (1973), the latter track featuring Vandross in an uncredited duet with Hall. Additionally, Vandross's songwriting drew attention from Ken Harper, who was developing an all-black musical version of *The Wizard of Oz*. When *The Wiz* debuted in January 1975, starring a seventeen-year-old Stephanie Mills in the lead role of Dorothy, Vandross's "Everybody Rejoice" was one of the original songs that appeared in the groundbreaking musical. The production would eventually earn seven Tony Awards, including the award for best musical.

Vandross's biggest break occurred in 1974, when he joined David Bowie's tour as a backup singer. Vandross also provided backing vocals and arrangements on Bowie's American breakthrough recording, *Young Americans* (1975), an album recorded in Philadelphia's famed Sigma Studios. During the *Young Americans* sessions Vandross and Bowie reworked a Vandross original, "Funky Music (Is a Part of Me)" and transformed it into "Fascination," which appears on *Young Americans*. Impressed with Vandross's voice, Bowie eventually asked Vandross to become his opening act, giving the singer his first taste of the limelight as a solo artist. Though a tremendous opportunity, the request animated Vandross's lifelong anxieties about his weight, which at various times during his career was more than three hundred pounds. Referring to Vandross's weight, the saxophonist David Sanborn, who was part of Bowie's studio and touring band, told

Seymour, "he seemed to be very self-conscious. . . . He seemed to not want to have the spotlight on him. He would've preferred to be behind a curtain."[3] Vandross's stint on Bowie's tour gave him needed exposure, and the actress Bette Midler was quick to hire him as an arranger and background vocalist for her show *Clams on the Half-Shell Revue*, which opened in April 1975. Bowie's "Young Americans" and Bobby "Blue" Bland's "Ain't No Love in the Heart of the City" were among the songs that Vandross arranged for the show, which ran for ten weeks.

Vandross's apprehensions about being up-front were manifested when he transitioned from Bowie and Midler and became leader of the vocal ensemble Luther. The group released two recordings, *Luther* (1977) and *This Close to You* (1978), for the Cotillion label. The opening track on the group's debut album was "Funky Music (Is a Part of Me)," the song that Vandross and Bowie had earlier transformed into "Fascination." Though the group was clearly an embodiment of Vandross's musical sensibility, the ensemble allowed him to remain in the background of his own project. According to Vandross, "I love background vocals so much I can't breathe. . . . When I get the chance to do background vocals on a professional level, in my mind, I had made it."[4] Vandross's comments put into some context his professional choices after the demise of Luther shortly after the release of their second album.

Vandross earned a stellar reputation for his work as a session singer, arranger, and guest vocalist, and his resume in the late 1970s includes work with a virtual who's who of pop and soul music. Between 1978, the year of the last Luther album, and 1981, the year that Vandross's debut, *Never Too Much,* was released, he appeared on recordings by Chic, Roberta Flack, Garland Jeffreys, Cat Stevens, Carly Simon, the Average White Band, Cher, Evelyn Champaign King, Ben Sidran, Sister Sledge, Mandrill, the Brecker Brothers, Irene Cara, Cissy Houston, Chaka Khan, Mtume, the Brooklyn, Bronx, & Queens Band, the J. Geils Band, Stephanie Mills, the Spinners, and Bernard Wright. Two particularly notable appearances by Vandross during this period set the groundwork for his burgeoning career as a solo artist. In 1978 Vandross was a featured vocalist on Quincy Jones's 1978 recording *And . . . Stuff Like That*, providing co-leads with Gwen Guthrie on a remake of the Doobie Brothers' classic "Taking It to the Streets," and sharing leads with Patti Austin on "I'm Gonna Miss You in the Morning." Vandross met Jones when the latter was working on the soundtrack for the film version of *The Wiz*, while also in the studio recording *And . . . Stuff Like That*. Like the Broadway production of *The Wiz*, the film version featured Vandross's "Everybody Rejoice." The experience with Jones provided Vandross with one of his largest artistic platforms; three years after the release of *The Wiz*, Vandross would be a label-mate with the movie's scarecrow, Michael Jackson.

Two years after the success of Jones's *And . . . Stuff Like That*, Vandross went into the studio with the producer Jacques Fred Petrus, becoming the featured vocalist for a studio band simply known as Change. After initially balking at Vandross's financial demands and his desire for billing on the album cover, Petrus relented and Vandross provided lead vocals on the tracks "The Glow of Love" and "Searching" from Change's debut, *The Glow of Love* (1980). The songs, which became club favorites, earned Vandross his first recognition as a soloist, though he remained invisible to most audiences. As Seymour writes, Vandross's voice was "now more ubiquitous than ever. Radio announcers started crediting 'Searching' and 'The Glow of Love' to Change *featuring Luther Vandross*. Sometimes they would just say Luther Vandross. People now knew his name."[5] Vandross was initially disappointed that his visibility with Change didn't immediately translate into a solo deal with a label—he finally signed with Epic in the spring of 1981—but, as in the past, many labels didn't quite know what to do with Vandross's body. In an industry that was increasingly drawn to image—the groundbreaking music video network MTV hit the airwaves the year before the release of *The Glow of Love*—Vandross was simply known as a "voice," perhaps portending the concepts of disembodiment that would mark the singer's career.

The Labor of Luther's Voice

Though relatively unknown at the time of his debut, *Never Too Much*, by the time of his death in July 2005 Vandross was easily the best-known black male vocalist of his generation. The irony of Vandross's success is that little was known about his personal life, though he would be the subject of a level of rumor, innuendo, and speculation rivaled only by his industry peers the late Michael Jackson and R. Kelly, both men whose private lives were mainstream fodder. As Craig Seymour queries, "How did Vandross go from being a new artist about whom little was known to becoming an international superstar about whom much was suspected but little was spoken?"[6] This particular dynamic suggests that Vandross was valued not so much for who he was, but for his function as a singer and artistic icon. Seymour puts it another way, suggesting that "Vandross is not so much singing *to* his female fans, asking them for love, as he is singing *for* them or commiserating *with* them."[7] The key to understanding Vandross's appeal as an artist is unpacking the labor he provided on behalf of his core audience and the black public at large.

As mentioned above, Vandross's body size was a major impediment to his achievement of mainstream crossover success, and it was also a challenge for him in the early days of his solo career, when his music primarily circulated to black audiences. At the time of his debut, Vandross was frequently compared to Barry White, the plus-sized baritone singer who was popular in the 1970s with tracks like "Can't Get Enough of Your Love" and "You're the First, You're the Last, My Everything." Though White and Vandross shared body type and a preference for lush, ornate musical production, there was little else that connected the two. White's reputation was as a "love man" in the tradition of his peers Marvin Gaye, Teddy Pendergrass, and perhaps most notably the 1960s balladeer Solomon Burke. Burke, who was also plus-sized—at various times in his career he has tipped the scales at close to four hundred pounds—is perhaps best known for his excesses: his weight, regal attire (he frequently wore a crown and robe on stage), and seemingly insatiable sexual appetite (he fathered more than twenty children). In the 1960s Burke, along with others like Otis Redding, Wilson Pickett, and Aretha Franklin, was one of the most successful purveyors of southern soul, a genre of music noted for its earthiness, references to the black Pentecostal tradition, and improvisational energy. Southern soul music was the embodiment of the Chitlin' Circuit, the network of clubs, dance halls, theaters, and after-hour clubs that black performers and audiences were dependent upon prior to the 1960s, particularly in the South.

In the era when Vandross emerged, a period defined, in part, by the emergence of a "new" black middle class and gestures toward residential and educational racial integration, the Chitlin' Circuit was thought to be passé by some, and for others it was a vulgar reminder of a segregated past that many wanted to forget. L. H. Stallings suggests that the Chitlin' Circuit might have also been read as queer in black communities. As Stallings explains, "the chitlin' circuit reconfigures elements associated with camp to include issues of race. Though the chitlin' circuit and its sister avenues, traveling tent shows and the TOBA (Theater Owners Booking Association), did not explicitly perform for sexually queer audiences, they did address the needs of Black people consistently ascribed to the realms of non-heternormativity."[8] In that Vandross's girth became a visual stand-in for the pathological excesses of the Chitlin' Circuit and segregation, in order to find success Vandross's voice had to do a cultural work that undermined the meanings associated with his body. Eschewing the familiar church and Chitlin' Circuit influences that propelled earlier generations of black artists, Vandross performed an iteration of black respectability—his music and voice embodied the refined, corporate sensibilities of the new black middle class. Indeed, Vandross's attention to, and even obsession with, elements of presentational style in his music and his appearance in many ways mirrored the consumerist desires of a black middle class poised to purchase the mainstream acceptance that the civil rights movement hoped would be legislated. The R&B sound that Vandross came to personify was aspirational, in sync with a decade that featured the first black Miss America pageant winner in Vanessa Williams (who would become an R&B star in her own right), Jesse Jackson's two presidential campaigns (which laid the groundwork for Barack Obama's success in 2008), the emergence of *The Cosby Show* and its upper-middle-class Huxtable family as the quintessential American family, and the rise of Michael Jackson as the first and most lasting icon of the video age.

Examples of Vandross's strategy are found on his debut, *Never Too Much*, which featured his seven-minute revision of the late Hal David and Burt Bacharach classic "A House Is Not a Home," a song originally recorded by Dionne Warwick in 1964. "A House Is Not a Home" established Vandross as a balladeer extraordinaire and revealed his exceptional talents as an arranger. "A House Is Not a Home" also helped establish Vandross's music as a staple of the "Quiet Storm" radio format—a late-night urban radio format that features soft ballads. The programming format was conceived by a staffer, Cathy Hughes (now known for her ownership of the Radio One network), and popularized by the late Melvin Lindsey when they worked at Howard University's WHUR in the mid-1970s. Vandross's reputation as the premier black male balladeer of his generation was so pronounced that he quickly became even more synonymous with the "Quiet Storm" than Smokey Robinson, whose recording *Quiet Storm* (1974) originally inspired the format.

Vandross's style harked back to an era when black men such as Duke Ellington, Billy Eckstine, Miles Davis, and Nat King Cole embodied a visual representation of black respectability, but there was also a sprinkling of post-soul glam (courtesy of his early apprenticeship with David Bowie). A quick survey of some of Vandross's signature album covers—*The Night I Fell in Love* (1985), *Give Me the Reason* (1986), *Never Let Me Go* (1992) —illustrates this point. The stylishness of men like Eckstine and Davis countered a black masculinity that in their era was often depicted as ragged, rugged, buffoonish, and dangerous in Hollywood cinema and elsewhere. Although the sexuality of the aforementioned men bubbled hotly just below the surface of their images (and in the case of Davis a propensity for violence against women), they were a far cry from the crazed "Gus" (actor Walter

Long in blackface), whose desire for the "sweet whiteness" of Flora (actress Mae Marsh) forced the latter to jump off the side of a cliff in *Birth of a Nation* (1915), D. W. Griffith's cinematic treatment of Thomas Dixon's novel *The Clansman*. As such, Vandross's performance of "black respectability" was a throwback of sorts; had he emerged in the 1940s and 1950s like, say, Johnny Mathis or Jimmy Scott, two singers with whom he also shares a vocal lineage, perhaps little would have been made of his emotiveness or his hyper-stylishness.

Instead Vandross emerged during an era when public performances of black masculinity were dominated by the notion of the black macho, an ideologically constructed masculine identity, thought to be in sync with the psychic energies of the Black Power movement. In her controversial book *Black Macho and the Myth of the Superwoman*, Michele Wallace offers a critique of the "black macho," suggesting that "his" appearance was motivated by "revenge. It was not equality that was primarily being pursued but a kind of superiority—black manhood, black macho —which would combine the ghetto cunning, cool, and unrestrained sexuality of black survival with the unchecked authority, control, and wealth of white power."[9] The late filmmaker and activist Marlon Riggs was even more explicit in his critique of the "black macho," a critique that pivots on his identity as a "black gay man." According to Riggs, "by the tenets of Black Macho, Black Gay Man is a triple negation. I am consigned, by these tenets, to remain a Negro Faggot. And as such I am game for play, to be used, joked about, put down, beaten, slapped and bashed, not just by illiterate homophobic thugs in the night, but by many of Black American culture's best and brightest."[10]

In the context of the recording industry of the late 1960s and 1970s, the black macho was not an explicitly political construct. While Marvin Gaye's recording *What's Going On* is generally thought to be a significant example of politicized soul music, the political undercurrents of songs like "Inner City Blues" or "What's Happening Brother" didn't necessarily translate into Gaye being thought of as any more of a political figure than most of his musical peers. Most audiences understood that Gaye's cultural politics could not be easily conflated with traditional notions of political struggle. Yet popular culture was a critical site for the contesting of ideological discourses that sought to marginalize black masculinity, particularly in the realm of heterosexuality. One would be hard pressed, for example, to identify figures in 1970s soul who would be comparable to Eldridge Cleaver and George Jackson or their cinematic counterparts, Sweetback and Shaft (though Isaac Hayes's Truck Turner comes close), unless the hypersexual antics of the aforementioned figures are isolated from their more explicitly political activities of challenging "the man," as it were. When black macho's role is reduced to that of a hypersexual archetype of black masculinity, as was the case in much black popular culture during the era, then artists such as Marvin Gaye, Barry White, Isaac Hayes, Al Green, and Major Harris (whose "Love Won't Let Me Wait" was covered by Vandross) easily subscribed to such roles. Gaye's sexual opus *Let's Get It On* (1973) is paramount here, establishing Gaye as the quintessential "sex man" of the soul era.

Black macho was a performance for which Vandross was ill-suited, as he had little interest in the kind of political discourses associated with the era, and because of his size, he would not be taken seriously as a hypersexualized object of desire (indeed, part of Barry White and much later Notorious B.I.G.'s genius was their ability to play such a role). Vandross's nuanced, refined, and, as Jason King suggests, "sentimental" masculine performance was at odds with the available notions of black masculinity that existed in the late 1970s. The same could be said about Vandross's musical performances, as King writes that the "singer's soulfulness, the authenticity of his 'blackness,' comes under fire because of his lack of 'masculine' funk. Precisely, Vandross comes to represent the loss of funk in Soul."[11] King's observations contextualize the comments of the rap artist KRS-One, who in the song "Ya Strugglin'" (quoted in the epigraph above) essentially deems R&B a queer and inauthentic black space. The rapper's critique of R&B music anticipates rap music's own debates about queerness and authenticity a generation later, particularly when the R&B artist and Jay-Z and Kanye West collaborator Frank Ocean gestured toward his bisexuality on his 2012 release *channel* ORANGE. As Riggs notes, according to the "tenets of Black Macho, true masculinity admits little or no space for self-interrogation or multiple subjectivities around race. Black Macho prescribes an inflexible ideal."[12] Thus Vandross is doubly queered for not being *man enough* and not being *black enough*—queered, to use the language of John Nguyet Erni, for embodying "surplus representations" of black masculinity (both in concert with and in contrast to the "excess" representations of his body).[13] While the black macho and the black queer represent a logical dichotomy, it is useful to remember that not all queer bodies are constructed the same. The queer sexuality that Marlon Riggs embodied in his life is not the sentimental queerness—that which could be thought as strange or oppositional —that marked Luther Vandross's performance of masculinity at the beginning of his solo career.

Critical to contextualizing Vandross's "queerness" in the early 1980s is to read him against the dominant black male soul singers of that era, including Al Green, Teddy Pendergrass, and the disco diva, Sylvester. Pendergrass, who was arguably the most commercially bankable black male singer of the late 1970s with the exception of Stevie Wonder, offers the most interesting and useful contrast to Vandross. The former lead singer of the hugely successful Harold Melvin and the Blue Notes, Pendergrass began his solo career in early 1977 with the release of *Teddy Pendergrass*. Aided by his label's "Teddy Is Ready" campaign, where Pendergrass did radio station drop-ins and recorded phone messages for women fans in the various cities on his promotional tour, and the lead single "I Don't Love You Anymore," which rode the crest of the disco wave, Pendergrass became a dominant commercial success. Pendergrass succeeded in part because of an emerging black consumer base that his label, the legendary Philadelphia International Records (PIR), itself helped to cultivate. With crossover historically deemed the most likely route to success in the recording industry, PIR tapped into the increasing buying power of a post–civil rights–era black middle class that was just beginning to flex its economic might, an audience interested not in watered-down crossover blackness, but in something more "authentic" (owing in part to the obvious anxieties produced by their newfound class status). In the late 1970s Teddy Pendergrass was that voice of authenticity, and the proof was in the sales; Pendergrass's first five studio albums all went platinum or multi-platinum (he was the first black male artist to achieve the feat), selling primarily to black audiences and garnering little if any airplay on mainstream pop stations.

Perhaps more powerfully, Pendergrass represented an idealized black masculinity in the late 1970s. Though his work with Harold Melvin and the Blue Notes had political connotations, Pendergrass's popularity as a solo artist lay in his performance of a masculinity that was virile and potent and tailor-made for a cultural discourse that had moved beyond the struggles for civil rights and fixated on establishing acceptable images of black masculinity in an integrated society. Though such images existed in black macho cinematic figures like Super Fly (Ron O'Neal) and Shaft (Richard Roundtree), Pendergrass made such performances real and accessible, in an era partially defined by cartoonish performances of black masculinity in popular culture, like Antonio Fargas's Huggy Bear and Jimmie Walker's J. J. Evans. What made Pendergrass's performance of black masculinity palpable was, in part, the physical limits of his vocal instrument. Though he was never technically strong as a singer—he never possessed the vocal dexterity of his peers Marvin Gaye, Al Green, or Vandross—there was an earnestness in Pendergrass's baritone that helped soften a hypermasculinity that was off the charts. Pendergrass was still in his late twenties when he became an icon, but his full beard and sonorous voice evoked a man twice his age.

Pendergrass was also part of the first generation of black male performers who could publicly express a distinct sexual identity, with examples ranging from Richard Roundtree to Marvin Gaye and even Sylvester. With the sexual revolution in full swing, sex (as opposed to romance) became Pendergrass's primary calling card. As such, Pendergrass's rise coincides with communal anxieties produced in response to Al Green's rejection of the very secular sexuality that helped establish the popularity of the male soul singer, dating back to Sam Cooke's emergence in the 1950s. If Al Green was no longer invested in the hypersexualized black masculinity that he and an aging Marvin Gaye (who would later see Pendergrass as a rival) helped cultivate in the 1970s, Pendergrass was a suitable and unequivocally (hetero) masculine (by the standards of the era) replacement.

Pendergrass was primed for greater success and perhaps even the crossover appeal that had thus far eluded him, when a car accident in 1982 left him paralyzed. Officially, Pendergrass was driving his 1981 Rolls Royce, late in the evening of March 18, 1982, with a companion, Tenika Watson, when he lost control of his car. Pendergrass and Watson were trapped in the car for more than forty-five minutes, with Pendergrass sustaining spinal cord injuries that would leave him paralyzed from below the waist and confined to a wheelchair for the rest of his life. If Pendergrass's hypermasculine and sexually potent body previously served as a salve for the anxieties produced in the midst of disco's decided queering of popular music, Pendergrass's broken body became the site for a new set of anxieties about black masculinity. The source of that angst was the revelation that Pendergrass's companion that night, Tenika Watson, was transsexual. Well before there was remotely a politically correct way to address transsexual and transgendered people in the public realm (as if that's the case even now), Watson was immediately positioned as some sort of freak. As Watson told the *Philadelphia Tribune* two months after the accident—which she escaped with minor injuries—"I can't get over how people treat you, how they turn everything around. . . . What really made me upset was the fact that the papers made me seem as though I was some kind of animal or demon and that I was not a God fearing person."[14]

The accident subsequently generated whispers about Pendergrass's own sexuality. Pendergrass's accident marks a shift in black masculine performances in R&B, best exemplified in the increasing popularity of figures like Prince, Rick James, El DeBarge, Michael Jackson, and Vandross, who all trafficked in androgynous and asexual performances of masculinity that were the antithesis of Pendergrass's version of the black macho.

Vandross's ascendance as the dominant male R&B vocalist of the 1980s and early 1990s occurs in the context of Pendergrass's symbolic fall from black masculine "grace." Accordingly, as Vandross's popularity increased, so did speculation about his sexual identity. A bachelor throughout his life and never publicly linked to any romantic interest (male or female), Vandross was intensely protective of his private life, and his silence about his sexuality created anxieties among his audiences. Vandross was equally invested in distancing himself from overly "feminine" masculine performances. In this regard, a figure like the late dance artist Sylvester, who personified a more flamboyant black gay style, was as much a threat to Vandross's "sentimental" masculinity as the "black macho." To sample from Joshua Gamson's book *The Fabulous Sylvester: The Legend, the Music, the Seventies in San Francisco*, Vandross needed to be a "plausibly masculine rhythm-and-blues" singer.[15] Vandross often undercut perceptions of his "queer" identity by buttressing a "fierce masculinity," drawn from notions of a hypermasculine diva. The ongoing behind-the-scenes tensions when Vandross toured nationally with Anita Baker in 1988 and the vocal group En Vogue and a fairly contentious spat with Aretha Franklin in the mid-1980s provided the first public insight into this aspect of Vandross's identity. En Vogue would later dub Vandross "Lucifer," which became a marker of how he negotiated his masculinity in private, but publicly he remained silent about his sexual identity.

And then there was (again) Vandross's body. In a broad cultural sense, with his increased popularity, Vandross's body became a source of anxiety for some black audiences, initially because of his girth (complicated by the hypervisuality of blackness in the era) and later with the advent of the AIDS/HIV crisis. Once the source of communal apprehension and humor —Eddie Murphy's comic routine about Vandross from his *Delirious* stand-up recording stands out—Vandross trimmed down significantly in 1986 (losing more than a hundred pounds), just prior to the release of *Give Me the Reason*. This weight loss generated intense scrutiny and speculation. Rumors that Vandross was in ill health gained traction when the British magazine *Blues and*

Soul erroneously reported that Vandross had contracted AIDS.[16] Vandross's body became the site of a corporeal and diseased queerness. It is important to put the Vandross AIDS rumors in a historical context. As the political scientist Cathy Cohen writes in her important study, *The Boundaries of Blackness: AIDS and the Breakdown of Black Politics*, when the first coverage of the disease emerged in 1981, there was "little attention to its impact on African-American gay men, African-American injection drug users, or other members of the black community. . . . The absence of a specific focus on AIDS in African-American communities led many to believe that this disease was not about them."[17] The rumors about Vandross and AIDS were the first to circulate regarding a relatively prominent African American figure, a few years before the television journalist Max Robinson (1988), Sylvester (1989), and the tennis legend Arthur Ashe succumbed to the disease, and more than five years before the basketball player Magic Johnson's admission that he was HIV-positive. As Seymour states rather plainly, "for many African-Americans, AIDS was still considered something white folks got."[18]

Cohen suggests that there was much more at work than simply the belief that it was a white, gay disease, particularly in light of black political leadership, which initially ignored the threat of HIV and AIDS in black communities. As Cohen points out, during the Reagan era "constructed images of a black community in disarray were used to legitimize the neglect of state and federal governments and the flight of corporations, individual whites, and some economically successful blacks from black and brown cities."[19] Cohen adds that as the impact of AIDS on black communities became more pronounced and public, "many black leaders pursued a more aggressive program of denial and distance, employing strategies of secondary marginalization to negate the relationship between those black people with AIDS and the larger black community. . . . Code words like *junkie*, *faggot*, *punk* and *prostitute* were deployed both inside and outside of black communities to designate who was expendable."[20] Cohen's reading anticipates the shift in black communal discourse regarding homosexuality in the 1990s and the early twenty-first century

—"queer" black bodies were no longer simply to be tolerated, excused, and humored, but were now going to be culturally and politically quarantined as diseased black bodies. What did this new state of affairs mean for Vandross, who was doubly marked as potentially gay and HIV-positive?

Seymour opines that Vandross's ability to remain popular was premised on his black audience's willingness to maintain a "code of secrecy" about prominent figures who might have been suspected of being "textual[ly] gay." That code of secrecy was itself related to the very issues of black respectability that Cohen outlines above. As Seymour observes, "gay people, far from being marginal in black communities, are often central to their cultural makeup." With regard to Vandross's relationship with black audiences, Seymour adds, "It is a widely acknowledged, if unspoken, assumption that he is gay yet he is also considered the predominant voice of black heterosexual courtship. Therefore his widespread acceptance as a cultural figure in many black communities hinges upon his sexual orientation remaining a secret."[21] That code of secrecy was tested shortly after the rumors about Vandross's health circulated, when he was in an automobile accident in January 1986 with a teenage singer, Jimmy Salvemini, and his older brother and manager, Larry Salvemini. The elder brother was killed in the crash. Rumors circulated at the time that Vandross, who was producing Jimmy Salvemini's debut album, was romantically linked to one of the brothers. As Seymour observes, Vandross dutifully obliged his audience by never publicly commenting on the Salvemini brothers or the charges of misdemeanor manslaughter and reckless driving (Vandross was driving) that were associated with the accident.[22]

Vandross and his audiences were complicit in their desires to simply treat the rumors about him with silence. Indeed, silence became a defining metaphor for the fears and apprehensions about homosexuality and AIDS/HIV in some black communities, mirroring the "don't ask, don't tell" strategy of the US armed forces during the Bill Clinton presidency in the 1990s. Vandross's ability to remain commercially viable can be contrasted to the career of the rapper Big Daddy Kane, who at the height of his career in the late 1980s, when he was a paragon of hip-hop masculinity, was also rumored to be dying of AIDS; Big Daddy Kane was hip-hop's version of the black macho. In that discourses surrounding hip-hop culture at the time, as now, heavily trafficked in a hypermasculinity that Vandross was already outside of, it was not surprising that Big Daddy Kane's career, as Marc Lamont Hill observes, was not able to withstand speculation about Kane's sexuality. As Hill writes, "After the rumors began to circulate, . . . Kane's image was placed in serious peril. Hip-hop's Goliath of masculinity had been slain by a disease presumably preserved for 'punks,' 'fags,' and 'queens.'"[23]

Vandross owed some of his sustained popularity to the aforementioned Quiet Storm radio format, the late-night urban radio programming that featured romantic R&B ballads, leading to the widely circulated notion that Vandross specialized in "baby making" music. Vandross's voice became a centerpiece of black heterosexual desire. The same could be said about Melvin Lindsey, the Washington, DC, radio personality who popularized the Quiet Storm format in the late 1970s and 1980s. In an interesting twist, Lindsey, described by the journalist Jacqueline Trescott as "synonymous with romance," died in 1992 of complications from AIDS, the consequence of unprotected sexual encounters with men.[24] Ironically, it was sexual discourses about Vandross and Lindsey's core audience—heterosexual black women—that brought the issue of AIDS to the forefront of concerns about sexuality in black communities via the spectacle of the "down low." Whether or not Vandross was gay or HIV-positive, he became a comforting sign in some black communities who were trying to negotiate this new sexual terrain.

For some heterosexual audiences Vandross became the dominant trope for heterosexual romantic relationships, at a time when black marriage rates were in decline. Vandross's original music video for "Here and Now" is instructive. Originally included as a "new" track on the Luther Vandross collection *The Best of Luther Vandross: The Best of Love* (1989), "Here and Now" became Vandross's first major pop hit. In order to promote the single and the album, Vandross's label partnered with New York

City's leading black-owned radio station, WBLS-FM, in a contest in which the winning couple would be serenaded by Vandross at their nuptials. Video of Vandross's performance of "Here and Now" at the winning couple's wedding served as the basis for the song's initial music video. The fact that the video was quickly re-shot, featuring an animated head shot of Vandross and heterosexual white lovers, speaks volumes about Vandross's struggles to cross over, but of particular interest was the intent of the initial video to actively portray Vandross as an element of black marriage practices, as if Vandross, and the code of silence around him, represented last stands for the institution in black communities. Indeed, when Vandross appeared on Oprah Winfrey's show shortly thereafter, she specifically requested that he sing "Here and Now" in the event that she got married.[25] In addition, Vandross functioned as a trope of black respectability, warding off a new generation of soul and R&B singers that emerged in the 1990s, led by R. Kelly, who melded the sound of contemporary R&B with the more urgent and profane sexual desires expressed in rap music.

As Seymour explores, in addition to Vandross's role as a "virtual gay friend" for some black women, Vandross also became a trope for black queer men negotiating their liminality in black publics that were fearful of the impact of AIDS and homosexuality on black domestic life. One index of Vandross's discursive impact is his presence in the burgeoning genre of popular fiction marketed to black women, of which the work of Terry McMillan and the late E. Lynn Harris are prominent. McMillan is best known for her series of popular novels, *Disappearing Acts* (1989), *Waiting to Exhale* (1992), and *How Stella Got Her Groove Back* (1996), which were turned into motion pictures or television films. The openly gay Harris self-published his first novel, *Invisible Life* (1991), which helped instigate the fascination among black publics with closeted black men. Harris's books were particularly popular among black women who were either in relationships with black men on the so-called down low or seeking signs that their male partners might be on the DL. Harris's work marked the beginnings of a cottage industry of products aimed at the spectacle of DL sexuality. Because Harris was openly gay, he became a trusted confidant for many black female readers, functioning in the literary world much the way Vandross did in the musical realm.

Inevitably, given the audiences Vandross shared with figures like McMillan and Harris, he would also be present in their literary works. Seymour, in fact, identifies at least thirty-six popular novels in which Luther Vandross is mentioned. According to Seymour, in these novels, most geared toward black women readers, Vandross's music is used to "establish a character's romantic longing or loneliness; to provide the background for a moment of private escape or relaxation; or to set the mood for a romantic encounter."[26] Vandross's presence was more pronounced in the novels of the writer James Earl Hardy, whose B-Boy Blues series might be singularly responsible for the emergence of the so-called homo-thug, or what Hardy refers to as "homiesexuals," in black popular culture and media. As Seymour notes, Hardy used variations of Vandross's song titles for his book titles. In some ways, Hardy's titles are as much a tribute to Vandross's artistry and prominence in African American life as they are a knowing wink, even an affirmation, to an artist who might have wanted to remain closeted. As such there is an organic quality to Hardy's use of Vandross, in contrast to others who worked earnestly to reproduce Vandross as an element of a normative, heterosexual reality for many black Americans.

Luther Vandross and the Heterosexual Frame

In December 1986, Luther Vandross was asked to perform at the nineteenth annual NAACP Image Awards ceremony, at the Wiltern Theater in Los Angeles. The NAACP (National Association for the Advancement of Colored People) has a long history of advocacy on behalf of African Americans, including its role in the seminal *Brown v. Board of Education* case, which successfully challenged segregation in schooling. By the mid-1980s, the Image Awards, which were founded in 1967 by the Hollywood branch of the association, may have been the most visible aspect of the organization's work. Born out of historical efforts to force mainstream media to depict "Negroes"—African Americans— in a more positive light, the Image Awards "honor companies and individuals who contribute positively to the images of black people."[27] A seemingly innocuous endeavor, the Image Awards have at times courted controversy, as was the case when the so-called gangster rapper Tupac Shakur was recognized for his acting at the Image Awards in 1993. Several organizations threatened to boycott and protest the event.[28] The NAACP had made a practice of recognizing only "art" that offered a positive view of the lives of black Americans, refusing to sanction performances —no matter their artistic value—that essentially made black folk look bad. As such, the NAACP, through its annual Image Awards, became one of the most visible and effective arbiters of black respectability.

The Image Awards show in 1986 drew special attention because it was the first to be broadcast by one of the major networks, NBC, which was then riding the wave of the hugely successful and groundbreaking sitcom *The Cosby Show*. The mainstream crossover success of *The Cosby Show*, which featured an upper-middle-class African American family, is one of the reasons that NBC president Brandon Tartikoff felt compelled to broadcast the program. According to Tartikoff, "We at NBC are proud to play a part in the broadcast of 'The Image Awards' and to support the NAACP in its effort to show appreciation for those who fulfill their moral and legal responsibilities to civil rights."[29] In many regards *The Cosby Show* was the logical conclusion of the impact the NAACP hoped the Image Awards would create. The nineteenth annual Image Awards also celebrated the success of Steven Spielberg's film adaptation of Alice Walker's novel *The Color Purple*, which was nominated for eleven Academy Awards the year prior, despite the NAACP's initial criticism of the film's depiction of black men. The ceremony was cohosted by the actors Denzel Washington and Debbie Allen.

Vandross was asked to participate in the awards ceremony by performing a tribute to Dionne Warwick, who was feted as Entertainer of the Year, in large part because of her efforts on behalf of AIDS research. Proceeds from Warwick's 1985 single "That's What Friends Are For," which featured Gladys Knight, Elton John, and Stevie Wonder, were donated to the American Foundation for AIDS Research. The song also earned Grammy Awards for "Best Pop Single by a Duo or Group" and "Song of the Year" for its writers, Carole Bayer Sager and Burt Bacharach.[30] Vandross was a logical choice, given his admission of Warwick's influence on his vocal stylings as well as his production work with her in the early 1980s. Vandross chose to sing "A House Is Not a Home," easily his most recognizable and popular tune and a song that Warwick recorded during her heyday in the mid-1960s. Jason King argues in his essay "Any Love: Silence, Theft, and Rumor in the Work of Luther Vandross" that there is a "refined majesty about Vandross' version. . . . Indeed the drama and intentional stakes of Vandross' version seem higher, more explicit, as the domestic melodrama becomes amplified."[31]

Vandross's performance of "A House Is Not a Home" was a tour de force, evidence of an artist at the peak of his performative powers, a fact that was reinforced by SONY/Legacy's decision to include the performance as a bonus feature on *From Luther with Love: The Videos* (2004), a video music retrospective of the singer's career. Despite the artistic value of Vandross's performance, the video provides insight into the ways that the show's producers reinscribed (perhaps inadvertently) heterosexual norms via their framing of Vandross and Dionne Warwick, who was sitting in the audience at the Wiltern Theater that evening. Throughout Vandross's performance, the camera cut back and forth between Vandross and Warwick's reaction to his performance. On a purely logical level, such framing made sense, since Vandross was performing a tribute to her. The overall effect of the shots was to create the impression that Vandross was singing for Warwick. Vandross, however, wasn't just any black male singer, but a singer whose queerness was tacitly expressed for many of his fans and the black public at large. Given the rumors that had circulated about Vandross in the year and a half before his performance at the NAACP Image Awards and given the stakes associated with the first network broadcast of the show, the heterosexual framing of Vandross and Warwick seems more than incidental. Even if such framing wasn't consciously pursued, it speaks to the hegemony of heteronormativity, particularly in black popular culture. Who else could Vandross have been singing to, if not a woman? As such, Warwick was the logical subject.

As Jason King writes, Vandross's version of "A House Is Not a Home" is a "narrative of male vulnerability, if not outright submissiveness. No longer actively in control of destiny, the male performer of 'A House Is Not a Home,' must sit and wait for his partner to 'turn his house into a home.'"[32] Given this reversal of traditional black male-female gender expectations, Vandross is always/already queered in his performance of the song, even without the possibility that he could be singing to a male partner. In the midst of the *Cosby* era, the camera could not risk the possibility of Vandross's desire for a male partner, thus the more mature Warwick assumes the role of the knowing older lover, which in effect normalizes Vandross's always/already queer performance of the song. Rather than providing a passive gaze of Vandross, the camera actively, even aggressively, works to silence competing narratives—the rumors—of Vandross. Indeed, the camera becomes more explicit at several points during Vandross's performance, when the producers present split screens showing Vandross and Warwick side by side, as if attempting to literally couple the duo. In another example, as Vandross begins the song's bridge, the camera shot is from behind Warwick's head, presenting an image of Vandross singing directly to Warwick. When Vandross sings the lyric "your face appears" from the bridge, the producers again present the split screen.

Interesting in the camera's framing of Vandross and Warwick are the other audience members whom the camera chooses to capture. Notable is the relatively long time—about five seconds—of a close-cropped view of a very young and animated Janet Jackson and frequent views of two older African American women, who likely caught the producers' attention because of their gaudy sequined gowns. Incidental to the camera's gaze was the capturing of the actor Paul Winfield and the actress and comedian Marsha Warfield, who was sitting behind the aforementioned women. Winfield was sitting in the row directly behind Warwick and about two seats to her left. Given the camera's focus on Warwick, Winfield becomes a regular feature of the frame. Winfield and Warfield are curious spectators, in that their reaction to Vandross's performance is subdued, even dismissive in that they seem unwilling to give in to the heterosexual scripting that is taking place. Winfield and Warfield present looks of *silence*, which suggest that they possessed alternative knowledge in which to read Vandross's performance of "A House Is Not a Home." With regard to silence and queerness in black communities, Jason King argues that "Silence is a realm of possibility unto itself. In the supposed gap between official discourses which work to silence and make invisible public displays of queerness and those underground discourses circulated by marginalized audiences, silence is reconstructed not only as knowledge, but also as sentimental kinship."[33]

Indeed, Vandross, Winfield, and Warfield might have been symbolic kin. An accomplished stage, television, and film actor who was nominated for an Academy Award for his role in the film *Sounder* (1972) and who won an Emmy Award (after several nominations) for his role in the television series *Picket Fences* (1994), Paul Winfield was a closeted gay man for most of his career. Many were unaware of Winfield's sexuality until he was "outed" in obituaries following his death in 2004.[34] Though Warfield has never come out, she has been read as queer because of her performances of "butch femininity" in her stand-up routines and most notably in her role as Roz on the NBC sitcom *Night Court* (1986–1992). Winfield, Warfield, and Nell Carter, who was also feted at the nineteenth annual Image Awards and was similarly "outed" after her death in 2002, were of a generation of black performers who, like Vandross, were on the cusp of unprecedented crossover success in the 1980s and thus guarded their privacy—anything that would mark them as pathological —with a vengeance. And that is exactly what the look on Winfield's face conveys during Vandross's performance, as he seemingly begrudgingly accepts Vandross's ability to follow the heteronormative script—on that occasion.

Though the cultural terrain would change later in Vandross's career, he would continue to subject himself to such heteronormative scripting in order to reach the widest audiences possible. Such was the case in 2001, when a fifty-year-old Vandross was on the comeback trail after leaving the Epic label and recording a one-off project with Virgin Records that was under-promoted. Signed to Clive Davis's J label, *Luther Vandross* (2001) was one of Vandross's strongest records in nearly a decade, but by the time of its release, Vandross was an aging balladeer who was being displaced on so-called urban radio by the likes of R. Kelly, Usher Raymond, and Brian McKnight. Davis and his staff sought to give Vandross a cutting-edge hip-hop sheen, styling him in Sean Combs's Sean John clothing line and pairing him in the video for the lead single, "Take You Out," with the Haitian American actress Garcelle Beauvais, who was perhaps best known for her role as Fancy on *The Jamie Foxx Show* (1996–2001) and her role in the music video for R. Kelly and Ronald Isley's "Down-Low" (1995).[35] Though J Records was concerned with making Vandross relevant to hip-hop–generation audiences, Vandross's comeback also occurs after a second round of virulent rumors about his contraction of AIDS. With the onset of the Internet and twenty-four-hour media outlets, rumors about Vandross's sexuality and health had a viral quality that was not possible in the mid-1980s.

During the summer of 2000, urban radio stations erroneously reported that Vandross, who had recently lost more than a hundred pounds, had died of AIDS. As Seymour writes, Vandross "finally heard about the false death rumors while en route to the Essence Music Festival in New Orleans, where he was scheduled to perform" and famously addressed the crowd by saying "And I sound real good for somebody who's dead."[36] Whereas Vandross's earlier performance at the NAACP Image Awards had a modicum of credibility, footage of Vandross wooing Beauvais at a restaurant with his "crew," including the retired NBA star John Salley, comes off as simply camp. Fifteen years later, Vandross's performance could not be taken seriously, especially by a generation that had grown up with Vandross's always/already queerness and particularly as narratives of DL sexuality began to propagate. Ironically, Vandross's performance of coy romanticism marked him as an outlier at the close of the black macho era and late in his career, as hip-hop came to dominate black cultural terrains, yet he remained wedded to a performance of black masculinity that was pitched to notions of black respectability and aspiration largely formulated in the 1980s, when he emerged as the dominant male voice in black popular music.

Postscript

Looking for Denzel, Finding Barack

Throughout his career, Denzel Washington has been a paragon of a well-mannered, good-intentioned, and deftly committed "race man," a term from the beginning of the twentieth century that describes black men of stature and integrity who represented the best that African Americans had to offer in the face of Jim Crow segregation. The term has lost some of its resonance in a post–civil rights, post-race, post-blackness world, but it remains an unspoken measure of commitment to uplifting the race. Race men inspire pride; their work, their actions, and their speech represent excellence instead of evoking shame and embarrassment. Thus the pundit Roland Martin and the Reverend Jesse Jackson (even with an illegitimate child) can be race men, whereas the comedian Dave Chappelle and the rapper/mogul Jay-Z can never be. Washington's hero and mentor Sidney Poitier had impeccable race man cred. The legendary black actor was one of the first to achieve mainstream success, and he never wavered. In films such as *The Defiant Ones* (1958), *In the Heat of the Night* (1967), and even *Guess Who's Coming to Dinner* (1967), he made black audiences proud to be black. At the height of the Black Power movement, when his articulate, educated, and even affable characters were often measured against fiery political icons such as Malcolm X and the Black Panther leader H. Rap Brown, some blacks felt ambivalent about Poitier. But the actor's willingness to support the civil rights movement appeased those who wanted a more radical image. It was an image that Poitier himself was heavily invested in: on the occasion of receiving an Honorary Award from the Academy of Motion Picture Arts and Sciences in 2002, Poitier remarked, "My love and my thanks . . . to those audience members around the world who have placed their trust in my judgment as an actor and filmmaker."[1]

There's little doubt that Poitier and contemporaries such as James Earl Jones and Raymond St. Jacques influenced Washington in his choice of roles. Early in his career, he was often drawn to the part of the heroic do-gooder; his roles in *Cry Freedom* (as the martyred anti-apartheid hero Steve Biko) and the Civil War epic *Glory* (which earned him a 1990 Academy Award for best supporting actor) displayed his gravitas. The tear he shed when his character, Private Trip, was flogged in *Glory* lent black men a depth of humanity not seen in American cinema before or, arguably, since. In his collaborations with the director Spike Lee, Washington complicated the race man ethos. No longer defined solely by their willingness to stand up for their race, characters such as Bleek Gilliam (*Mo' Better Blues*), Jake Shuttlesworth (*He Got Game*), and Detective Keith Frazier (*Inside Man*) represented the new race man, whose main emphasis was on being manly. These characters were self-absorbed and selfish and demanded the respect they thought they deserved. Still, many black audiences embraced them, if only because Washington had earned their trust, especially after his signature collaboration with Lee on the film *Malcolm X*.

That trust—so crucial to Poitier's career—began to erode with Washington's portrayal of Alonzo in *Training Day* (2001). When he finally won the coveted Best Actor Oscar for that role, on the same night that Halle Berry won Best Actress, much was made of their being rewarded for portraying characters who demeaned African Americans. And yet it was still easy to give Washington a pass, because the Motion Picture Academy had ignored his more celebrated roles as Rubin "Hurricane" Carter and Malcolm X.

The cultural landscape had changed considerably by the time Washington appeared in the films *American Gangster* and *The Great Debaters* in late 2007. In the aftermath of the Don Imus debacle, rap music and urban reality television in particular became litmus tests for the perceived erosion of black culture's prestige.

Washington's desire to portray the gangster Frank Lucas in

the film *American Gangster*—the kind of character who has become a staple of so much commercial rap music—understandably raised eyebrows. In an interview with *Men's Vogue*, the actor defended his choices: "It's not about the black experience. It's more specific and selfish than that. It's what I feel like doing, not what I feel like people need."[2] In his review of the film, Alex P. Kellogg notes that "By taking on such a role, Washington is reinventing the conventional villain, and the black villain in particular," highlighting the sophisticated and nuanced aspects of his performance of a drug dealer and thug, including resonances of Avery Brooks and his character Hawk.[3] Washington's portrayal of Lucas also resonated with Jay-Z, who, after screening the film before its release, recorded a companion project, also titled *American Gangster*, in which he compared the career trajectory of the cinematic Frank Lucas with his own career.

When Washington agreed to direct and star in *The Great Debaters*, released a month after *American Gangster*, he may have been seeking redemption. Produced by Oprah Winfrey's Harpo Productions and opening on Christmas Day 2007, *The Great Debaters* tells the feel-good story of Melvin B. Tolson, who coached the debate team at historically black Wiley College in the 1930s. At a time when black intelligence was under assault, Wiley's team challenged conventional wisdom by successfully competing against its white peers (imagine *Akeelah and the Bee* or *Pride* taking place in a debate hall). In his portrayal of Tolson, a celebrated if largely forgotten modernist poet, Washington reasserts his claim to the race man mantle. In fact, he may have chosen to do *American Gangster*, which reportedly earned $46 million on its opening weekend, because it would give him the bankability to make an African American period piece that most Americans—including quite a few blacks—would ignore. Call this the "Danny Glover effect," after the way Glover has often chosen roles in high-revenue–generating films such as the *Lethal Weapon* franchise in order to earn the financial flexibility to produce politically minded films such as *Bopha!* or *The Black Power Mixtape*. There are many who might make critical distinctions between a Harlem drug lord and a celebrated modernist poet who happened to coach one of the most accomplished college debate teams in the 1930s. I argue, though, that both men, and the worlds they inhabited, provide a rich entrée into the nuanced and complicated lives that everyday black folk lead, lives that are rarely depicted in Hollywood cinema.

Ironically, the comfort that many audiences derived from their consumption of Melvin Tolson, as opposed to Frank Lucas, underscores the fine line between legibility and illegibility that both men—and their cinematic depictions—possess for their audiences. The treatment of Tolson in *The Great Debaters* is instructive in this regard, as the film takes liberties with historical realities, often solely for the effect of creating a classic Hollywood tale, making Tolson more legible to mainstream audiences. In his own right Tolson is a figure deserving closer cinematic examination. Throughout *The Great Debaters*, though, his story is too often dwarfed by the need for his character to power the "little engine that could." Thus in the name of adhering to "feel-good movie-of-the-year" clichés, *The Great Debaters* offered little insight into Tolson's significant reputation as a black modernist poet.

More alarming was the way Tolson's involvement with southern tenant farmers was employed in the film to elevate his—and by extension Washington's—race man status, providing little insight into how deadly and underappreciated labor and farmer organizing was in the South, particularly when such organizing aimed to bring together farmers and workers across the color line. Tolson's truly engaged political work wasn't simply about instructing black college students (largely drawn from the middle class) in the fine art of debate or in producing a body of literature that ranked with the best of his more celebrated Harlem Renaissance peers, but rather the more concrete, roll-up-your-sleeves labor that he did on behalf of the tenant farming movement. But of course the reality of that struggle is not as exciting as a group of students from a tiny historically black college in Texas successfully competing against students from the very paragon of American higher education, Harvard University. In this regard the film —despite the earnest intentions of the director (Washington)

and producer (Oprah Winfrey)—does a disservice by being dismissive of the real political struggles engaged by those depicted
in the film.

And yet the film's signature moment is another example
of where the film takes liberties, as the presumed debate with
Harvard actually took place against the University of Southern
California (USC). Understandably, having Wiley slay the mighty
Harvard is a more compelling story, particularly for a black period film trying to compete for holiday dollars. Wiley's real defeat
of the USC debate team is no less a significant achievement at a
historical moment (and some say contemporary moment) when
the very concept that blacks possessed intellectual capabilities
on par with whites was under assault. The tweaking of history in
Hollywood cinema is of course a time-tested practice, where the
sanctity of the narrative is often privileged at the expense of real
historical events and people. It is not surprising, then, that the
characters Henry Lowe (played by Nate Parker) and Samantha
Booke (played by Jurnee Smollett) were composite characters.
The fact that the film's producers needed audiences to invest in
the lives and futures of these characters led to their decision to
create biographies for "fictional" characters after test audiences
reacted negatively to vague descriptions of Lowe's future.

Ironically, the story of James Farmer Jr. (Denzel Whitaker),
one of the real historical figures in the film and arguably the
most compelling on the debate team, was often a backdrop to
the steamy relationship between Lowe and Booke. Highlighting the on-screen sexual tension between Smollett and Parker
(think about the bare-chested Parker in another feel-good
movie, *Pride*) obviously helps make the film more accessible
to hip-hop–generation audiences, but Farmer's own story as a
teen who was drawn into the critical political movement of his
era should have been equally attractive to the film's producers.
Farmer, who was a frequent debater of Malcolm X in the 1960s,
became an important figure in his own right as a founder of the
Congress of Racial Equality (CORE). Figures like Farmer are
often footnotes to the "magic" Negro narratives that mainstream
audiences find so damn fascinating—those stories of black folk

who with their superior talents or superhuman capacity for for-
giveness help whites salve their guilt about this country's racist
past. The success of *The Help* in 2011 is yet another example of
that phenomenon.

The Great Debaters makes little effort to connect the future political engagement of Farmer—CORE organized some of the first
southern "freedom" rides nearly two decades before the more
well-known freedom rides of the 1960s—with the visceral struggles that he witnessed following Tolson to a meeting with black
and white tenant farmers. Instead, that experience with Tolson
and the dramatic lynching scene that serves as the film's emotional turning point are used simply as inspiration for Farmer's
anecdotal usage in his debate with the fictional Harvard debate
team. That the film's producers make little effort to connect the
historical dots here is particularly egregious at a contemporary
moment that demands that American youth imagine themselves
as potential agents of social justice. Films like *The Great Debaters* often revel in the ability of blacks to transcend racist realities
and their own moral deficiencies, but provide little inkling of the
real political struggles that create the victories and successes that
these films promote. It is of course in this context that the race
man is rendered illegible, even to black publics, particularly as
embodied by the figure of Barack Hussein Obama, who roughly
a year after the releases of *American Gangster* and *The Great Debaters* was elected the first black president of the United States.
As a community organizer and later Illinois state senator, Obama
was rendered more legible to black publics under the tutelage of,
arguably, one of the last "race men" in America.

Years before Barack Obama emerged as a national political
figure, his mentor and minister at the Trinity United Church of
Christ in Chicago, the Reverend Jeremiah Wright, appeared on
a 1989 recording, *Majesty of the Blues*, by the Grammy Award–
winning trumpeter Wynton Marsalis, which paid tribute to the
legacy of New Orleans jazz. The centerpiece of the recording was
a three-part suite called "The New Orleans Function." Arranged
as a traditional New Orleans funeral on the occasion of "The
Death of Jazz," the suite features a sixteen-minute sermon aptly

titled "Premature Autopsies." Though "Premature Autopsies" was written by the noted jazz critic and curmudgeon Stanley Crouch, the sermon is delivered by Reverend Wright. Unknown to most in America prior to the 2008 Democratic primary season, at the time he recorded "Premature Autopsies" Reverend Wright was already regarded among the black cultural vanguard as one of black America's—if not America's—greatest preachers. Like the music that Marsalis "re-created" for *Majesty of the Blues*, Reverend Wright's preaching was the embodiment of what some might call "classical" black American culture—easily invoking examples like the Fisk Jubilee Singers, Louis Armstrong, Mahalia Jackson, Bessie Smith, Katherine Dunham, Langston Hughes, and Duke Ellington, the latter of whom serves as the primary referent throughout "Premature Autopsies."

Crouch composed "Premature Autopsies" in response to his sense that classical black American culture was under assault in the marketplace and by a dismissive generation of young Americans. The sermon gives the best insight into what drives Crouch's very public criticisms of rap music and hip-hop culture. But I also submit that the passion with which Reverend Wright delivers the sermon also explains the sense of indignation that was on display during the question-and-answer portion of Wright's talk at the National Press Club in April 2008. As Crouch wrote prophetically more than twenty years ago, "we must understand that the money lenders of the market place have never ever known the difference between an office and an auction. . . . They'll tell you that everything is always up for sale. They recognize no difference or distance between the sacred and the profane. For them everything is *fair* game to be used in their game."[4] While there were clearly forces that designed to have the legacy and rhetoric of Reverend Wright undermine the legitimacy of then Senator Barack Obama's campaign, what perhaps offended Wright and others was the mainstream press's unwillingness to treat black theological beliefs—and I'm not saying all black theological beliefs—with the respect that sacred beliefs deserve. What seems to have offended Wright—and rightfully so—is the legions of mainstream commentators and casual observers who feel compelled to comment on and judge Wright and his theological foundations without even a fleeting understanding of or interest in the tradition of black liberation theology that he espouses.

It is white privilege that allows mainstream media to presume that that which they don't know is illegitimate, as was the point of Reverend Wright's thesis of "different, but not deficient" at the Detroit NAACP Freedom Fund dinner the night before his National Press Club address. Like Crouch, who traces the "majesty of the blues" and the "noble sound" of jazz to an "artistic language that uttered its first words way back on that first day that a slave sang a new song in this new and strange land," Wright views the religious beliefs he espouses as a "faith tradition" that has its roots "past Jim Cone, past the sermons and songs of Africans in bondage in the transatlantic slave trade."[5] The mention of Jim Cone is a reference to the groundbreaking work of Dr. James Cone, whose scholarly contributions to black Christian thought began with the publication of *Black Theology and Black Power* (1969). Cone explained to the journalist Kelefa Sanneh in a 2008 *New Yorker* article that he was motivated by the violence that erupted in Detroit and Newark in the summer of 1967 to create a theological framework that "speaks to the hurt in my community. I want a theology that would empower people to be more creative."[6] Cone also understood, as Sanneh further describes, that the "black Christian church" (broadly defined here) had a public relations problem with regard to attracting young converts who were being drawn instead to Islam, Marxism, and various incarnations of black nationalism. According to Sanneh, the "urgency of [Cone's] prose reflected his anger but also his fear that the black Church was becoming obsolete."[7] It was this tradition that Reverend Wright embraced when he ascended to the leadership of Trinity in 1972, trying to create a place and space of worship where the black church's role was as much about sacred concerns as it was secular ones—a church as committed to saving souls as it was advocating for the political and social well-being of those souls.

If one were to have found a VHS of one of Reverend Wright's speeches in March 1984, perhaps it wouldn't have raised an eyebrow, particularly in contrast to the rhetoric emanating at the time from the Nation of Islam leader Minister Louis Farrakhan, who was thought to have doomed the Reverend Jesse Jackson's largely symbolic 1984 presidential campaign (though it brought a host of new voters to the polls, impacting other national, state, and local elections). Reverend Wright's rhetoric then, as in 2008, would have been perfectly in sync with the theological race man who has always been at the center of African American and black politics, so much so that calling one a "theological" race man is an oxymoron. Wright reads as out of touch with mainstream black Christianity only in the context of a "black" church that is seen as being largely devoid of any real political engagement. In the era of black televangelists like Bishop T. D. Jakes, Bishop Eddie Long, and Minister Creflo Dollar, who espouse a "gospel of prosperity" (hence Marc Lamont Hill's brilliant turn of phrase "I bling because I'm happy"), real political engagement takes a backseat to wealth accumulation and at times crass materialism. This is not to negate the importance of building wealth in black America—and the "rappers" understand this as well as anybody in the pulpit—but it helps explain why Jeremiah Wright might seem odd or even anachronistic; Wright remains the unrepentant race man, even as his fifteen minutes disappeared into YouTube's archives.

Reverend Wright's support for Barack Obama as "race man" ran counter to the pragmatic race politics that the candidate espoused throughout the campaign and in his later governing style as president. Indeed, one of the prevailing theses of the 2008 election season was that Barack Hussein Obama was not the round-way-brand of black man. Such a premise is palpable only to the extent that one chooses to read Obama against the image of marketplace confections of black masculinity—thugs—particularly those that legibly erect centuries-old tropes of danger, bestial behavior, and sinister eroticism. The idea that we should distinguish between the candidate and the thug(s) is one of the defining truisms of polite society—less a measure of the candidate's humanity and more an index of the tolerance in said polite society. But black men do not live in polite society—however effectively they earn their keep in those spaces—and even the candidate's wife understood this, telling *CBS News* in April 2008 about her fears that her husband might get shot at a gas station in Chicago as opposed to being assassinated on the campaign trial by some desperate political actor (or birther) yelling "traitor" or "liar." As Chris Rock surmised some time ago, to paraphrase, "niggas don't get assassinated, they get shot"—and there has always been more of a chance that Barack Obama's fate would be decided by a bullet intended for a nigga, as opposed to that intended for the president, because quiet as it's kept—Harvard pedigree notwithstanding—Obama never stops being a black man. And this was perhaps the implicit message of Byron Hurt's film short *Barack & Curtis: Manhood, Power and Respect.* The film is a brilliant and thoughtful intervention on the subject of black masculinity at a moment when Barack Obama was poised to re-define black manhood for much of the world.

There is a telling sequence early in Hurt's *Barack & Curtis,* where the radio journalist Esther Armah states that "Barack equaled Harvard, someone like 50 Cent equaled hood; hood equaled virility, Harvard equaled impotence." That Armah's compelling observation is rarely disturbed speaks to the extent to which many of our perceptions about black masculinity have been finely shaped by a market culture that makes it easier for us to go to sleep at night because we can so effectively distinguish the niggas from the black men. As such, Barack Obama and Curtis Jackson are little more than brands in a highly volatile and fabulously lucrative and politicized marketplace. As Nikhil Singh observes, "If the ideal inhabitants of the nation-state are citizen subjects, abstract, homogeneous, and formally equivalent participants in a common civic enterprise, then the ideal inhabitants of the market are private individuals endowed with a knowable range of different attributes and engaged in competition and personal advancement."[8] The concept of 50 Cent—Curtis Jackson—as brand is a no-brainer, as a commodity who implores us to believe that he is a highly dangerous and highly sexualized (to all comers, I might add) embodiment of contemporary black masculinity. The obviousness of Barack Obama-as-brand (as the historian William Jelani Cobb suggests we think of him in the film) is less pronounced, presumably as running for political office doesn't immediately translate into the salaries associated with being a highly compensated gangsta rapper—or a professional social menace. But Obama's political success was largely premised on his ability to brand himself as a beacon of hope, as an alternative to the Clinton aristocracy, and as a black man we don't have to fear. Branding helps make these men legible to very diverse and often competing constituencies. In a widely circulated cover story in *Fast Company* magazine, a veteran advertising executive matter-of-factly stated that "Barack Obama is three things you want in a brand: . . . new, different and attractive."[9]

What branding doesn't help illuminate is the extent to which the candidate and the thug(s) are dependent upon each other to lay claim to that which their brand doesn't—and quite frankly, can't—allow. This is the point that the literacy expert Vershawn Ashanti Young makes when he suggests, "That black men who display hypermasculine characteristics fetishize—that is, simultaneously love and loathe—those considered less masculine or, to be explicit, that niggas covet faggots has been unmasked in insightful criticism. That faggots desire to be niggas has occasioned less critique."[10] Jackson's ability to wear $2,000 suits establishes a mainstream upper-middle-class identity that his G-Unit clothing largely undermined. Obama's feigned performance of "Dirt on My Shoulder"—the Jay-Z song that Obama appropriated in response to tactics by the Clinton campaign—pivots on hypermasculine tropes easily accessed by those who would think otherwise. Where the candidate and the thug(s) find common ground is perhaps more nuanced and may be observed in the "I don't give a fuck" look that Obama so brilliantly deployed in the waning months of the presidential campaign or in response to Joe Wilson's outburst ("you lie") during an Obama address to both houses of Congress. As Young notes in his book *Your Average Nigga: Performing Race, Literacy, and Masculinity*, "What the phrase 'I don't give a fuck' really does is convert racial and gender anxiety into a mask of nonchalance. . . . That niggas carry it off so well, however is exactly why [black middle-class professionals] are drawn to them." Young adds that "whereas rappers exaggerate their blackness and masculinity, [black middle-class professionals] are required to underplay ours."[11] Both Barack Obama and Curtis Jackson are fictions that are the products of the larger culture's inability to imagine anything but radical dichotomies for black men.

Notes

Introduction

1 Robert Reid-Pharr, *Once You Go Black: Choice, Desire, and the American Intellectual* (New York: New York University Press, 2007), 170.

2 Seth Clark Silberman, "'Youse Awful Queer Chappie': Reading Black Queer Vernacular in Black Literatures of the Americas, 1903–1967" (PhD diss., University of Maryland, 2005), 34.

3 Andrew Ross, "The Gangsta and the Diva," in *Black Male: Representations of Masculinity in Contemporary American Art*, ed. Thelma Golden (New York: Whitney Museum of American Art, 1994), 159.

4 Michelle Alexander, *The New Jim Crow: Mass Incarceration in the Age of Colorblindness* (New York: New Press, 2010).

5 Ibid., 2.

6 Bryant Keith Alexander, *Performing Black Masculinity: Race, Culture, and Queer Identity* (Lanham, MD: Altamira, 2006), 74.

7 Herman Gray, "Black Masculinity and Visual Culture," in *Black Male*, ed. Golden, 177.

8 Topos Partnership, "Literature Review: Media Representations and Impact on the Lives of Black Men and Boys" (New York: Opportunity Agenda, 2011), 13–14.

9 Ibid., 22–28.

10 David Dante Troutt, "A Portrait of the Trademark as a Black Man: Intellectual Property, Commodification, and Redescription," *U.C. Davis Law Review* 38 (2004–2005): 1152.

11 Ibid., 1146.

12 Hank Willis Thomas, interview by the author, *Left of Black,* season 1, episode 19 (January 31, 2011).

13 René de Guzman, "Nothing Better," in *Pitch Blackness: Photographs by Hank Willis Thomas* (New York: Aperture Foundation, 2008), 98–99.

14 Anna-Katarina Gravgaard, "Visual Slang," *FLYP*, October 24–November 6, 2008, 25.

15 "Strange Fruit: Interview with Hank Willis Thomas," by Ilysha McMillian, *Art Nouveau Magazine,* March 23, 2012, http://www.an-mag.com/hank-willis-thomas/.

16 See Mark Anthony Neal, "Confessions of a ThugNiggaIntellectual,"

Popmatters.com, March 27, 2003, http://www.popmatters.com/pm/column/criticalnoire030327/.

Chapter 1

1 Kay Jarvis-Prokop, "Parker: The Real-Life Spenser," *San Diego Union-Tribune*, June 28, 1985, D-1.

2 William L. Van Deburg, *Hoodlums: Black Villains and Social Bandits in American Life* (Chicago: University of Chicago Press, 2004), 110.

3 David Mills, "The Pride and the Passion: Avery Brooks and His Mythology of Rage," *Washington Post*, December 9, 1990, G-01.

4 Ibid.

5 Vershawn Ashanti Young, *Your Average Nigga: Performing Race, Literacy, and Masculinity* (Detroit: Wayne State University Press, 2007), 142.

6 Martha Southgate, "Avery Brooks: Not Just a Pretty Face," *Essence*, April 1989, 114.

7 Jill Nelson, "Avery Brooks: The Artist behind the Enforcer's Mask," *Washington Post*, April 27, 1987, Y7.

8 Beth Turner, "Avery Brooks: A Powerful Voice for Black Culture," *Black Masks*, August 31, 1994, 5.

9 Mills, "The Pride and the Passion."

10 Ronald A. T. Judy, "On the Question of Nigga Authenticity," *Boundary 2*, 21, no. 3 (Autumn 1994): 225.

11 Ibid., 219.

12 Southgate, "Avery Brooks," 76.

13 Mills, "The Pride and the Passion."

14 *A Man Called Hawk*, episode 2, "A Time and Place."

15 *A Man Called Hawk*, episode 9, "Never My Love."

16 Bryant Keith Alexander, *Performing Black Masculinity: Race, Culture, and Queer Identity* (Lanhan, MD: Altamira, 2006), 74.

17 Mills, "The Pride and the Passion."

18 Gloria T. Hull, *Color, Sex and Poetry: Three Women Writers of the Harlem Renaissance* (Bloomington: Indiana University Press, 1987), 165.

19 Ibid., 178.

20 Mills, "The Pride and the Passion."

21 Mark Dery, "Black to the Future: Interviews with Samuel R. Delany, Greg Tate and Tricia Rose," *South Atlantic Quarterly* 92, no. 4 (1993).

22 Alondra Nelson, "Future Texts," *Social Text* 20, no. 2 (Summer 2002): 9.

23 Harry F. Waters with Jeanne Gordon, "Star Trek Sets a Bold New Course," *Newsweek*, January 4, 1993, 40.

24 Jefferson Graham, "Brooks' 'Deep Space' Adventure," *USA Today*, February 23, 1993, 3D.

25 Ibid.

26 It should be noted, of course, that much of that anxiety is produced in response to households parented by single black mothers. In this regard, *Deep Space Nine* offers an interesting alternative view of single parenthood in black communities that potentially represents a progressive intervention on the subject.

27 Sandra Grayson, *Visions of the Third Millennium: Black Science Fiction Novelists Write the Future* (Trenton, NJ: Africa World Press, 2002); and Sheree Renée Thomas, ed., *Dark Matters: A Century of Speculative Fiction from the African Diaspora* (New York: Warner Books, 2000).

28 Richard J. Powell, *Cutting a Figure: Fashioning Black Portraiture* (Chicago: University of Chicago Press, 2008), 63.

29 Ibid., 64.

30 Sekou Sundiata, "Urban Music," *Longstoryshort* (Righteous Babe Records, 2000.

31   " 'Words Don't Go There': An Interview with Fred Moten," by Charles Rowell, *Callaloo* 27, no. 4 (2004): 966.

32 Fred Moten, "The Case of Blackness," *Criticism* 50, no. 2 (Spring 2008): 204.

33 James T. Jones IV, "Brooks Flies against Odds with *Hawk*," *USA Today*, February 3, 1989, 3D.

Chapter 2

1 Manthia Diawara, "Homeboy Cosmopolitan," in *In Search of Africa* (Cambridge: Harvard University Press, 1998), 238.

2 Ekow Eshun, "Battle of the Brands," *New Statesman*, January 17, 2005, 40–41.

3 Ifeoma Kiddoe Nwankwo, *Black Cosmopolitanism: Racial Consciousness and Transnational Identity in the Nineteenth-Century Americas* (Philadelphia: University of Pennsylvania Press, 2005), 10.

4 Jayna Brown, *Babylon Girls: Black Women Performers and the Shaping of the Modern* (Durham: Duke University Press, 2008), 9.

5 Dereka Rushbrook, "Cities, Queer Space, and the Cosmopolitan Tourist," *GLQ* 8, nos. 1–2 (2002): 188–89.

6 John L. Jackson Jr., *Real Black: Adventures in Racial Sincerity* (Chicago: University of Chicago Press, 2005), 177.

7 Jasbir Kaur Puar, "Circuits of Queer Mobility: Tourism, Travel, and Globalization," *GLQ* 8, nos. 1–2 (2002): 110–11.

8 Bakari Kitwana, "Jay Z: Hip-Hop and High Society," *Black Book Magazine*, Spring 2004.

9 Jay-Z, "30 Something," *Kingdom Come* (Island Def Jam / Roc-A-Fella, 2006).

10 Jay-Z, *Decoded* (New York: Spiegel & Grau, 2010), 76.

11 Nwankwo, *Black Cosmopolitanism*, 72.

12   My thinking here was provoked by the work of the political scientist
     Cathy J. Cohen in her essay "Deviance as Resistance: A New Research
     Agenda for the Study of Black Politics," *Du Bois Review* 1, no. 1 (2004):
     27–45. Cohen writes,

> I continue to be interested in the possibility of constructing a field
> of investigation based in African American Studies and borrowing
> from queer theory and Black feminist analysis that is centered in the
> experiences of those who stand on the (out)side of state sanctioned,
> normalized White, middle- and upper class, male heterosexuality. I'm
> talking about a paradigmatic shift in how scholars of Black politics
> and more broadly African American Studies think and write about
> those most vulnerable in Black communities—those thought to be
> morally wanting by both dominant society and other indigenous
> group members.

13   Richard Iton, *In Search of the Black Fantastic: Politics and Popular Cul-
     ture in the Post–Civil Rights Era* (New York: Oxford University Press,
     2008), 200.

14   Alexis De Veaux, *Warrior Poet: A Biography of Audre Lorde* (New York:
     Norton, 2004), 179.

15   Ibid., 55.

16   Ibid., 311.

17   Ibid., 300.

18   Audre Lorde, *Zami: A New Spelling of My Name* (Freedom, CA: Cross-
     ing, 1982), 255.

19   Christopher Holmes Smith, "'I Don't Like to Dream about Getting
     Paid': Representations of Social Mobility and the Emergence of the
     Hip-Hop Mogul," *Social Text* 77 21, no. 4 (Winter 2003): 82.

20   Lorraine Ali, "The Coolest Mogul," *Newsweek*, December 4, 2006, 63.

21   Jay-Z refers to this exchange with Simon on the track "Flow" from the
     mixtape *S. Carter—The Remix.*

22   Kelefa Sanneh, "Getting Paid: Jay-Z, Criminal Culture and the Rise of
     Corporate Rap," *New Yorker*, August 20, 2001, 60.

23   See Zack O'Malley Greenburg, *Empire State of Mind: How Jay-Z Went
     from Street Corner to Corner Office* (New York: Portfolio/Penguin,
     2011), 67–69, 75–77.

24   Young Jeezy featuring Jay-Z, "Go Crazy (remix)," *Let's Get It: Thug
     Motivation 101* (2005).

25   Houston A. Baker Jr., *Blues, Ideology, and Afro-American Literature: A
     Vernacular Theory* (Chicago: University of Chicago Press, 1984), 152;
     see also Jennifer C. Lena, "Voyeurism and Resistance in Rap Music
     Videos," *Communication and Critical/Cultural Studies* 5, no. 3 (2008):
     264–79.

26   I was among those 493,000 consumers.

27 Fred Moten, *In the Break: The Black Radical Tradition* (Minneapolis: University of Minnesota Press, 2003), 69.

28 http://www.hp.com/personalagain/us/en/index.html?product=prod1.

29 Kanye West, featuring Jay-Z, "Diamonds from Sierra Leone" (remix), *Late Registration* (Roc-A-Fella, 2005).

30 Judith Halberstam, *In a Queer Time and Place: Transgender Bodies, Subcultural Lives* (New York: New York University Press, 2005).

31 Imani Perry, *Prophets of the Hood: Politics and Poetics in Hip-Hop* (Durham: Duke University Press, 2004).

32 See bell hooks in *Black Is, Black Ain't* (dir. Marlon Riggs, 1994).

33 In her insightful review of *The Black Album*, the journalist Elizabeth Méndez Berry recalls Jay-Z's awareness that some of his lyrics might be interpreted the wrong way: "When during a listening session, he played the track '99 Problems' for a group of journalists, he took great pains to explain that the word *bitch* as used in the song doesn't refer to a woman, and therefore isn't misogynistic. Either he thought we were a very gullible bunch or he felt conflicted about his use of the term, embarrassed even." See Elizabeth Méndez Berry, "The Last Hustle," *Village Voice*, November 26, 2003.

34 Many thanks to Ingrid Banks for initially helping me work through this particular analysis of Jay-Z's work.

35 Shanté Paradigm Smalls, "'The Rain Comes Down': Jean Grae and Hip-Hop Heteronormativity," *American Behavioral Scientist* 55, no. 1 (2011): 89.

36 In addition to his role on *The Wire*, Lance Reddick also portrayed James Baldwin in a brief scene from Rodney Evans's film *Brother to Brother*, which linked the coming-out narrative of a contemporary black male (portrayed by Anthony Mackie) to the queer legacies of a group of Harlem Renaissance–era writers, including Zora Neale Hurston, Langston Hughes, Richard Bruce Nugent, and Alain Locke. The film costarred Larry Gilliard Jr., who also costarred with Reddick in the first two seasons of *The Wire*. Though *Brother to Brother* was released two years after the "'03 Bonnie and Clyde" video (though they were in production at the same time), Reddick's portrayal of Baldwin speaks to the general ways that queer bodies are often in conversation with each other.

37 Martin Edlund, "Turning the Turntables," *New York Sun*, February 17, 2004, 18.

38 Kanye West, "Last Call," *College Dropout* (Roc-A-Fella Records, 2004).

39 C. Liegh McInnis Jr., *The Lyrics of Prince Rogers Nelson: A Literary Look at a Creative, Musical Poet, Philosopher, and Storyteller* (Jackson, MS: Psychedelic Literature, 2000), 214.

40 "If I Was Your Girlfriend" was also covered by TLC on their album

CrazySexyCool (1994). The lead singer T-Boz's deep voice also has the effect of challenging notions of gender address.

41 The scholar and journalist Craig Seymour notes a similar shift in gender address in Beyoncé's later duet with Luther Vandross on their performance of Donny Hathaway and Roberta Flack's "The Closer I Get to You." See "'Searching' for Luther: The Politics and Performance of Studying an African-American Icon" (PhD diss., University of Maryland, 2005).

42 Jay-Z, "My First Song," *The Black Album* (Roc-A-Fella / Island Def Jam, 2003).

43 See Jason King, "Any Love: Silence, Theft and Rumor in the Work of Luther Vandross," *Callaloo* 23, no. 1 (2000).

44 KRS-One, "Ya Strugglin'," *Edutainment* (Jive Records, 1990).

45 McInnis, *Lyrics of Prince*, 247–48.

46 "Dead on It" is also seemingly a reference to a James Brown session from the mid-1970s. According to Rickey Vincent in his book *Funk: The Music, the People, and the Rhythm of the One* (New York: St. Martin's, 1996), on "Dead on It" Brown chides other funk artists who had appropriated his sound without giving him proper credit (85–86).

47 McInnis, *Lyrics of Prince*, 251.

48 Jay-Z, *Decoded*, 192.

49 Smalls, "'The Rain Comes Down,'" 87–88.

50 Bill Werde, "Defiant Downloads Rise from Underground," *New York Times*, February 25, 2004.

51 Albert McCluster III, "Jay-Z, the Grey Album & DJ Dangermouse," *HipHipDX.com*, March 3, 2004, http://www.hiphopdx.com/index/features/id.277/title.Jay-Z-the-grey-album-dj-dangermouse.

52 According to Edward M. Jones at the Dallas-based consulting firm Strategic Initiatives Group, "Some of the urban brands have already morphed into being 'lifestyle brands' and the next stop will be 'mega,' if that is defined as a strong brand message that resonates with many groups, cross-category product extensions and international expansion." Quoted in Lisa Lockwood and Julie Greenberg, "The Mega Branding of Hip-Hop," *WWD*, February 11, 2004, 28.

53 Nicole Fleetwood, "Hip-Hop Fashion, Masculine Anxiety, and the Discourse of Americana," in *Black Cultural Traffic: Crossroads in Global Performance and Popular Culture*, ed. Harry J. Elam Jr. and Kennell Jackson (Ann Arbor: University of Michigan Press, 2005), 330.

54 Nicole Fleetwood, *Troubling Vision: Performance, Visuality, and Blackness* (Chicago: University of Chicago Press, 2011), 151–52.

55 Ibid., 152.

56 Ibid., 165.

57 In this regard Jay-Z's anxieties about his newfound celebrity are palpable on a track like "Hollywood" from *Kingdom Come* (2006), where he laments both the multiple gazes he now faces as well as his deference to his wife, Beyoncé, who is clearly the more visible celebrity.

58 Mark Simpson, "Here Come the Mirror Men," *Independent* (UK), November 15, 1994.

59 Maurice Wallace, *Constructing the Black Masculine: Identity and Ideality in African-American Men's Literature and Culture, 1775–1995* (Durham: Duke University Press, 2002), 75.

60 Quoted in Erik Parker, "Hip-Hop Goes Commercial," *Village Voice*, September 11–17, 2002.

61 Deborah A. Thomas, *Modern Blackness: Nationalism, Globalization, and the Politics of Culture in Jamaica* (Durham: Duke University Press, 2004), 260.

62 Kitwana, "Jay Z: Hip-Hop and High Society."

63 See Julie Creswell, "Nothing Sells Like Celebrity," *New York Times*, June 22, 2008.

64 Moten, *In the Break*, 160.

65 Jay-Z, "Cashmere Thoughts," *Reasonable Doubt* (Roc-A-Fella Records, 1996).

66 Jay-Z's query "What's your name?" made me think of the recording "I Wanna Know Your Name" by the Philadelphia-based soul group the Intruders. Recorded nearly thirty years earlier, the song's spoken-word performance becomes the site where the lead singer, Little Sonny, bares his "soul" while ostensibly trying to find out the identity of a young woman he is attracted to.

67 Marlon B. Ross, "Beyond the Closet as Raceless Paradigm," in *Black Queer Studies: A Critical Anthology*, ed. E. Patrick Johnson and Mae G. Henderson (Durham: Duke University Press, 2005), 161.

68 Wallace, *Constructing the Black Masculine*, 115.

69 Mark Waid and Alex Ross with Tom Klein, *Kingdom Come* (New York: DC Comics, 2008), 68.

70 Toure, "The Book of Jay," *Rolling Stone*, December 15, 2005, 80–89.

71 Eric Konigsberg, "Why Damon Dash Hates Mondays," *New York*, June 19, 2006, 48–55.

72 See Byron Hurt's film *Hip-Hop: Beyond Beats and Rhymes* for a thoughtful and provocative examination of how various rappers feminize each other in so-called rhetorical battle.

73 Tim'm T. West, "Keepin' It Real: Disidentification and Its Discontents," in *Black Cultural Traffic*, ed. Elam and Jackson, 168–69.

74 Michael Ivey, "Beanie Sigel Rips Pharrell and Kanye West," *NobodySmiling.com*, May 22, 2007.

75   West, "Keepin' It Real," 170.

76   Michael Eric Dyson, *Holler If You Hear Me: Searching for Tupac Shakur* (New York: Basic Civitas, 2001), 227.

77   See Eva Tettenborn, "'Will the Big Boys Finally Love You': The Impossibility of Black Male Homoerotic Desire and the Taboo of Black Homosexual Solidarity in Thomas Glave's 'Whose Song?'" *Callaloo* 26, no. 3 (2003): 855–66, for some commentary on "social death" and black masculinity.

78   Armond White, "Feature," *New York Press*, May 11, 2004.

79   Taiye Tuakli-Wosornu coined the term Afropolitan in his essay "Bye-Bye Babar," originally published in *LIP Magazine* in 2005.

80   White, "Feature."

81   The film *Fade to Black* offers a fascinating view of the process by which Jay-Z recorded "99 Problems" with the producer Rick Rubin. Notable is that Jay-Z performs the perspective of both himself and the law enforcement officer who stops him.

82   Dyson, *Holler If You Hear Me*, 227.

83   Jay-Z, "What More Can I Say," *The Black Album*.

84   Jay-Z quoted in Elizabeth Méndez Berry, "The Last Hustle," *Village Voice*, November 26, 2003.

85   Ibid.

86   John Norris quoted in Jeffrey Rotter, "Jay-Z Wants to Kill Himself," *New York Times*, May 9, 2004.

87   Greg Dimitriadis, *Performing Identity / Performing Culture: Hip-Hop as Text, Pedagogy, and Lived Practice* (New York: Peter Lang, 2004), 105.

88   Mark Healy, "Renaissance Mogul," *GQ*, December 2006, 286.

89   Hua S. Hsu, "The New Jay-Z: A Man of the World," *Los Angeles Times*, October 23, 2006, E4.

90   kris ex, "Jayhova's Witness," *Vibe Magazine*, December 2000; Jay-Z, "Kingdom Come," *Kingdom Come*.

91   Jay-Z discusses at length his exchanges with Méndez Berry in *Decoded*, 22–24.

92   Jeff Chang, "Moving On Up," *Nation*, January 22, 2007.

93   Common, "It's Your World (parts 1 and 2)," *BE* (MCA, 2005).

94   Talib Kweli, "Beautiful Struggle," *Beautiful Struggle* (Rawkus/Geffen, 2004).

95   Steve Stoute, *The Tanning of America: How Hip-Hop Created a Culture that Rewrote the Rules of the New Economy* (New York: Gotham Books, 2011), 7.

96   Sekou Sundiata, "Urban Music," *Longstoryshort* (Righteous Babe Records, 2000).

97   William DeVaughn, "Be Thankful for What You Got" (Roxbury Records, 1974).

98 See David Levering Lewis, *When Harlem Was in Vogue* (New York: Oxford University Press, 1989), 109–10; Daphne Brooks, *Bodies in Dissent: Spectacular Performances of Race and Freedom, 1850–1910* (Durham: Duke University Press, 2006), 66–130.

99 The Notorious B.I.G. (Christopher Wallace), "Big Poppa," *Ready to Die* (Bad Boy Entertainment, 1994).

100 "Got Next: A Roundtable on Identity and Aesthetics after Multiculturalism," in *Total Chaos: The Art and Aesthetics of Hip-Hop*, ed. Jeff Chang (New York: Basic Civitas, 2007), 42.

101 Bakari Kitwana, "Zen and the Art of Transcending the Status Quo: The Reach from the Hood to the Suburbs," in *Jay-Z: Essays on Hip-Hop's Philosopher King*, ed. Julius Bailey (Jefferson, NC: McFarland, 2010), 100–101.

102 Robin D. G. Kelley, *Race Rebels: Culture, Politics and the Black Working Class* (New York: Free Press, 1996).

103 Jonah Weiner, "Hova Goes MoMa," *Slate*, January 13, 2010.

104 Thanks to Rizvanna Braxton for reminding me of this colloquial gem.

105 "*Watch the Throne* Artwork Designed by Riccardo Tisci," http://multivu.prnewswire.com/mnr/prne/givenchy/50537/.

106 Yale Breslin, "Watch the Throne: Riccardo Tisci," *Life + Times*, September 14, 2011.

107 Ohm Youngmisuk, "No Sleep Till Brooklyn: Jay-Z Won't Rest Until Nets Take Over Town," *New York Daily News*, November 15, 2005.

108 Douglas Century, "Jay-Z Puts a Cap on Cristal," *New York Times*, July 2, 2006, sec. 9, p. 1.

109 And not to belabor the Superman references much longer, but I am struck by Jay-Z's allusions to "fortresses," suggesting that his foray into political discourse is much like Superman's return from his "fortress of solitude."

110 Jay-Z's Gulf region politics offer yet another way to view his relationship with Beyoncé or, more concretely, the ways that she has impacted his worldview. See Daphne Brooks, "'All That You Can't Leave Behind': Black Female Soul Singing and the Politics of Subrogation in the Age of Catastrophe," *Meridians* 8, no. 1 (2007): 180–204.

111 Thomas, *Modern Blackness*, 15.

112 Ibid., 13.

Chapter 3

1 Rafael Alvarez, *The Wire: Truth Be Told* (New York: Pocket Books, 2004), 13.

2 Margaret Talbot, "Stealing Life: The Crusader behind *The Wire*," *New Yorker*, October 22, 2007.

3 Ibid.

4   Alvarez, *The Wire*, 11.

5   Ibid., 47.

6   Earl Byrd, "Why I'm Glad 'Little Melvin' Williams Is Home," *Baltimore Afro-American*, January 31, 2003, 47.

7   Diane Anderson-Minshall, "Sonja Sohn Taps into *The Wire*," *Curve Magazine*, http://www.curvemag.com/Curve-Magazine/Web-Articles-2008/Sonja-Sohn-Taps-Into-the-Wire/.

8   Judith Halberstam, *Female Masculinity* (Durham: Duke University Press, 1998), 180.

9   Ibid., 229.

10 Ibid., 229–30.

11 Quoted in Teresa Wiltz, "The Role of Her Life," *Washington Post*, March 16, 2007, C01.

12 Ibid.

13 Ibid.

14 Ibid.

15 Joel Barraquiel Tan, "Homothugdragsterism," in *Total Chaos: The Art and Aesthetics of Hip-Hop*, ed. Jeff Chang (New York: Basic Civitas, 2007), 210.

16 Guy Trebay, "Homo Thugz Blow Up the Spot," *Village Voice*, February 1, 2000.

17 Jason King, "Remixing the Closet," *Village Voice*, June 24, 2003.

18 José Esteban Muñoz, "Queer Minstrels for the Straight Eye," *GLQ* 11, no. 1 (2005): 102.

19 John Nguyet Erni, "Queer Figurations in the Media: Critical Reflections on the Michael Jackson Sex Scandal," *Critical Studies in Mass Communication* 15 (1998): 160–61.

20 Quoted in Alvarez, *The Wire*, 85.

21 Ibid.

22 Williams quoted in Mike Goodridge, "Criminal Lover," *Advocate*, September 2, 2003, 67.

23 See Elaine Scarry's classic work, *The Body in Pain: The Making and Unmaking of the World* (New York: Oxford University Press, 1987).

24 Marona Love, "Michael K. Williams' Hot Wire Act," *MOSAEC*, August 2002.

25 See Davarian Baldwin, *Chicago's New Negroes: Modernity, the Black Migrations and Black Urban Life* (Chapel Hill: University of North Carolina Press, 2007), esp. 91–120.

26 St. Clair Drake and Horace A. Cayton, *Black Metropolis: A Study of Negro Life in a Northern City* (Chicago: University of Chicago Press, 1993), 489.

27 Francis A. J. Ianni, *Black Mafia: Ethnic Succession in Organized Crime* (New York: Simon and Schuster, 1974), 69.

28 In this particular iteration, Omar's crew included his lover, Dante (Ernest Wadell), as well as Tosha and Kimmy (Kelli R. Brown), who were also lovers.

29 Alford A. Young Jr., *The Minds of Marginalized Black Men: Making Sense of Mobility, Opportunity, and Future Life Chances* (Princeton: Princeton University Press, 2004), 147.

30 Ibid., 58.

31 Ibid., 59.

32 Alvarez, *The Wire*, 47.

33 Janice Roshalle Littlejohn, "London Chill," *Savoy Magazine* 1, no. 2 (Spring 2005): 70.

34 Ibid.

35 Spike Lee's 1995 adaptation of Richard Price's novel *Clockers* was an attempt to intervene in the genre of urban films that *Scarface* and *New Jack City* inspired. Simon has cited Lee's film as an influence on *The Wire*, for which Price has been a regular writer. See also S. Craig Watkins, *Representing: Hip-Hop Culture and the Production of Black Cinema* (Chicago: University of Chicago Press, 1998).

36 Littlejohn, "London Chill," 70.

37 I say "presumed" because knowledge of Elba's English and African roots more than hints at the reality of a generation of African Americanized children of African immigrants.

38 Littlejohn, "London Chill," 70.

39 Jeannine Amber, "Sexy Talk with Idris Elba," *Essence.com.,* August 2009, http://www.essence.com/news_entertainment/entertainment/articles/idris_elba_covers_essence.

40 James S. Williams, "The Lost Boys of Baltimore: Beauty and Desire in the Hood," *Film Quarterly* 62, no 2 (Winter 2008–2009): 59.

41 Ibid.

42 Ibid.

43 Ibid.

44 Ric Curtis and Travis Wendel, "'You're Always Training the Dog': Strategic Interventions to Reconfigure Drug Markets," *Journal of Drug Issues* 37, no. 4 (Fall 2007): 871.

45 Ibid., 876.

46 Ibid., 880.

47 Ibid., 883.

48 Young, *Minds of Marginalized Black Men,* 194.

49 Ibid., 170.

50 Ibid., 45.

51 Notable here is that the murder of Omar's lover, Brandon, was largely intended as a public recognition of Barksdale's ruthlessness.

52 Walton Muyumba, *The Shadow and the Act: Black Intellectual Practice,*

Jazz Improvisation, and Philosophical Pragmatism (Chicago: University of Chicago Press, 2009), 24.

53 Ibid., 25.

54 Clay Davis's character is loosely based on Clarence Mitchell III, a former Maryland state senator who was convicted in 1988 of criminal conspiracy in relation to his association with the Baltimore drug dealer Melvin Williams. Mitchell is the son of the late NAACP lobbyist Clarence Mitchell Jr. and the nephew of the former Maryland congressman Parren Mitchell.

55 Steven Holmes, "As Farrakhan Groups Land Jobs from Government, Debate Grows," *New York Times*, March 4, 1994.

56 "David Simon Answers Fans' Questions," http://www.hbo.com/thewire/interviews/david_simon.shtml.

57 Lola Ogunnaike, "Whacked! Another HBO Main Player Meets His End," *New York Times*, December 13, 2004, E1.

58 Stuart Jeffries, "The Midas Touch," *Guardian*, May 5, 2009.

Chapter 4

1 Saidiya Hartman, *Scenes of Subjection: Terror, Slavery, and Self-Making in Nineteenth-Century America* (New York: Oxford University Press, 1997), 79.

2 *TP-3: Reloaded* is the conceptual follow-up to two of Kelly's most popular recordings, his solo debut, *12 Play* (1993), and *TP-2* (2000).

3 Angela Davis, *Blues Legacies and Black Feminism* (New York: Random House, 1998), 4.

4 Candice M. Jenkins, *Private Lives, Proper Relations: Regulating Black Intimacy* (Minneapolis: University of Minnesota Press, 2007), 163.

5 Austin Scruggs, "Q & A: R. Kelly," *Rolling Stone*, August 25, 2005, 24.

6 See Daphne Brooks, *Bodies in Dissent: Spectacular Performances of Race and Freedom, 1850–1910* (Durham: Duke University Press, 2006); and Fred Moten, "The Case of Blackness," *Criticism* 50, no. 2 (Spring 2008).

7 Jenkins, *Private Lives*, 19.

8 John Ridley, "The Manifesto of Ascendancy for the Modern American Nigger," *Esquire,* December 2006.

9 C. Riley Snorton, "Trapped in the Epistemological Closet: Black Sexuality and the 'Ghettocentric' Imagination," *SOULS* 11, no. 2 (2009): 108–9.

10 See Mark Anthony Neal, "'You Remind Me of Something': Toward a Post-Soul Aesthetic," in *Soul Babies: Black Popular Culture and the Post-Soul Aesthetic* (New York: Routledge, 2002), 1–22; and idem, "The Tortured Soul of Marvin Gaye and R. Kelly," in *The Best Music Writing 2004* (New York: Da Capo), 222–29.

11 Robert Reid-Pharr, *Once You Go Black: Choice, Desire and the Black American Intellectual* (New York: New York University Press, 2007), 123.

12 See "The Firing of Jimmy" from *Dreamgirls: Original Cast Album* (Geffen Records, 1982).

13 Bobby Womack with Robert Ashton, *My Autobiography: Bobby Womack, Midnight Mover* (London: John Blake, 2006), ix-xiii.

14 Jonathan L. Walton, *Watch This! The Ethics and Aesthetics of Black Televangelism* (New York: New York University Press, 2009), 111–14.

15 Chuck Klosterman, "The Guide: Sex, Lies and Videotape," *Guardian*, August 25, 2007.

16 Snorton, "Trapped," 107.

17 Kevin Gaines, *Uplifting the Race: Black Leadership, Politics, and Culture in the Twentieth Century* (Chapel Hill: University of North Carolina Press, 1996), 170.

18 Evelyn Brooks Higginbotham, *Righteous Discontent: The Women's Movement in the Black Baptist Church, 1880–1920* (Cambridge: Harvard University Press, 1993), 202.

19 Lisa B. Thompson, *Beyond the Black Lady: Sexuality and the New African American Middle Class* (Urbana: University of Illinois Press, 2009), 3–4.

20 Thomas Shevory, *Notorious H.I.V.: The Media Spectacle of Nushawn Williams* (Minneapolis: University of Minnesota Press, 2004), 5.

21 Cathy Cohen, "Black Sexuality, Indigenous Moral Panics, and Respectability: From Bill Cosby to the Down Low," in *Moral Panics, Sex Panics: Fear and the Fight over Sexual Rights*, ed. Gilbert Herdt (New York: New York University Press, 2009).

22 Kelefa Sanneh, "Outrageous Farce from R. Kelly: He's In on the Joke, Right?" *New York Times*, August 20, 2007.

23 Jody Rosen, "R. Kelly Gets the Joke," *Slate*, August 22, 2007.

24 Hartman, *Scenes of Subjection*, 27.

25 Jane Gaines, "The Scar of Shame: Skin Color and Caste in Black Silent Melodrama," *Cinema Journal*, Summer 1987.

26 Cathy Cohen, "Deviance as Resistance: A New Research Agenda for the Study of Black Politics," *Du Bois Review* 1, no. 1 (2004): 29.

27 Snorton, "Trapped," 100.

28 Anne-Lise Francois, "Fakin' It / Makin' It: Falsetto's Bid for Transcendence in 1970s Disco Highs," *Perspectives of New Music* 33, nos. 1–2 (Winter–Summer 1995): 448.

29 Snorton, "Trapped," 102.

30 On this point, I think that it is critical that Bridget, the white woman, is the one with the most credible knowledge about Big Man's sexuality, given historical narratives that have suggested that white women would be the most curious about black male sexuality.

31 Louis Chude-Sokei, *The Last "Darky": Bert Williams, Black-on-Black Minstrelsy and the African Diaspora* (Durham: Duke University Press, 2006), 30.

32 Hartman, *Scenes of Subjection*, 29.

33 Vivian Barrera and Denise D. Bielby, "Places, Faces, and Other Familiar Things: The Cultural Experience of Telenovela Viewing among Latinos in the United States," *Journal of Popular Culture* 34, no. 4 (2001): 1-18.

Chapter 5

1 Michele Wallace, *Black Macho and the Myth of the Superwoman* (London: Verso, 1999).

2 Craig Seymour, *Luther: The Life and Longing of Luther Vandross* (New York: HarperCollins, 2004), 36.

3 Ibid., 72.

4 Quoted in ibid., 95.

5 Ibid., 134.

6 Craig Seymour, "'Searching'" for Luther: The Politics and Performance of Studying an African-American Icon" (PhD diss., University of Maryland, 2005), 47.

7 Ibid., 108.

8 L. H. Stallings, *Mutha' Is Half a Word: Intersections of Folklore, Vernacular, Myth and Queerness in Black Female Culture* (Columbus: Ohio State University Press, 2007), 127.

9 Wallace, *Black Macho and the Myth of the Superwoman* (New York: Dial, 1978), 34–35.

10 Marlon Riggs, "Black Macho Revisited: Reflections of a Snap! Queen," *Black American Literature Forum* 25, no. 2 (Summer 1991): 390.

11 Jason King, "Any Love: Silence, Theft and Rumor in the Work of Luther Vandross," *Callaloo* 23, no. 1 (2000): 435.

12 Riggs, "Black Macho Revisited," 394.

13 John Nguyet Erni, "Queer Figurations in the Media: Critical Reflections on the Michael Jackson Sex Scandal," *Critical Studies in Mass Communication* 15 (1998).

14 Barbara Faggins, "Teddy's Friend Thought Crash Would Kill Them," *Philadelphia Tribune*, May 14, 1982, 6.

15 Joshua Gamson, *The Fabulous Sylvester: The Legend, the Music, the Seventies in San Francisco* (New York: Holt, 2005), 124.

16 See Seymour, "'Searching' for Luther," 57.

17 Cathy Cohen, *The Boundaries of Blackness: AIDS and the Breakdown of Black Politics* (Chicago: University of Chicago Press, 1999), 79.

18 Seymour, "'Searching' for Luther," 57.

19 Cohen, *Boundaries of Blackness*, 90.

20 Ibid., 90.

21 Seymour, "'Searching' for Luther," 45.

22 See Seymour, *Luther*, 205-6.

23 Marc Lamont Hill, "Scared Straight: Hip-Hop, Outing, and the Peda-
    gogy of Queerness," *Review of Education, Pedagogy, and Cultural Studies*
    31 (2009): 29.

24 Jacqueline Trescott, "Shelter from a Fatal Storm," *Washington Post*,
    March 18, 1982, B1.

25 Seymour, "'Searching' for Luther," 229–30.

26 Ibid., 116.

27 Mike Boone, "NAACP Image Awards Buried in Late Night Slot,"
    Gazette (Montreal, Quebec), January 17, 1987.

28 Marisa Leonard, "Jackson Surprise Presenter at NAACP Awards," *Los
    Angeles Times*, January 6, 1994.

29 "NAACP Image Awards Get First Network Airing," *Washington
    Informer*, December 17, 1986, 22.

30 "That's What Friends Are For" was originally recorded by Rod Stewart
    in 1982.

31 King, "Any Love," 427.

32 Ibid., 428.

33 Ibid., 430.

34 Shola Adenekan, "Obituary: Paul Winfield," *Guardian*, April 2, 2004.

35 Beauvais's roles in the Isley/Kelly video and in Vandross's "Take You
    Out" offer one of the most striking contrasts between the latter's view
    of R&B and that of his contemporaries in the late twentieth and early
    twenty-first centuries.

36 Seymour, *Luther*, 268–69.

Postscript

 1 Retrieved from the Academy of Motion Picture Arts and Science data-
    base of acceptance speeches, http://aaspeechesdb.oscars.org/ics-wpd/
    exec/icswppro.dll?AC=qbe_query&TN=AAtrans&RF=WebReport
    PermaLink&MF=oscarsmsg.ini&NP=255&BU=http://aaspeechesdb
    .oscars.org/index.asp&QY=find+acceptorlink+%3d074-26.

 2 Alex P. Kellogg, "How American Gangster Re-Invents the Black Vil-
    lain," *American Prospect*, November 9, 2007.

 3 Ibid.

 4 Stanley Crouch, "Premature Autopsies," in Wynton Marsalis, *Majesty of
    the Blues* (1989).

 5 "Reverend Wright at the National Press Club" (transcript), *New York
    Times*, April 28, 2008.

 6 Kelefa Sanneh, "Project Trinity: The Perilous Mission of Obama's
    Church," *New Yorker*, April 7, 2008.

 7 Ibid.

8   Nikhil Pal Singh, *Black Is a Country: Race and the Unfinished Struggle for Democracy* (Cambridge: Harvard University Press, 2004), 25.

9   Ellen McGirt, "The Brand Called Obama," *Fast Company*, April 2008, 87.

10 Vershawn Ashanti Young, *Your Average Nigga: Performing Race, Literacy, and Masculinity* (Detroit: Wayne State University Press, 2007), 53.

11 Ibid., 63.

Index

About the Author

Mark Anthony Neal is Professor of African & African American Studies at Duke University. He is the author of several books, including *New Black Man* (2005), *Songs in the Key of Black Life: A Rhythm and Blues Nation* (2003), *Soul Babies: Black Popular Culture and the Post-Soul Aesthetic* (2002), and *What the Music Said: Black Popular Music and Black Public Culture* (1998).